The Author

Born in Iran, Siba Shakib grew up in Tehran and attended a German school there. A writer and maker of documentaries and films, she has travelled to Afghanistan many times in recent years, visiting the north as well as the territory commanded by the Taliban. Several of her documentaries have won awards, including the moving testimonials she has made of the horrors of life in Afghanistan and the plight of the Afghan women. She is currently writing the script to a film about Afghanistan, and when not travelling the world with her work, she lives in New York and Germany.

Afghanistan, Where God Only Comes To Weep

Siba Shakib

Century · London

First published by Century in 2002

Translated from the German, *Nach Afghanistan kommt Gott nur noch zum Weinen*,
first published in 2001 by C. Bertelsmann Verlag,
an imprint of Verlagsgruppe Random House, Munich.
© 2001 by Siba Shakib
© 2001 by C. Bertelsmann Verlag, Munich, inder
Verlagsgruppe Random House GmbH

First published in the United Kingdom in 2002 by
Century, Random House, 20 Vauxhall Bridge Road,
London SW1V 2SA

Random House Australia (Pty) Limited
20 Alfred Street, Milsons Point, Sydney,
New South Wales 2061, Australia

Random House New Zealand Limited
18 Poland Road, Glenfield,
Auckland 10, New Zealand

Random House South Africa (Pty) Limited
Endulini, 5a Jubilee Road, Parktown 2193, South Africa

The Random House Group Limited Reg. No. 954009
www.randomhouse.co.uk

A CIP catalogue record for this book is available
from the British Library

Papers used by Random House are natural,
recyclable products made from wood grown in sustainable forests.
The manufacturing processes conform to the environmental
regulations of the country of origin

Typeset in Fairfield by SX Composing DTP, Rayleigh, Essex
Printed and bound in the United Kingdom by Mackays of Chatham plc

ISBN 0 7126 2339 6

The writing of all Afghan and Persian names accords to the local pronunciation
and is intentionally not written in the Western style.

For Rahela.
For my mother.
The free.
The unfree.

'Peace cannot be kept by force.
It can only be achieved by understanding.'

Albert Einstein

آری این کلمات همه جا پراکنده شود،
زنان فرزندان خود را با نفرت از جنگ به دنیا اورند.
دنیا به دست قهرمانان خراب شده،
با ماست که بسازیمش!
نوای شادی و غم هر دو بسرائید.
دنیا تا بنگرید ویران است.
درود بر آن که بسازد،
درود بر آن که بیارد جهان آبادان!

بهرام بیضا یی

There have been many wars, many dead.
To bring peace to her land Aybanu sacrificed herself.
She became the wife of the mogul ruler.
Do you have anything to say? she is asked.
Yes, she says.

Yes, spread these words.
Women should give birth to their children with hatred of war.
The world has been destroyed by the hand of heroes.
It is to us to build it up!
Play both, songs of joy and songs of grief.
As far as eyes can see the world is shattered.
Praised shall be those who build it up.
Praised shall be those who bring a fruitful world.

Bahram Beyzaie

How It Came About

What's your name?

Shirin-Gol.

Is that your child?

Bale. Yes.

And that one?

Bale.

And what about that one?

Bale.

Those two boys there? Are you telling me they're brothers?

Yes. My sons, Navid and Nabi. I gave birth to them myself.

The official, Malek, looks dubious, but he still brings his stamp down on the thin paper, sweat-drenched and floppy from being clutched for so long in the woman's hands.

Go down to the back there, Malek tells her self-importantly. Show my colleagues this piece of paper, tell them Mr Malek's sent you, and there'll be no problems and you'll get your sacks of wheat. One for your husband, one for you and one for each of your children. You understand? A sack each.

The woman's face is completely veiled, the fine net in front of her eyes is too dense to give even the faintest impression of her eyes. But despite her facelessness her fury, her shame, the feeling of humiliation is palpable. Although I don't know if she's looking at me, I smile, express my sympathy, show that I'm not on Malek's side but hers.

Did you see that? asks Malek, as though we were old friends or relations or in-laws. Familiar. He and myself on one side and the people around us, his compatriots, on the other. I take a step backwards and avoid looking at him.

Malek knows very well that it's pure good fortune that he's not standing on the side of fate where he would have to hope for a hand-out of wheat. Where he would need a stamp, a permit, the mercy of one of his fellow countrymen. This time, this time he's lucky. This time he has a job and is thus one of a tiny handful of privileged people.

Since the United Nations set up this transit camp for Afghans returning from Iran, he has earned the equivalent of about sixty dollars a month, which means that he's able to feed both his own family and his brother's. Particularly since at least once a week a sack of wheat, which is supposed to make life easier for the ones coming home, doesn't make its way to its proper owner, and Malek sells it for good hard cash.

Did you see that? he repeats, with the same attitude of self-importance.

Yes, I say dryly, as though I hadn't the slightest interest in the fate of Shirin-Gol, the woman with the damp piece of paper and the four children who look as though they were born to different mothers and fathers. Malek is disappointed, and his lecherous expression makes way for an almost childish defiance.

I can imagine what he would like to talk to me about while his compatriots crouch in an endless queue on the sandy ground in the blazing sunshine, waiting for him to give them a stamp.

He probably wants to explain to me that Shirin-Gol only borrowed the children to get more wheat than she's allowed. Then she'll put the poor things out on to the street, and he, Malek, will have to gather them up and find somewhere for them to stay. Or he'll tell me Shirin-Gol has, like many other Afghan women, sold her body and had herself impregnated by different men.

Mr Malek, I say in anticipation, please forgive me. It's too hot and windy here, I'm going to look for a shady spot. Thank you very much for allowing me to watch you at work.

But you haven't seen a thing, Malek protests.

I'll come back later, I lie, disappearing between the blue plastic tents. I don't want Malek to find out where I am and who I'm talking to.

It's just as I feared. The children who look as though they have different mothers and fathers have vanished into thin air, and I didn't look at Shirin-Gol's shoes. Women's shoes are the only way of recognising them. A blue, pleated cloth covers the women from head to foot, making them all identical, dehumanising them. How could I find Shirin-Gol? The place is swarming with blue *burqas*, blown by the wind against the women's thin bodies, then inflating like balloons as though the women were about to rise into the heavens and float away. Again and again I try to make out human faces through the finely-woven net before the eyes of these living ghosts.

I stand undecided in the middle of all the cloths, staring straight ahead. I've had enough. I've been back in

Afghanistan for a month and a half. I'm tired, I'm exhausted. The constant, dusty wind and the dry air, heated by the sun, make even breathing a terrible effort. Call me whatever you want. I just don't want to hear any more stories about people who have lost everything, everything except their fear, their hunger, their pain, their misery, their poverty, their illnesses and a little bit of hope that things might get better again.

Perhaps I should just withdraw into the shadows somewhere. Perhaps I should find myself an empty tent, lie down and sleep. Then again I could also climb into one of the empty lorries driving back to the border to collect more new refugees. By evening I could be back in my homeland, Iran, where I was born and grew up. From there I could finally return to my comfortable, western world of luxury.

Unable to take so much as a single step further, I stand there in the heartless sun, my body leaden, just staring straight ahead. Suddenly, a blue cloth comes towards me. *La-elah-ha-el-allah*. What do you want of me? Those are my children. Leave me in peace in the name of God.

My senses react in slow motion, I can hear myself saying, forgive me. I can say nothing more than that, my tongue sticks to the roof of my mouth. I stare at the cloth in front of me until I can finally regain my ability to speak: I'm just standing around here. I don't work for the United Nations, or for any other aid organisation. I'm just here because I . . .

Because I what? Because I want to see your misery, film it and write about it? Because we Westerners can only feel our own hearts beating if we see the far-off suffering of the world? Because I think it might help you if someone told about the cruelty of the life you lead?

Particularly if the Lord your God sent you into the world as girls. Because I . . .

Are you all right? the cloth asks. A hand emerges from underneath it, pushes my sleeve back and settles on my arm.

This can't be happening, I think. I'm standing in the middle of the desert, watching hundreds and thousands of people being crammed like cattle on to the backs of trucks, and this woman is asking me if I'm all right?

I'm watching people coming from a home that never was, and returning to a home that will never be. Women, children, men who know nothing but constant flight. People who have buried daughters and sons, their fathers, mothers, husbands, wives, brothers, sisters. People who have no houses, nowhere to sit down, to eat, to sleep. Little girls and boys with only one arm, one leg, no arms or legs at all. People who are thin and rickety, sick, under-nourished, nothing but skin and bones. Men who have killed other men, who have looked death in the face themselves. Women who would rather be dead than watch another of their children die.

That's what I was thinking, says Shirin-Gol in a calm voice that falls on my heart like soft velvet.

What? I still don't quite understand. What were you thinking?

That you didn't belong to a relief organisation. You speak our language. Who are you? What are you doing here?

Shirin-Gol's strong hand is still on my arm. She squats down and pulls me down to sit next to her on the sandy ground.

I'm writing a book, I say, and try to make out the woman's eyes through the finely woven net. I get the usual explanations ready in my mind.

A book about Afghanistan, about us? people laugh. A book about a country where there's nothing but hunger and misery, wars and corpses? What's there to write about? Who wants to read a book like that?

I can read too, Shirin-Gol says instead. When the Russians were here I went to school and learned to read. Apart from my school books I've read three and a half proper books. The first I bought myself. The second my teacher gave me, the third was only half a book. I found it in the bombed-out ruins of the capital. A shame I never found the other half. I'd have liked to read the whole story to the end, it was such a lovely story, about a girl who . . . oh, I can't remember. And the other book was given to me by my friend, the only real friend I've ever had. She was a doctor. I met her in one of the many villages where we have lived, and worked for her.

The Shirin-Gol-cloth looks at me and I have the feeling that she's reading me, too, like one of her books. That she doesn't need any of my words to understand me.

Finally she takes her hand off my arm. A little damp patch remains on my skin. I don't wipe it away. Let it dry in the sun.

A book, says Shirin-Gol, without moving her cloth-covered head. I smile at the blue fabric.

Should I tell you my story for your book? asks the cloth. Would you like that?

Her question sounds like a warning, there's something threatening about it. While I don't know why I don't say yes, why instead my eyes sweep into the distance, to the trucks, bringing the dusty Afghan home-comers back from Iran, and spewing them out into the midst of blue plastic tents, while my thoughts have no beginning and no end, Shirin-Gol takes my chin in her hand, turns my head towards her, forces me to look at her cloth-covered head and asks once again, Would you like that?

Only years later would I understand that Shirin-Gol knew even then that if I said yes, if I got involved with her and her story that morning, we would be bound together for years. Perhaps for ever.

Yes, I'd like that, I say, smile, and put my hand on hers, which is still holding my face.

I'm glad I said yes.

Shirin-Gol is different from all the other women I've met in all my years in Afghanistan. Shirin-Gol is like a tree. Like a powerful, slender poplar that withstands the strongest winds and storms, seeing everything, understanding everything, knowing everything and passing everything on.

No other Afghan woman I know has talked so readily, so openly and so honestly about her life, let alone about her relationship with her husband. Shirin-Gol talks about everything she can remember, precisely and in detail, as though she wanted to be sure that at least her stories would remain when she herself had passed away. She doesn't care whether I ask her any questions or not. Shirin-Gol has her own rhythm, her own tempo for telling the stories of her life. Shirin-Gol's words are like the weather, sometimes they all sweep away like a storm, sometimes they settle on the heart like a soft, light breeze, sometimes they warm the heart like a tender spring sun, sometimes they burn like the heartless desert sun, sometimes they cool the senses like a little shower, sometimes they drum down like a rainstorm, become a rushing river and demolish everything that stands in their way.

Shirin-Gol's story isn't unusual, it relates the very normal madness that thousands of women and other people have experienced and continue to experience in Afghanistan, either like this or in a very similar way.

The camp where we first met, the cities, villages, the whole country, is full of women, children and men who are constantly in search of hope, constantly leaving where they live, constantly believing that everything will be sorted out. And time and again it looks at first as though everything will indeed be fine.

Chapter One

Red Blood, Sweet Flower

In Afghanistan almost all names have a meaning. Shirin-Gol means Sweet Flower. To claim that her mother saw a sweet flower, smelled the scent of a flower or even thought of a sweet flower the moment she was born would be to exaggerate, a romanticised invention of the Western imagination.

In all likelihood Shirin-Gol's mother, like all mothers in the world, suffered terrible pains at the birth of her fourth daughter, her ninth child, and in all likelihood she wondered at that moment how she would feed another child with her already weakened body and her empty breasts. And she was probably glad when she pulled the child from her body and saw that it was only a girl, because if Shirin-Gol had been a boy, that boy would have needed even more milk, even more attention. His mother would have had to carry him more often in her arms, they would have had to give a party to celebrate his birth and slaughter a sheep, rustle up some money for his circumcision and send him to the mullah to learn the Koran.

No, Allah is merciful, and this time he only sent her a daughter. To be precise, God has always been merciful to

Shirin-Gol's mother. He made her first child a son, so that her husband could feel like a real man, and wouldn't have to knock her teeth out or divorce her, or take her back to her father's house.

For safety's sake, so that everything would stay as it was, God sent her another boy just after the first. And the third child was a son as well.

Then God thought about Shirin-Gol's mother and sent her three daughters in a row. That meant she finally had some help with all the work she had to do for her husband and her three sons, tilling the field, baking bread, sewing clothes, tending the sheep, milking the cows, making meals, weaving carpets and whatever other tasks came her way.

The next two children were boys again, and for each of them Shirin-Gol's father slaughtered a sheep. Each one had to be circumcised, but at least these two didn't have to go to the mullah, because the first three sons in the family had learned the Koran.

And the year after these not-so-important brothers, Shirin-Gol suddenly comes into the world. As far as her father's concerned it's neither good nor bad. For her mother it's good.

Shirin-Gol is a quiet child, and her life is good. When she is a little girl everyone leaves her in peace. She sits in the shade by the corner of the mud hut on the sandy ground, watching her mother and father, her elder brothers and sisters, tilling the little field, milking the few sheep they have, watering the donkey, sweeping the dust out of the hut, weaving carpets, fetching food, baking bread, ensuring the survival of the family afresh each day. Shirin-Gol is set down at the corner each morning by her sister with the mole on her cheek, given a piece of bread in her hand, and given no other task but to behave as quietly as possible, to look, and to understand a girl's role in life: to be inconspicuous, to work, and to obey the orders of the boys and men.

It is only when she is about two years old that Shirin-Gol stands up by herself for the first time, comes out of her corner in front of the hut, takes a few steps, goes over to Mole-sister, who is crouching in front of the hut and washing clothes, crouches beside her, splashes her little hand around in the soapy water, gets a smack on the fingers, pees on the floor, is carried back to her place by Mole-sister and set back down again.

God sees all that and at that moment he remembers Shirin-Gol's mother. He suddenly remembers that for two years he has forgotten to give Shirin-Gol's mother a new child in her belly. So merciful God hurries to catch up on what he has missed, and before Shirin-Gol is quite three years old she has two brothers at once put in her lap, and from that point on, day in, day out, she is busy with the twins.

She rarely raises her head now, no longer knowing what her mother and older sisters, her father and other brothers are doing all day.

The next time Shirin-Gol looks up and sees what is going on in the world around her is the day the twins take their first steps without her holding them by the hand. One of them walks straight from right to left and the other from left to right, they crack their heads together, fall over, start howling and both look to their sister Shirin-Gol for help. Then, very close by, a rocket explodes, the first, but by no means the last, that Shirin-Gol will hear in her lifetime. The twins fall silent, both stagger anxiously over to their sister, burying their heads in her little skirts. Their mother looks up in horror, the older brothers run back from the field, the older sisters howl, their father looks concerned and says, more to himself than to anyone else, then it's true. The Russians are here.

The Russians? Who are the Russians? Our neighbours? Why have they turned up? What do they want from us? We haven't got anything ourselves, says Shirin-Gol's mother in a loud, high voice.

Her father looks at his sons and says, we'll have to go into the mountains. In the past the English occupied our country and decided our fates, now the Russians are having a go. In the past the English cast an eye on our wives and daughters, now it is the turn of the Russians. In the past the English dishonoured and sullied our country and our religion, took away our power and responsibility for ourselves, robbed us of our freedom and polluted the soil of our homeland, now it is the Russians. We have no other way, it is time for us, too, to join the Mujahedin, go to war against the Russians, and, if it has to be, fight them to the last drop of our blood. To the last drop.

Those are the last paternal words that Shirin-Gol remembers. Her father lines up with her older brothers, prays, gives each of the brothers a rifle and ammunition, and vanishes from Shirin-Gol's life and the mud hut, leaving a lot of room for eating, for sitting, for looking after the twins, for picking lice from their hair, for spinning wool, sewing clothes, weaving carpets, chopping sugar into small pieces, grinding corn, sitting together and talking about the war, the wounded, the dead, the Russians, spreading out the sleeping mats and blankets at night.

From then on Shirin-Gol and the twins no longer sleep

in the corner behind the fireplace in the ground, get more to eat and are allowed to talk more than before. Only the shots, rocket attacks and bomb explosions in the mountains remind them of their brothers and their father, who only ever appear occasionally, stay for a short time and then vanish again.

Shirin-Gol is in the field collecting the last puny *kachalou*, potatoes, when a man quickly runs past her. He is carrying another man on his shoulders, covered in blood all over. The man with the bloody man on his shoulders stops and turns to look at her. She recognises him as one of her older brothers and smiles. Her brother does not smile back, asks, why aren't you wearing your *burqa*? walks on and disappears behind the mud hut.

Shirin-Gol's mother comes out of the hut, her face drained of colour. *Madar*. Mother.

Madar-with-no-colour-in-her-face stands in front of the hut, holds the clay water jug in front of her belly with both hands and says a lot of little words that Shirin-Gol can't hear, because Madar-with-the-drained-face has also lost her voice.

Shirin-Gol stands there, staring at Madar-with-no-colour-in-her-face-and-no-voice-in-her-mouth. Shirin-Gol wonders who has stolen the colour from *Madar*'s face and the voice from her mouth, whether it was the bloody man or whether *Madar* herself put them in the niche and forgot to bring them back out again. Shirin-Gol is wondering this, when Madar-with-no-colour-in-her-face-and-no-voice-in-her-mouth hurls the clay water jug on to the ground, so that it breaks and becomes a thousand and one little shards of clay.

Colour gone. Voice gone. Water jug gone.

14   Siba Shakib

Shirin-Gol takes the twins by the hand, turns around without looking at Madar-with-no-colour-in-her-face-and-no-voice-in-her-mouth-and-no-water-jug-in-her-hand again, and goes back to the field, to the puny *kachalou*, which are under the earth and have a good life because it's cool there and there is no mother there to go around breaking clay water jugs.

More men come at night, familiar and unfamiliar, her father and her other elder brothers. Shirin-Gol hears them chopping up the soil behind the hut, goes out, sees the bloody man her brother had been carrying on his shoulder being put into the hole and the hole filled up again. The men weep, put their rifles and Kalashnikovs over their shoulders and vanish back into the dark of the night.

The next morning only Shirin-Gol's mother is crouching by the filled hole. She has a black cloth over her head, her body rocks back and forth as though she were in pain, she keens and laments and doesn't even stop when Shirin-Gol brings her a fresh glass of tea.

Shirin-Gol thanks God that *Madar* has recovered her voice, says a quick prayer for God to bring the colour back to her face, and to make sure that she hasn't pulled the black cloth over her head because she's lost her eyes, her nose and her mouth as well. But if she had lost her mouth, she wouldn't be able to lament, Shirin-Gol thinks to herself, and decides to behave as though she hadn't seen Madar-with-no-colour-in-her-face-and-no-voice-in-her-mouth-and-no-water-jug-in-her-hand the day before.

What's wrong? the little girl asks, putting as much unconcern into her voice as God is willing to grant her.

What do you think is wrong? *Madar* sighs, taking the cloth from her head to take a sip of tea. Then Shirin-Gol sees it with her own eyes. During the night *Madar* has lost the colour from her hair.

And then Shirin-Gol learns that God killed the bloody man in the hole for that very reason, so that *Madar* would lose the colour from her face, the voice from her mouth, the clay water jug, the colour from her hair, and so that her mother's heart would break and her mother's hair would turn white.

Shirin-Gol still doesn't understand how everything connects, but the further the sun travels to sink in the west at the end of the day, the more Shirin-Gol learns about the man in the hole, and what he has to do with her mother's suddenly white hair.

The man on her brother's shoulder, the man now lying in the hole in the ground behind the hut, is actually a martyr, fallen in the name of the Prophet, the Koran and of Islam.

Shirin-Gol has heard of martyrs many times, but always firmly believed that martyrs dwelt in the company of God, in Paradise, and not in holes in the ground. But now she has seen it with her own eyes, in the hole behind the hut there is a flesh-and-blood martyr. A *shahid*.

Shirin-Gol also learns that he will not be the last *shahid* in her life by any means, and that this *shahid* had previously been a real man, someone that Shirin-Gol had known, even someone from her own family, one of her brothers, to be precise, the second son that God had granted to her mother, the first he had taken back for himself, and precisely for that reason her mother has terrible pains that may kill her and it is for that and no other reason that her hair turned white overnight. Shirin-Gol takes the twins by the hand, sits down by the filled hole in the ground and does as her mother and everyone else, she weeps, doesn't understand, closes her eyes and asks God why he does that. First he sends mothers sons that they grow to love, sons they get used to. Then he makes the little sons turn into big sons, sends the Russians into their homeland and the sons into the mountains, where they die and become *shahid* and break their mothers' hearts – and all for them to have white hair in the end? It would be much simpler, wouldn't it, if he didn't send them any sons in the first place, and just gave the mothers white hair from the beginning.

And just in case he plans to do the same thing with Shirin-Gol, when she is grown up and a mother, then frankly she'd rather he didn't, because she doesn't want all the work that boys bring with them, after all she's already learning from the twins how much effort and attention boys need, and how much responsibility they mean, and nor does she want, if God intends to make her sons die as *shahid* as well, to have to endure the pain. And the eyes swollen from all the crying and the white hair – she doesn't want any of it.

God's ways are endless, says Shirin-Gol's eldest sister every day from this point onwards. On the fourteenth day after her brother's death she paints her lips red and her eyes black and goes down into the village.

Where are you going? Why are you painting your lips? Why aren't you wearing a veil? What will people say? They'll talk behind your back. You're sullying the honour of our father, our living brothers and our dead martyr brother. In the name of the Prophet, the Koran and Islam, you are bringing shame and misfortune upon us.

Shirin-Gol says all that and everything else she has learned to believe and obey, but her sister doesn't listen to her, she goes into the village and doesn't come back until the following morning, when she has four Kalashnikovs with her, a box of hand grenades, one of ammunition, four pairs of trousers, four helmets and a horse to carry it all.

How many were there? asks her mother. Four, says Shirin-Gol's sister, lowering her eyes.

I want to go, too, calls Shirin-Gol two weeks later, when her sister and now the next eldest paint their lips red again and go back into the village. No, you don't, says the eldest, draws a knife from under her skirt, holds it to Shirin-Gol's breast, looks her straight in the eyes and asks, or would you dare to carve up Russian soldiers?

I want to go, too, calls Shirin-Gol a few weeks later, when the two elder sisters and Mole-sister as well, go back to the village and she herself does nothing but go to the field, sweep the floor of the hut, cook meals, wash the blood from her sisters' clothes, keep an eye on the twins and comfort them when they crack their heads together.

You'll have to do that soon enough, says Mole-sister, looking Shirin-Gol in the eyes, chokes back her tears, kisses her on the forehead, pulls her veil over her face and vanishes into the village.

But I want to go now, Shirin-Gol complains, crouching over the washing bowl when her sisters come back in the evening and throw their bloody frocks into the soapy water, sending the water and the bubbles jumping into the air, drenching Shirin-Gol. The sisters pay no attention to Shirin-Gol, sigh wearily, squat down and sort and hide the Russian Kalashnikovs, ammunition, hand grenades, mines, boots, helmets and whatever else they have taken from the Russian soldiers.

It was only two this time, says one sister.

They were careful, says the other. Word has gone around about how dangerous it is to go into the villages and violate Afghan women. Thanks be to Allah. They're frightened.

Frightened? The Russian soldiers? The enemies of the homeland, of the Prophet, of the Koran, of Islam and freedom? Who turned her brother into a *shahid* in a hole in the ground? The men in the uniforms, with the heavy boots, with the rifles, the mines, are frightened of her sisters? Fairy tales, the sisters are inventing them to make themselves important and Shirin-Gol envious.

Shirin-Gol creeps secretly behind her sisters, sees everything with her own eyes. But only years later will she understand that they weren't fairy tales.

Her brothers, her father, the other men from the village are in the mountains fighting against the Russians and the government soldiers. Other Russian soldiers come into the villages, plunder, rob, steal, carry off women and even little girls.

The soldiers are still boys themselves, eighteen, nineteen, twenty years old, no notion of life, of war, of killing – let alone of being killed.

Two days before they were still in their barracks, in Kazakhstan, Leningrad, Uzbekistan, slurping borscht from metal bowls and writing letters to their mothers and the girls who promised to wait for them until they were released from military service, until they came home and married them.

The call comes suddenly, as it always does, boots on, combat pack on their backs with Kalashnikov, ammunition and helmet, lashing everything down, with stamping boots, into the plane, flying in darkness, seeing nothing, believing they're being flown to Siberia or somewhere, to shovel coal or whatever. Disembarking, with no idea where they are.

Nothing but mountains all around, pitilessly rocky, unimaginably high. Snow-covered, the massif of the Hindu Kush soars into the sky. How much is seven thousand metres? Who are the Mujahedin? How many of them have hidden out in the mountains, what have they done to us, why are we killing them, why are they enemies of the Soviet people, of the Socialist Party? How many enemies have we killed already, how many more will we have to kill, how long are we staying, why can't I send that letter to my mother?

Hashish and opium silence the questions, the anxiety, the hunger. Afghan girls with black hair that looks like silk, eyes like coals, big white teeth like pearls, soft lips like plums awaken lust, assuage sad, young Russian hearts.

What they don't get given freely they take by force. Afghan food, clothes, money, Afghan women, girls, the honour of Afghan men, fathers, sons, the dignity and pride of the nation, faith and trust in God.

Russian boys in uniform obey orders, overcome fear, perform military rituals, muster courage, demonstrate power, strength and superiority. They fall upon villages, carry off women, rape, cut breasts off, carve stomachs open, sling foetuses into the sand with a slap. They part children's necks from children's bodies, kiss girls' mouths, lick girls' stomachs, grab girls' breasts, satisfy young Russian cocks in virgin Afghan vaginas.

Afghan teachers, peasants, shoemakers, butchers, bakers, tradesmen, pupils and students become freedom fighters, take to the mountains, kill, are killed, lay mines before they step on one themselves, carve up Russian soldiers before they themselves are carved up.

The Afghans call it 'taking off their shirts' when they cut around the waists of the Russians and pull the skin over their heads, leaving the skinned men in the sun, that the Afghan flies can feast upon their exposed red Russian flesh.

In Kazakhstan, Leningrad and Uzbekistan, the Russian mother feels a pang in her heart, two weeks later a letter arrives, an officer, two soldiers, a zinc coffin: Do not open.

Everything is different in war, things are permitted that are forbidden by faith and tradition, ancient values and personal morality, things are permitted that only death would otherwise atone. Unveiled, red-lipped, well-behaved Afghan girls sit in the corner, in the place where the Russians have occupied an Afghan hut, smoking a gift of hashish, losing their senses, bereft of all desire save for one thing, the giggling, nudging girls with their kohl-rimmed eyes and bodies that no man has ever seen, let alone touched.

From her hiding place Shirin-Gol sees it with her own eyes, hears it with her own ears, but still can't believe it. Befogged Russian boys stare with their blue eyes at her unveiled sisters, slaver, lecherously lick their lips, stretch out their hands, lay them on her sisters' breasts, grasp her sisters' hips, kiss her sisters' necks, pull her sisters' backsides to them, groaning ever louder, saying words in a language that Shirin-Gol doesn't understand.

A cry, not of satisfaction but of death. A carved-up Russian boy in uniform lies at her sister's feet, bent double and wriggling, tries to pull the knife from his stomach, hasn't the strength, claws his bloody hand into her sister's skirt, begs for mercy with his blue Russian eyes and gets it.

After all, he is only a human being with a mother waiting somewhere on this goddamn earth for her son to come back, her sister says, wiping tears from her kohl-rimmed Afghan eyes. Bending over the dying man she pulls the knife from his stomach and frees him from his torments. With a quick slice to the throat.

For freedom, for honour, for faith and with the aim of staying alive herself.

Even after twenty years or more these images have still not fled, they lie heavy and blood-red in Shirin-Gol's heart and won't let her forget.

Since those days Shirin-Gol's Mole-sister has had *djinn*, evil spirits, in her body. She will be sitting somewhere peacefully, talking, eating, cooking, washing or just staring ahead when she will suddenly start gulping for air, start screaming and crying. She gets yellow foam around her mouth, clenches her teeth together so hard they crack, and she pulls her hair out.

Another one driven mad by war, the people say.

Even Shirin-Gol's father knew what his daughters did for honour, for their homeland, the Prophet, the Koran and Islam. With the passing of the years he spoke less and less until he was finally mute, until he stopped talking altogether. Never again, to no one. He never looked anyone in the eye again, not his daughters or his sons, not even his wife.

Chapter Two

A NAKED WOMAN, A LETTER, A WORD AND A LITTLE FREEDOM

The twins are still wetting themselves, still nursing, still crouching in Shirin-Gol's skirts, still having titbits stuffed in their mouths. They've been talking for a long time now, saying words and whole sentences, bread, water, hungry, Shirin-Gol, give me that, leave me alone, come here, go away, tired, carry me and lots more, when Shirin-Gol's life changes once again. The sun is just casting its first light over the top of the hill above the village, the weapons of the Mujahedin, the brothers and fathers of the village and the Russians are silent in the mountains, the cock is crowing, one of the twins presses his little, sleeping, rigid body against his sister's, the other twin places his hand tenderly on his sister's cheek, when a deafening explosion tears through Shirin-Gol's sleep and the silence of the early morning.

A moment later the sky is full of roaring, humming, massive iron birds whose like Shirin-Gol has never seen before.

God has sent the flying monsters, her mother says, to punish us for our sins.

What sins? asks Shirin-Gol.

They aren't birds or monsters, the older brother says, they're Russian helicopters and they're called Antonovs.

Antonov, Shirin-Gol whispers. A pretty name, what a shame they're so coarse and horrible.

From her hut, set outside the village, Shirin-Gol watches the fire-spewing, horrible monsters with the pretty name flying low over the village, wheeling in a broad arc and coming back, flying lower and lower, so close you could touch them, with fire-spitting metal rods that make a horrendous din. In less time than it would take to say half a prayer, all the mud huts are in ruins, and more than half the village population have been turned into martyrs.

Shirin-Gol, the twins, her mother, the brother who had emerged from her mother's stomach shortly before Shirin-Gol and her three sisters, all grab as many of their things as they can carry and flee into the mountains. From there they watch the Russians descending on one side of the village in tanks, trucks, jeeps and on foot, killing anything or anyone left alive, setting everything alight and leaving on the other side.

Shirin-Gol, the twins and the rest of the family scrabble a hole in the ground and hide the Russian Kalashnikovs, rifles, mines, helmets and everything else that has to stay here. Shirin-Gol wonders whether the rifles and everything else that has to stay here are martyrs as well, finds no answer, hurries not to be left behind and heads north towards Kabul, the capital, with the others.

Where is Kabul? Why Kabul? Why not to the south? Why not to the east, to the west, back to the village? Why not build the huts back up again? Why? Why this, why that?

Be quiet, order her brothers, her father, her mother, when Shirin-Gol asks.

Be quiet, orders Shirin-Gol when the twins ask.

*

Noise and hubbub and asphalt, stone houses the size of mountains, people in a hurry, cars belching black smoke, stinking air, dirty trees, unveiled women, bare-armed girls, boys shouting stupid mountain people and meaning Shirin-Gol and her family. Shirin-Gol's father, who is suddenly shrunken and smaller than he was in the mountains of home, lowers his eyes in shame. Shirin-Gol's brothers picking up stones and dropping them again. Shirin-Gol's sisters, peering secretly out from under their veils. Shirin-Gol's mother, smacking them on the back of the head with the palm of her hand – Kabul, the capital.

Russian administration. Shirin-Gol cannot believe her eyes. But she can see it right there in front of her. A woman, an Afghan woman, her hair back-combed and as much paint on her face as if she were a bride, sits unveiled opposite her father. The skin and flesh of her arms and legs, her neck, are bare and visible to all. She doesn't lower her gaze, she looks Shirin-Gol's father straight in the eyes, addresses him directly so that her teeth and her tongue can be seen, asks him a thousand and one questions that have nothing to do with her.

Questions to which she gets lies in reply. Profession? Farmer. No, he's never fought in the mountains. Mujahed? What's that? Russians? Good people, here to help the homeland. Money? No, nothing. Possessions? None.

The only true words her father utters that day are when he says that neither he nor his wife and none of their children can read or write.

The naked woman gives Shirin-Gol's shrunken father a piece of paper and says the laws of the new government state that all men, even Shirin-Gol's father and her brothers, must report immediately to the nearest headquarters, to enter the service of the noble army, it is the prime task of every patriotic Afghan to fight for the father-land against all enemies of the state and resistance fighters. In addition, it is the duty of every Afghan, man or woman, old or young, to join the honoured and beloved, newly founded People's Party. Further, the laws of the new government decree that anyone seeking lodging or a tent must send his children to school, anyone who wishes to eat must send his children to school.

In short, anyone who doesn't want to go to prison has to join the army and the Party and send his children to school and also forbid his wife and his daughters to wear the whole-body veil in public.

Shirin-Gol feels dizzy under her cloth, and she is glad that the naked woman can't see her face, or she would probably be sent straight to jail. Shirin-Gol waits excitedly to hear what her father will reply to the naked woman's blasphemous and outrageous words. But her father says nothing. He rises from his chair, knocks it over, not being used to chairs, and starts to go. Just like that. Without punishing the naked woman with so much as a harsh word for her brazen godlessness.

And then something happens that makes Shirin-Gol think she's imagining and possibly dreaming it all. The naked woman gets up, holds out her hand, looks her father in the eye, holds her hand outstretched in the air until her father holds out his hand in turn and actually briefly touches the naked woman's finger-tips.

Shirin-Gol utters a faint cry, gets a slap on the back of the head from her mother, hurries to pull the twins under her cloth so that at least their innocent, childish eyes are not forced to look upon the incredible things that are happening there, but it is too late, they've seen everything, and will clearly remember the naked woman, and talk about her, for a long time to come.

School? says Shirin-Gol's father when they are back in the noisy, dirty, crowded, stinking street, and spits. His spittle doesn't drain away, it stays where it is on the hard, grey ground called asphalt. While Shirin-Gol is looking at her father's spittle to see what will happen to it her father says, Army? Never. I'm going back into the mountains and my daughters aren't going to go to school. It's the devil's work. These infidels want to dishonour us. Girls who go to school become confused and curious, they know too much, they get greedy, they start demanding things, they become choosy, and what kind of man is going to marry a woman like that? And in the end, Allah is my witness, these infidels only want to steer us from the right path, stuff our heads full of this godless nonsense, destroy our dignity and our faith and turn our daughters into what that, that, that . . . Her father can't find the word, but goes on, then her father finds the word and says, that WHORE? Never.

Disgrace and shame, a hundred times shame, God damn all infidels, Shirin-Gol murmurs under her cloth, and she almost feels ill at the idea of having to go to school, to end up like the naked woman.

What is school, in fact? What is a whore? Shirin-Gol bites her lips, shuts her eyes, prays to her God to protect her from that terrible fate. Shirin-Gol is about to say something, maybe something along the lines of, I'd rather be dead than end up like the naked woman, or, I'm going back into the mountains to kill Russians, but then she keeps her mouth shut after all, because her father is so worked up that she'd probably get a clip around the ear for daring to raise her girlish voice, unasked and in public, and say what she thinks.

*

The place where Shirin-Gol, the twins and the rest of the family are staying is made of stone, the walls and the floor are smooth and cold. There's a button on the wall that you can press, then a globe under the ceiling lights up and makes more light than four oil lamps. The room has two doors, one takes you out on to the street, the other takes you to a tiny room with a hole in the floor. To her horror Shirin-Gol learns that the hole is there for you to do your business in.

Gradually Shirin-Gol starts to feel sorry for the people who have to live in the city. It's really incredible, the women run about naked and half-naked, the streets are so hard that your feet hurt, the men's spittle lies where it falls, it stinks, it's noisy, and on top of everything you're supposed to piss and shit where you sleep and eat and spend your days and nights?

Shirin-Gol keeps a tight grip on the hands of the twins, stays by the door and waits to go back to the mountains. But instead of going, her mother spreads out the blankets on the cold, hard floor, her sisters make a little fire, her brothers go out with a pot, fetch water, someone makes tea, someone else unpacks the dry bread, everyone eats, her mother clears everything aside, one by one they lie down and they all sleep.

During the night Shirin-Gol has a dream. She dreams her brothers were wrong and the Russian helicopters weren't helicopters but wonderful Antonov birds that didn't fire fire-spewing rods. In the fat belly of the Antonov birds there are little sheep that the birds give Shirin-Gol, and deposit in the field in front of her hut. Little white sheep with soft, fluffy wool that tickles when Shirin-Gol cuddles them. Little white sheep that grow into big sheep and give milk. Milk that her sisters can turn into cheese. Milk that Shirin-Gol can drink. Little white sheep that you can eat.

A shame it was only a dream, thinks Shirin-Gol when she wakes up.

On the third or fourth day in the capital a man in uniform comes to see them and talks to Shirin-Gol's father outside the door. Four days later another man in uniform comes, but this time he doesn't talk, he shouts at her father behind the door. There's a rustling noise in the night, and in her half-sleep Shirin-Gol hears voices. In the morning when she wakes up her elder brothers aren't there, her father isn't there, her elder sisters aren't there, even Mole-sister has disappeared. They've all gone back to the mountains to do what Shirin-Gol can never mention to a soul because her mother would tear out her tongue and God the merciful would blind her.

There is a knock at the door, Shirin-Gol gives a start, a woman in uniform comes in, talks to her mother, sits down on the floor with Shirin-Gol, her mother, the twins, smiles, takes the twins by the hand, gestures to Shirin-Gol to follow her, politely bids her mother goodbye and goes into the street with the three children.

The woman in uniform is not as naked as the naked woman on the first day, but neither is she dressed like Shirin-Gol's mother, her sisters, herself and all the other women who have been in Shirin-Gol's life so far.

Nonetheless, at least the half-naked woman covers her hair with a headscarf, her face isn't painted, her arms are covered, her skirt is long enough to cover her knees, she wears stockings, flat shoes, she keeps her head bowed, doesn't look men in the eyes in the street, makes way for them as one is supposed to do, stepping to one side if they walk towards her. When she looks at Shirin-Gol and the twins she always smiles. That's good, because at least it makes Shirin-Gol and the twins a little less frightened.

The half-naked woman with the pretty smile is called Fawzi, she is a teacher and Shirin-Gol will be seeing her every day from now on.

That is your school, says Fawzi, that is your classroom, those are your fellow pupils. You can keep your shoes on, take your veil off, sit down over there where there's a space free, no, not on the floor, there on the bench, this is an exercise book, this is a textbook, this is a pencil, this is a letter: Sh, the beginning of your name.

Sh-i-r-i-n-G-o-l, Sweet Flower.

W-a-r.

M-u-j-a-h-e-d, no, not freedom fighter, resistance fighter. Enemies of the people. Enemies of the Party and the honourable government.

We live in Kabul, the capital of Afghanistan. Kabul is 3,500 years old. More than a hundred and fifty years ago the British tried to conquer our country, they tried over and over again, and over and over again they were forced back by the brave men and women of our country. Now the freedom-loving people of the Russians have come to our aid.

This picture shows the honourable president and the father of our beautiful homeland.

Shirin-Gol sits up, opens her mouth, is about to speak, falls silent and thinks, my father's name is . . . he is . . .

S-i-l-e-n-t.

L-y-i-n-g.

F-e-a-r.

R-u-s-s-i-a-n-s.

N-a-k-e-d w-o-m-a-n.

*

Under no circumstances does Shirin-Gol want to become like the naked woman on the first day and all the other naked women she has seen on the street since then, but even worse than becoming a naked woman would be not going to school and going to jail for it. So Shirin-Gol tries as best she can to follow Fawzi's instructions and do her best by her teacher, so as not to end up in jail. Because she knows one thing very well, and that is that in jail people have their tongues torn out, their fingernails torn out, their arms and legs drilled through with hot metal rods, their fingers cut off, the bones in their arms and legs broken, their stomachs run through, their teeth knocked out, their eyes ripped out.

Every free minute Shirin-Gol squats somewhere, usually by the door to the room that she shares with the twins and her mother, reading, writing, practising words and sentences.

In the next room another girl lives with her mother, her other brothers and sisters, but without her father and older brothers who have also stayed behind in the mountains, but she cannot talk about that because her mother, like Shirin-Gol's, would tear out her tongue and Almighty God would rip out her eyes.

The girl is called Malalai and apparently she doesn't care that much if her mother tears her tongue out and Almighty God rips out her eyes, because she does the thing that's forbidden and tells Shirin-Gol about her father and the older brothers who have gone back into the mountains, joined the Mujahedin, and are now fighting. Against the damned Russians and the damned puppet government of Taraki and all the presidents after him who all have some name or other but all want the same thing, to betray the beloved homeland to the Russians, and hand it to them on a plate.

How do you know all that, and how come you have the courage to talk like that, aren't you frightened? asks Shirin-Gol, wide-eyed.

No, I'm brave, my name is Malalai, says the girl, stretching her thin body as though to show Shirin-Gol her little sprouting breasts, and then she asks, do you know who Malalai was?

Shirin-Gol shakes her head and looks at the floor.

She was a heroine, says Malalai, an Afghan heroine. And it is important that we should know who she was.

Again Shirin-Gol says nothing and just nods.

Malalai killed the cruel king, says Malalai and pauses to enjoy the effect of her important words. Shirin-Gol raises her eyes, looks at Malalai and can't believe what the girl is telling her.

A woman killed a man, a king? Why did she do that? asks Shirin-Gol, and how did she do it?

Malalai is pleased. Well, she replies, it wasn't easy, but she was a brave, strong woman, braver than all the men and all the warriors and even stronger than the cruel king.

Malalai points to the hill on the other side of the canal and asks, you see the wall?

Shirin-Gol sees the wall and wonders why, before today, she hasn't ever noticed such a long wall, which snakes its way all the way up the hill to the top.

Malalai opens her school book and says, here, look. It's written down here. The story of brave Malalai.

I cannot read, says Shirin-Gol, feeling ashamed and looking back down at the floor.

It doesn't matter, says Malalai, you will learn. If you want I can read you the story of Malalai.

Shirin-Gol does, and Malalai reads.

The cruel king is afraid of his enemies, of which he has

many, and wants to protect himself against them. So he engages all the men of Kabul to build this high, thick wall around the city for his protection. And he instructs his soldiers to kill any man who drops so much as a handful of mud on the ground. Malalai, who has married the previous night, puts on her husband's clothes in the morning and goes to the mud wall in his place.

Why did she do that? asks Shirin-Gol.

Because her husband was exhausted, replies Malalai.

Why was he exhausted, asks Shirin-Gol.

That's obvious, replies Malalai, he was the bridegroom and he was exhausted by his wedding night.

Shirin-Gol doesn't dare to ask why the bridegroom was exhausted but the bride wasn't.

The cruel king, Malalai reads on, comes to the wall every day to see how the men are working, whether they are working hard and fast enough with the building of the wall. When he comes to the hill on the morning when Malalai is building the wall in place of her husband, and notices that in spite of her man's clothes she is a woman, he is astonished and starts shouting, what is a weak woman doing working on his wall with her unclean hands? Malalai, brave Malalai, stands in front of the king and asks him, what advantage do these men have over us women? They are just as weak and cowardly as we are. If they were brave, would they simply put up with your injustices and cruelties, without standing up for themselves? The men hear what Malalai says and are insulted. No woman has ever humiliated them like this before. The men of Kabul won't have that, and want to prove that they are by no means as weak and cowardly as Malalai claims. The men summon all their courage, hurl themselves at the king, kill him and bury him under his own mud wall. The mud wall of Kabul.

A king is buried under the wall? Where? At what point in the wall? What became of Malalai? Why did the men go on building the wall anyway? Shirin-Gol doesn't know which of her thousand and one questions to ask first. Shirin-Gol isn't quite sure whether or not to believe her neighbour. How could Shirin-Gol know whether it is all written in the book? Maybe Malalai only made up the story of brave Malalai who killed the king to make herself look important. But whether she made it up or not, Shirin-Gol likes Malalai's story and regrets that Afghan history has no heroine with the name Shirin-Gol.

Are you as brave as that heroine? asks Shirin-Gol, filled with admiration.

Of course I am, replies Malalai, maybe I'll be a heroine too, one day, and kill a cruel king. She stretches again, shows off her girlish breasts and says, all Malalais are brave.

You're lucky, says Shirin-Gol.

Malalai has been in the city for months, she likes going to school, likes learning words, likes learning to write, read and do sums. In the morning she knocks on Shirin-Gol's door with a cheerful smile, collects her and the twins, takes them by the hand and walks to school with them. That is to say that Malalai actually skips rather than walking, past strange people, women, men, soldiers, tanks, trucks, past the canal, that gleams and glitters in the sun, past calling tradesmen, shops selling colourful fabrics, men beating pots from metal so that it sounds like a thousand songs, past shops with sacks full of rice, wheat, lentils, beans, past men selling herbs, powders and spices in all colours and fragrances that enchant Shirin-Gol's senses, past horse-drawn coaches with ringing bells, past brightly coloured coaches in gleaming colours, past horses proudly raising their heads and whinnying, past hooting cars, past pigeons pecking at grains on the ground and flying up when Shirin-Gol, the twins and Malalai reach them, past all that and much else besides, which will soon be a familiar and much-loved sight for her as well.

During her years in the city Shirin-Gol comes to understand that she is still a child, and that children's lives involve lots of things of which she has been completely unaware. The most important are: playing, not only with girls but with boys too, being allowed to speak un-prompted, running, jumping, not wearing a veil, not always holding your little brothers and sisters by the hand or in your arms or clinging to your apron strings, singing, being silly, shouting. Shirin-Gol enjoys being a child and would like to stay that way for ever.

C-h-i-l-d, g-i-r-l, writes Malalai.

C-h-i-l-d, g-i-r-l, writes Shirin-Gol.

F-r-e-e-d-o-m, writes Malalai

F-r-e-e-d-o-m, writes Shirin-Gol, thinking that it's a par-ticularly pretty word and making it her favourite. آزادی

Shirin-Gol learns that one and one is two, two and two are four. She learns that money is valuable and that you can buy things with it, she learns that there are countries that are far, far away, further than she can imagine.

Shirin-Gol stands in front of the class and sings a song with her beautiful, deep, full, soft voice, and the other girls and boys clap. Shirin-Gol draws a word on the board, the chalk squeaks and screeches, making her skin retract and odd little bumps appear on it. Shirin-Gol dips the rag in water and wipes the board clean. Shirin-Gol opens her exercise book, writes words on an empty page, white as the flower of a lily. Shirin-Gol recites a poem in which she sings the praises of her homeland, the Party and the father of the nation, and gets a medal fastened to her chest, and the other children clap. Shirin-Gol learns that there is always a man who is the head of the country, who promises to bring freedom for everyone, and that he used to be called Noor Mohammad Taraki, then Babrak Karmal, then Hafizulla Amin – or was it Karmal first and then Amin? Then he was called Haji Mohammad Chamkani, then Mohammad Najibullah. At any rate there is always some man who promises to bring freedom.

Come with me, says Malalai, smiling, we are going to the lake.

We? Who's we?

The boys and me and you.

For the first time in her life Shirin-Gol is going somewhere without the twins. For the first time in her life she does not tell her mother where she's going. For the first time in her life she lies to her mother. For the first time in her life she drives in a car, called a taxi. For the first time she sits next to a boy who is neither her brother nor her father.

Shirin-Gol lies on her back, her bare feet playing in the water of the lake. She looks into the blue sky, hums a song, falls silent, listens to the silence, feels the boy's hand next to hers, feels her girlish heart leaping in her girlish body, losing her girlish breath, blood flooding her stomach, then her head, her girlish breasts stiffening. Shirin-Gol's uncovered head lies next to the boy's head, she looks into his beautiful, dark, hot eyes, breathes his name, gives a start when she hears her own voice, jumps up, giggles, runs into the water, her skirt gets wet, her legs get wet, she cools her hands, scoops water, drinks from the cool lake.

Shirin-Gol doesn't remember the boy afterwards, but she does remember the lake, the blue, the thin, cool air, the clear view over the calm water, in the distance the mountains, the song of the birds, the cool air under the fir trees, the taste of the fresh lake water in her mouth and the way it runs down her throat, reaches her stomach, cools her from within. Shirin-Gol remembers the wind blowing through her hair, she remembers knowing how unique, valuable and forbidden this moment is. All that and much else remain in Shirin-Gol's memory.

And she also knows that she thought, God has seen me, he's gone to my brother and told him everything that happened that afternoon. That I was at that lake with a boy, and my stomach twisted and turned. That I was barefoot and had my sleeves rolled up. That I lay down before the eyes of a strange boy, stretched myself out. That my skirts and legs got wet. God saw all that and told my brother all about it, because otherwise there is no explanation for what happened the next day.

Chapter Three

SHIRIN-GOL AND MORAD

Shirin-Gol tries to avoid her mother's reproachful, sceptical looks, pulls on her school uniform as quickly as she can, doesn't plait her hair all over again from the start as she usually does, puts on her headscarf without argument, ignores the hot, fresh, tea and the dry breakfast bread left over from the previous evening, the bread that glues your tongue to your palate, runs to the door, pulls it opens, yells at the twins to get a move on, slips quickly into her shoes, bends down to tie them, blood runs to her head, she remembers the lake and the boy, the unfamiliar, wonderful, forbidden feeling, she's ashamed, raises her blood-red head and looks into the face of a man who looks like the ones who stayed in the mountains, to fight for . . . for what was it again? Shirin-Gol cannot remember for the moment.

What is your name? the man asks, smiling into Shirin-Gol's blood-red face.

Shirin-Gol.

The man smiles and asks kindly, where are you going?

Nowhere, says Shirin-Gol and smiles back.

Where is nowhere? asks the stranger.

School, says Shirin-Gol, regretting that she hasn't plaited her hair.

The man just goes on looking at her and doesn't say a word. Somehow Shirin-Gol likes him.

Who are you? she asks, looking him straight in his beautiful, honey-brown eyes like soft, tender winters in the mountains at home.

Morad.

Morad, a wish, that's a nice name. What is your wish and your desire, why are you here? asks Shirin-Gol.

Nothing, says Morad and smiles.

There is no such thing as nothing, Shirin-Gol replies, giggles, darts a startled glance at her mother, who does not see that she is giggling, and asks, what do you want from me?

How do you know I want something from you? asks Morad.

I just do, replies Shirin-Gol.

Your brother sent me, says Morad.

More blood shoots into Shirin-Gol's head, making her dizzy. Her knees turn to jelly and she thinks, another *shahid*?

My brother? she whispers, startled. Silence. Just don't say anything right now. Not here in front of my mother and the children.

The twins stand on either side of Shirin-Gol, staring at the stranger, look inquisitively at their sister, pull on her skirt. Let's go, they say.

You go on ahead, says Shirin-Gol and pushes them outside. I'll catch you up.

No, they say, you've got to come too.

No, says Shirin-Gol, you go and I'll catch you up.

No, say the twins and stay where they are.

You come too, says Shirin-Gol to Morad, pushing him into the street, takes the twins by the hand as she does every morning, and the four of them set off.

Shirin-Gol does not take her eyes off Morad for a moment, nor he his eyes off her.

Wait here, Shirin-Gol says to Morad when they reach the school. She takes the twins inside, then comes back out to Morad. Now, she says, you can tell me. Why has my brother sent you?

Let's go, says Morad.

What has happened? Has someone died? Been hurt? Wounded? Tell me. Say something.

No, Morad says reassuringly, nothing serious, do not worry. I bring good news.

Shirin-Gol wipes the sweat from her brow with the end of her headscarf, takes a deep breath, walks behind Morad and hopes he is telling the truth.

By the time they are near the bazaar Shirin-Gol cannot bear it any longer. I don't feel well, I've got to sit down, will you please tell me why my brother has sent you?

Morad takes a cloth from his pocket, brushes the dust from a stone at the edge of the street, puts the cloth on the stone, says sit down, squats down himself in front of Shirin-Gol, looks at her for a long time, smiles, gently touches the back of her hand with his finger as though it was a butterfly, and repeats, kindly and still with a beautiful smile on his full lips, your brother sent me.

You've said that before, Shirin-Gol insists, looking at her hand as though the strange man's finger had left a trace.

A Morad-trace on the back of her hand.

Your brother and I fought together, says Morad, inflating his chest. We fought in the unit under the command of the brave Massud, the Lion of Panj Shir, the Valley of the Five Lions.

Yes, says Shirin-Gol, you all fight in some unit or other.

Your brother and I became friends, says Morad. For a few years we fought side by side, then I said I don't want to fight any more, I want to get married. Your brother and I played cards, he lost, he had no money to pay the debts he had with me, he said, you want to get married, I have lots of sisters. And then he said that instead of getting the money I should marry one of his sisters. And I asked him which of his sisters he liked best, and then he said he liked Sweet Flower best, and I said, then I'll marry Sweet Flower.

He likes me best? I had no idea, says Shirin-Gol without looking at Morad, and with her finger she draws words in the dust of the street, l-i-k-e-s m-e b-e-s-t.

He does, says Morad, and absently erases what she has scribbled on the ground. And now I've come to marry you.

I don't know whether I want to get married, says Shirin-Gol, looking at Morad.

Your brother decided you would, says Morad, still smiling.

Shirin-Gol says nothing and looks at the rubbed-out dust in the street.

Some people have given me the name of a mullah. They say he doesn't need much money and he'll marry us. It isn't far from here and we are going there now.

Now?

Now or later, what difference does it make? asks Morad.

None, replies Shirin-Gol, no difference at all.

Two hours later Shirin-Gol and Morad are back sitting somewhere near the bazaar, once again Shirin-Gol draws words in the dust of the street, once again Morad smiles when he talks, everything is as it was two hours before, except that Shirin-Gol and Morad are married now. Once again Shirin-Gol thinks it makes no difference, no difference at all.

What else has my brother told you? she asks.

Your brother said you were the strongest of all your sisters.

S-t-r-o-n-g-e-s-t, writes Shirin-Gol in the dust of the street. Did he also tell you that I have defied my father's prohibition and gone to school?

No, he didn't say that, Morad replies, and for the first time he does not smile.

Those are words, you see? That's M-o-r-a-d.

So you can write and read as well?

Bale. Albatah. Yes. Of course.

I did not know that, says Morad, looking at what she has scribbled in the dust of the street. People say that girls who can read and write are cheeky and uppity. People say the more a girl knows the more a girl wants. They say that girls who go to school are not happy with anything or anyone. People say those girls do not respect their husbands. People say girls who have been to school are not to be trusted.

Shirin-Gol looks at Morad, smiles and says, I used to think that if I didn't go to school they would send me to jail. And I thought if I went to school I'd be a naked woman.

Naked woman? Who's that?

Shirin-Gol thinks for a moment, looks at Morad, says, it's . . . oh, I don't know, it's nobody. N-o-b-o-d-y, Shirin-Gol writes in the dust of the street.

Men do not want wives who are cleverer than they are, Morad says, looking down the street to the end of the bazaar.

Don't you want me any more? asks Shirin-Gol, wiping out the N-o-b-o-d-y in the dust of the street.

We are man and wife now, says Morad, smiling again, let's leave things as they are, and see how it all turns out.

Fine, says Shirin-Gol, let's leave things as they are, and see how it all turns out.

Two days later Shirin-Gol and Morad move into a room of their own. All in all life after the marriage is neither better nor worse than life before. Morad is nice to Shirin-Gol, and she no longer has to pay constant attention to the twins and listen to her mother's complaints about her awful life, the injustice of fate and all her illnesses and worries.

What are we going to live on? Shirin-Gol asks Morad one day.

That's not a question a woman should ask her husband, Morad replies.

Are you afraid of my questions?

It's not a question of fear, it's a question of honour. If you ask me what we're going to live on, you're telling me you're worried I will not be able to feed us.

Can you feed us?

I'll find work, Morad answers, don't worry. Earning money is man's work.

I want to keep on going to school, says Shirin-Gol.

That is out of the question, Morad replies, you're a married woman now, what would the neighbours think? From the very start it was a mistake for you to go to school, you see where it leads, school and all that stuff in your head have spoiled your character.

I want to be a doctor, says Shirin-Gol, without taking her eyes off her husband.

Morad smiles benignly, lights a cigarette, closes his eyes and dozes off.

Shirin-Gol sits down beside Morad, puts her hand on his arm, hums a song to herself, thinks, falls silent, sings again, falls silent, speaks in a deep, gentle voice. Morad opens his eyes, says nothing, blows the smoke of his cigarette into the room, looks benignly at Shirin-Gol, sometimes with his beautiful smile, sometimes without his smile, just listening.

Way back in the mountains, says Shirin-Gol, I sat by my corner in front of the hut, sure that the world was as big or as small as what I saw every day with my own eyes. All I knew was the hut, the open space in front of it, my washing bowl, the chickens, the two big trees on one side, the green of them, the rustling of the leaves in the wind. On the other side I could see the start of the path, the bushes, the big stone my mother sat on, the post the donkey, the cow and the sheep were tied to, and ahead of me in the distance I saw the peaks of the mountains. My mother, my father, my brothers and sisters lived in my big little world, and shortly after I started thinking, that is, after I had started understanding it all, learning what things were called, the twins came into my life.

At some point I understood that every day my brothers and my father left my world and did not come home until evening. So I realised that out there were other places in this world apart from my hut and the space in front of it.

Slowly, step by step, I dared to go out into that world and discovered the green, yellow, brown fields, the valley and the little sandy road. I saw that the mountains did not just consist of their peaks, and that they were far fatter at the bottom than at the top, that there were even more peaks than the one I had seen from my corner in front of the hut. I saw the big sandy road, the village, the desert, other people, strangers, friends, relations.

Then the Russians came, and I understood that there was another country apart from Afghanistan. Then we came to the capital. At first I was very afraid of this terribly big, noisy world full of hubbub and stench, full of people I didn't know, who were always in a hurry, who didn't look each other in the eye.

Shirin-Gol laughs, I was afraid of the naked women, afraid I would end up like them, afraid of ending up in jail. Time passed and I met Russians and came to understand that they are people like you and me. I learned that good and evil in people does not lie in whether they pray five times a day or cover their faces with cloths. I met women who were stronger and more intelligent than all the men I have ever known. I learned that women are no less valuable than men, and that they can do all things that men do.

Your head is full of Russian stuff, Morad says benignly, blowing out the smoke from his cigarette.

Shirin-Gol looks at her husband-of-a-few-days, smiles just as benignly as he does and says, call it what you will, what difference does it make, the important thing is that I have seen and learned all that, it is in my head, and I don't want to give it up again. I can't give it up. It is there. It has burned its way into my brain, ineradicably. Even if I wanted to, I wouldn't get it out of there. There is still so much in the world that I don't know, that I would still like to know. I want to see it, I want to smell it. Hear it. I want to put my feet on ground that I don't know. I want to hear voices I've never heard. Look into the eyes of people I don't know. I'd like to speak different languages, smell different air.

Morad looks at his wife-of-a-few-days, sees the sparks and life in her eyes, sits up, puts his hand on hers, feels his breath growing faster, feels something happening in him that he cannot control, something deep within him, a part of him that he no longer knows, which he remembers dimly, quietly, distantly from his childhood, growing a new life, running back and forth in his head, running in his stomach, a feeling of fear – of fear, but of pleasure, too.

Morad, I have become your wife because it is what my brother wanted. Shirin-Gol looks straight into Morad's beautiful, honey-brown eyes, which recall soft, tender winters in the mountains of home, and says in a deep and peaceful voice full of tender love, not knowing where it comes from, Morad, I like you. I like you, not because someone tells me to, but because it is what I want. I have seen the goodness and intelligence in your eyes. Please Morad, don't say no, I would like to keep on going to school. But I would like to do it with your agreement.

Morad says nothing.

Morad, do you like me?

Bale.

Why do you like me?

Morad shrugs his shoulders.

Because I'm the way I am. And I'm that person because I have seen and learned everything that I have seen and learned. Because I go to school. Because that longing is on fire within me. Because I left the corner in front of the hut. Because I came out of the mountains. Because I want to be a doctor. Morad, you have fought in the mountains and helped and served our country, I would like to be a doctor and help and serve our country.

I want to go to sleep, says Morad.

Will you think about everything I've said? asks Shirin-Gol.

Bale.

Will we talk about it some more tomorrow? asks Shirin-Gol.

Bale.

Shirin-Gol takes off her headscarf, turns down the oil lap, blows out the flame, lies down next to her husband-of-a-few-days, puts her hand on his shoulder, lays her head on his manly heart, draws up her thigh, lays it on Morad's stomach, closes her eyes, smiles in the darkness and says, fine, let's talk about it tomorrow and see what happens.

During the night there is a hammering on the door. Shirin-Gol opens up. Four armed men in uniform want to take Morad away, he's to join the army. Shirin-Gol lies. Morad isn't there. The soldiers push Shirin-Gol aside, raise their voices, pull Morad from his covers, drag him out and say to Shirin-Gol, from today your husband is a soldier in the honourable army of our homeland, he will be deployed further up in the north to fight the Mujahedin, do not wait for him. You will not see him again before a year is up.

Thank God it is in the north, thinks Shirin-Gol, then at least he won't be fighting his brothers and mine, my father and his.

The next morning Shirin-Gol puts on her school uniform, plaits her hair again, ties on her headscarf, goes to school, sits down in her place, does not say that she has got married in the meantime, that she has become a woman in the meantime, learns what she can learn, reads what she can read, writes, does her sums, is moved up to the next class, her stomach grows fat, her mother pulls a child from her body. It is a girl. Shirin-Gol calls her her sunshine, Noor-Aftab. Four days after the birth of her first daughter Shirin-Gol goes back to school. A year later her daughter is already walking and saying her first words when the door opens and Morad comes in.

He embraces Shirin-Gol, kisses his daughter on the forehead, sits down in the corner, drinks tea, stares straight ahead, weeps, shakes, will not be calmed, sobs, stammers words, calms down, embraces Shirin-Gol again and again, leans his head against her powerful, strong girl-woman shoulder.

Tell me, says Shirin-Gol with a gentle, deep voice. What have they done to you? What has happened? Find words, tell me, share them with me and then I'll carry half of your pain for you, and it will only hurt half as much.

Morad looks at his young wife, wipes tears from his manly eyes and says, your brother wasn't lying, you are strong.

I am, says Shirin-Gol. You can depend on me. Now and for ever.

Have you been going to school?

Yes.

Listen closely. I have to go back in two days. And I want a promise from you.

Tell me what you want of me and I will see if I can give it to you, says Shirin-Gol.

I've been thinking about it, says Morad.

What?

You should become a doctor. A doctor or whatever else your heart desires.

Why? asks Shirin-Gol.

My Sweet Flower, my heart, my queen, because you were right. The only reason our own government was able to betray our country and us and sell it to the Russians – our misery, this war – all of that could only happen because we are stupid, because we know nothing, we understand nothing, we cannot read or write, we believe anyone who stands in front of us and comes out with clever stuff, holds a piece of paper and says this is the law from today onwards. We are a nation of the blind. Anyone can do what he likes with us. Push us in the pond, leave us standing somewhere, lead us astray, even kill us. Only one who can see knows where he is, and can make up his own mind whether he wants to be there, and he sees where he is going all by himself. You were right, Sweet Flower, you have always been right. For me it's too late, but I want you and my children to learn to read and write. I want them to learn to make their own minds up about what is good and what is evil, who is lying and who is telling the truth, who is an enemy and who is a friend.

Well spoken, says Shirin-Gol, kissing Morad on the forehead.

After two days and two nights, during which Shirin-Gol and Morad make love as they have never made love before and will never make love again, Morad is picked up in a Russian jeep and goes back into the mountains, in the north of the country, to go on fighting under the Russian command, against his own compatriots, the Mujahedin, against his brothers in faith, in a war that neither he nor they wanted, that neither he nor they started. For a victory that neither these nor those will have. For a goal that they can neither know nor understand. In a war that has been going on until the present day.

For two days and nights Shirin-Gol weeps over the fifteen, sixteen, or perhaps even only fourteen – who knows how many – years of her life, for the husband she has come to love, not knowing whether she will see him again, for her daughter, who doesn't know her father.

On the third day Shirin-Gol washes her swollen eyes,

puts on her school uniform, plaits her hair, puts on her headscarf, takes her daughter to her mother, goes to school, sits down in her place, reads, writes, does her sums and has a thousand and one questions that she does not ask.

Who benefits from this war? When will enough soldiers have been killed, skinned, chopped to pieces? Who will tell the mothers, wives and daughters of the soldiers what the soldiers' last words were? Who will hold the dying man's hand? Who will hold the hand of the grieving mother, wife, daughter? Who wins? And how much is it worth to the winner? Are there wars in all the countries of the world? Are children dying in all the countries of the world, becoming martyrs, breaking their mothers' hearts and turning their mothers' hair white?

Shirin-Gol, you have lost your happy smile, says Fawzi, the teacher. Your edge, the innocent glow in your eyes and the joy, your questions and your curiosity. You have become a woman.

Chapter Four

A Capitulation and the Departure of the Russians

Shirin-Gol, Malalai, the twins, other girls and boys, women, men, children, cripples, soldiers, one-armed and one-legged men, crazy people, starving people stand by the side of the street, with a red carnation in one hand and in the other a red paper flag that flaps in the wind making a clattering sound as if people were quietly applauding. Huge Russian tanks rattle past them, their heavy caterpillar tracks sending the street under Shirin-Gol's feet trembling. Russian tanks growl and spew black smoke on to Shirin-Gol's uncovered hair, Russian music wafts around her ears. Tired blue Russian soldier eyes gaze down at her, Russian soldier hands catch their red carnation, wave back with little Russian flags. The famed army of the peace-loving neighbour capitulates and leaves Shirin-Gol's homeland.

For ten years Russians, Georgians, Kazakhs and Kirghiz have been firing missiles, throwing bombs, laying mines, attacking villages. For ten years they have been killing Afghans and been killed in turn. For ten years Russian and Afghan mothers and women have wept for their sons, men, brothers, fathers. For ten years Shirin-Gol thought the Russians would never leave, the war would never come to an end.

Chapter Five

THE MUJAHEDIN, A BROTHER-WAR AND ANOTHER FLIGHT

I don't want to go anywhere, shouts Shirin-Gol. I want to stay here, wait for the father of my two children and become a doctor. She looks her mother straight in the eyes, even when *Madar* clips her around the ear for the second time. Shirin-Gol says nothing, packs everything together, apart from her own things, her son's and her daughter's.

You cannot stay, the war is raging, her mother cries.

Stupid, uneducated mother, the Russians have gone. The war is over.

Stupid little schoolgirl with no notion of life. You think what you have been through for the past ten years was war? There was war in the mountains. There was war in the villages. There was war in the desert. They have spared the capital so far. My poor little girl. You think the war is over? The war has only just started. Come with me. Do it for the sake of your two little innocent children. Don't be stupid, little Sweet Flower, pack your things. Let us go. I cannot manage on my own. I need you.

What do you need me for? Where are you going? Shirin-Gol asks her mother. If the war continues in the capital, it will continue in the mountains and everywhere else as well.

Just God in Heaven, her mother cries and tears at her hair, what are you doing to us? What are you planning for us? What will become of us?

Shirin-Gol takes her mother in her arms, gently strokes her back with a strong hand. *Madar*. Poor, dear *Madar*. Calm down. I'm here. God is great. He will sort it out. Everything will be fine. The war is over. Believe me. You do not understand. You have only ever been here in your four walls. Everyone out there knows. The Russians have gone. We are free. Life is going to start now. The war is over.

Shirin-Gol unpacks her mother's things again, the twins put their school uniforms on, go to school, Shirin-Gol's daughter sits in the corner of the room, her brother is lying in her lap, Shirin-Gol lays damp cloths on her mother's feverish brow, hums a tune, smiles and wonders why the weapons outside aren't falling silent, now the war is over.

Even the next day, the day after that and for many days to come the room of the door stays shut. The twins have stopped going to school, Shirin-Gol has stopped going to school. There is a knock at the door, neighbours asking for tea, wheat, bread, the shops have shut. There is gunfire out there, worse than ever. There is another knock at the door at dead of night, brave Malalai slips inside, says, we are going to leave the capital as soon as possible.

Shirin-Gol's uneducated mother, who knows nothing but the four walls of her room, who has only been in the street four times, no more, since she has been in Kabul, her mother who can neither read nor write, knew: in Kabul, the capital, the war is only just getting started.

On one side of the street some Mujahedin fighters fight, on the other side others. Everyone is fighting everyone else. Hekmatyar against Gailani, Ahmad Shah Massoud against Dostum, one Moslem brother against another.

Street battles, missile attacks, mines, tanks and once again people being sliced open, foetuses torn out and landing with a slap in the road, women being raped again, veils again, everything Shirin-Gol has seen before and much more, except that this time it is in the capital, except that this time everything is more pitiless, except that this time it is her own people, except that this time it is their own war. A brother-war.

What the Russians did not destroy the Afghan warlords turn to rubble and ashes. For years they fight until one day a new power, the Taleban movement, comes to the city. Najibullah, the feared former head of the secret police, is now the last president loyal to the Russians. Along with his brother he seeks sanctuary in the United Nations building. The Taleban pull both men out, beat them up, insult them, drag them through the streets. Najibullah and his brother are publicly spat upon and shot, their corpses are dragged through the city. The next morning the people see the dead bodies of their president and his brother hanging from a street post.

Shirin-Gol is lucky. By now she has been away from Kabul for ages, and does not see or experience any of this.

Shirin-Gol, her daughter Noor-Aftab, her first son Nasser, the twins, Shirin-Gol's mother, her neighbour Malalai, her mother, sisters and brothers, other girls and their mothers, sisters and brothers, grab together as much of their belongings as they can carry and flee where many of their compatriots have fled before them. To Pakistan. In cars, cabs, wheelbarrows, on horses, camels. Shirin-Gol, her daughter, her son, the twins, her mother on foot. They flee the bombs and missiles that Afghans are firing on Afghans in a cruel fraternal war between Ahmad Shah Massoud, Hekmatyar, Dostum, Khalili, Gilani and all the other leaders of the various groups of the Mujahedin. The women, children, men are fleeing unemployment and hunger, mines and gunfire, the danger of being robbed and raped.

By day helicopters fly and fire on anything that moves. By day the Mujahedin are on the move, taking tolls, sheep, blankets, food, boys who are old enough to fight, women, girls.

Leave us alone, cries Shirin-Gol, my father and my brothers are Mujahed as well.

Where are they? ask the bandits.

In the mountains.

What mountains?

Where the fighting is.

What side are they fighting on?

On the side of the fatherland, the Prophet, the Koran and Islam.

The men laugh, take what they want to take, disappear.

For days and weeks they wander through the desert, through villages, over mountains and through valleys, crossing dried-up riverbeds and mined fields. Time and again they have to hide from the Mujahedin sentries, but time and again they are stopped, they still have to pay tolls.

On one occasion a sentry wants money, then he says he wants Shirin-Gol. Her mother says, my daughter? You want my daughter? Take her. I'm giving her to you. She's mad. She's ill. You would be doing me a favour. Take her, says Shirin-Gol's mother and gives her such a shove that she falls at the Mujahed's feet. Shirin-Gol lies there on the ground, uttering peculiar noises and screaming, then claws her hand into the Mujahed's trousers and acts as though to pull herself up with them.

Repelled and horrified, the Mujahed kicks Shirin-Gol away, spits, wraps himself in his *patu* and disappears.

Shirin-Gol's mother kneels down on the ground beside her daughter, by now trembling with fear, wraps her in her arms, says nothing, just presses her tightly to her chest.

From now on the little trek of women and children only moves at night. By the twelfth night Shirin-Gol stops counting the days and nights. By the fourteenth she has lost the strength to go on. By the fifteenth, though, she is still dragging herself and her children onwards, and on all the nights that follow as well. They are walking on the same road, the same paths and byways as hundreds, thousands, millions of Afghans. For more than two decades, until the present day. The same paths and roads on which kings and warriors have led their armies. Darius, the king of the Persians. Alexander, the king of the Greeks. The Mongols were here, the British, the Russians, the Americans, Bin Laden was here, the KGB and the CIA and now Shirin-Gol and her family. It is the road that leads from Kabul towards Jalalabad and from there on in steep and narrow bends through the free Tribal Areas, across the legendary Khyber Pass to Pakistan.

The closer they come to the border, the more crowded the road becomes. On both sides there are cars, trucks, military transporters, the corpses of tanks. More and more people are climbing down the hills. Before the border, tradesmen have set up their stalls, some men are sitting behind glass boxes holding mountains of money that they are exchanging at extortionate rates. Others crouch by old containers, selling rope, tyres, iron, scrap, hubcaps, engine parts, car doors, glass, wood, planks, weapons.

Shirin-Gol cannot remember how she had imagined a border to be. Maybe she thought a border was a big clean house where you walk in, are handed a glass of tea, greeted warmly by the people of the other country and welcomed. Maybe she thought a border was a big, tall wall with a door. Maybe she thought a border was a barrier. At any rate, she did not think a border was two little towers with a gate in between. Although now that she is standing here she thinks it is actually very practical to turn a gate into a border. You can open and close it, go through it and come back again.

Shirin-Gol smooths her veil and her skirts, stuffs her hair under her cloth, smooths her children's clothes, stands upright and prepares to cross a border for the first time in her life.

On either side of the gate stand dark-skinned beardless men in pretty uniforms, with their caps set at an angle. They are wearing boots and holding sticks. With their sticks they lay into everyone who comes through the gate, driving him on to go faster. Shirin-Gol stands there for a while and watches her compatriots going through the gate to work out how quickly you have to walk to avoid being beaten. It doesn't seem to make any difference how quickly or how slowly you walk. It turns out that everyone who passes through the gate gets beaten.

You don't need to worry, Shirin-Gol's mother says to her children and grandchildren. Deep down they are good people. They are doing their duty. You'll see, it doesn't hurt. Look how thin their sticks are. You are not cowards. We've been through worse. We'll manage.

I don't want to go to Pakistan, says Shirin-Gol.

So where do you want to go? asks her mother.

The dark-skinned, thin-bodied soldiers, thinner and smaller than the men that Shirin-Gol has seen in her life so far, lash into Shirin-Gol, her daughter, her son, the twins, her mother, to hurry up, get out their money, clear the way. One of the men grabs Shirin-Gol by her backside, licks his lips, another laughs, pulls her to him, kicks her, shoves her away.

Pull your veil over your face, says the cheekier of the twins, crossly. Shirin-Gol obeys.

On the Pakistani side of the border it is as full and noisy as it is on the Afghan side.

Shirin-Gol, her children, her mother and the twins stand around, jump out of the way to avoid being driven over. People, compatriots, Afghans jostle her, shout at her to get out of the way, a soldier swishes his thin rod through the air so that it hisses.

A girl-woman of Shirin-Gol's age, who has two daughters about the same age as Shirin-Gol's children, stops and asks, what is your name?

Shirin-Gol.

Are those your children?

Yes, answers Shirin-Gol, and that is my mother, and those are my brothers.

Come here, Shirin-Gol, if you stand around in the way like that you'll get beaten or run over by a car. Come on, sit with me in the shade. Is this your first time here? asks the girl-woman.

Yes.

Take off your *hejab* so I can see you, says the girl-woman, you are not in Afghanistan any more, no one here can force you to cover your face.

I know, says Shirin-Gol, pushes back her cloth and beams at the girl-woman. It's so full of people here, says Shirin-Gol. I have never seen so many people, so many trucks and cars in my life, not even in the capital.

I have been here lots of times, says the girl-woman,

putting one leg over the other. I have always gone back home again, then time and again something has happened and I have had to flee again. Sometimes from Afghanistan to Pakistan, then back from Pakistan to Afghanistan.

Shirin-Gol copies the girl-woman and puts one leg over the other, gets a jab in the ribs from her mother and puts both feet back on the ground.

The girl-woman throws back her head, laughs and says, the first time I fled I was fleeing from the Russians, I was still a little girl. Then people said life in Kabul wasn't bad and we went back. Then the Russians shot my father and we fled back here again. Then I got married and my husband said, we're going home. Then he stepped on a mine and was crippled, and after a few weeks he died. Then I fled back here again, and my husband's father took me as his wife, but he was so old that he soon died as well. My second husband's first wife, who had been my mother-in-law, and who saw me as a secondary wife when my father-in-law took me as his wife, didn't want me to stay in her house. She married me off to her youngest son, my first husband's brother, my second husband's son. He was a commander with the Mujahedin and brought me back to Afghanistan, but he himself went to the front. Then our village was attacked, everything was destroyed, and I had to flee again. I waited for my husband, but he didn't come. And when I had nothing more to eat, I fled back here, to Pakistan. The old woman, who was my mother-in-law first time around and who's now my mother-in-law all over again, still didn't want me in her house, and she didn't want my daughters either. She only took in my son, not my daughters or myself. That's why I came here, to the border. A hundred yards and a whole life away from home, I sit here hoping every day that my husband might come and find me.

What do you live on? asks Shirin-Gol.

I do this and that, to keep my children and myself from starvation.

What's this and that? asks Shirin-Gol.

This and that is this and that, says the girl-woman and smiles.

Do you make good money with this and that? asks Shirin-Gol.

The girl-woman laughs, so that Shirin-Gol can see her tongue, her teeth and the funny little tongue at the back of her throat, jumping back and forth. Look at me, says the girl-woman, I am beautiful, I am young and here at the border there are lots of Pakistani officials, lots of Afghan men. Men who have not had a woman's body for ages and whose mouths water when they see mine. By and large I earn enough, sometimes even more than enough.

Shirin-Gol opens her mouth and is about to say something, but spittle fills her throat and stays there. Shirin-Gol chokes and coughs.

The girl-woman looks at Shirin-Gol. She is not laughing and says, what am I supposed to do? Starve and let my children starve? Am I supposed to let us die?

Shirin-Gol looks at the ground, says nothing, her eyes are fixed on the bare feet of a girl walking past. The little girl is carrying a massive iron plate on her head, her felted hair pointing in all directions. Her clothes are in rags, and as she walks she sucks on her fingers, looks with dark eyes, neither happy nor sad, at each of them in turn, the girl-woman, Shirin-Gol, Noor-Aftab, little Nasser, Shirin-Gol's mother, the twins, and walks on.

The girl-woman puts her two daughters down next to Shirin-Gol, kisses them on the forehead and says, stay here with your auntie, I'll be back soon.

Before Shirin-Gol has grasped the girl-woman's intentions, she leaps to her feet and disappears behind one of the many tea-houses.

The two girls sit where they are, holding each other by the hand, and watch their mother go.

Shirin-Gol strokes them both on the head, pulls them closer to her and asks, what are your names?

They look at Shirin-Gol, smile, say nothing.

Are we staying here? asks Noor-Aftab, pushing her way in between the girls and her mother.

No, says Shirin-Gol, this isn't a place to stay.

By the love of God, this really isn't a place to stay, says Shirin-Gol's mother.

What are all those people carrying about? asks the shy twin.

It looks like rubbish, says Cheeky-twin.

People aren't stupid, says Shirin-Gol, why would they be carrying rubbish?

It's contraband, says the girl-woman, who has reappeared as suddenly as she vanished.

Contraband? asks Shirin-Gol.

The girl-woman laughs and repeats, contraband. Whatever people can carry they don't have to pay duty on. People carry oil, petrol, parts of cars, parts of tanks, tyres, opium, chickens, radios, cables, money, wheat, rice, fruit, just everything they can carry, from Afghanistan to Pakistan and sell it. They sell it to traders and they sell it on to other people. A man I know buys old iron, he sells it on to a third party who melts it down and casts new iron from it.

How much would you get for a plate like the one the girl in the green dress is carrying on her head? asks Shirin-Gol.

If you do that all day, says the girl-woman, by evening

you'll have earned enough to buy two or three loaves of bread and a pot of tea for yourself and your children.

That's sad, says Shirin-Gol.

It isn't sad, it's good. Lots of people get their stomachs filled with this kind of work, and we are grateful to the Pakistani border guards for letting us pass, says the girl-woman, looking towards the gate, where a girl is running past the border guards and getting a blow on her little backside from a soldier's rod. She pulls her backside in, still skilfully balancing the heavy load on her head, and walks on.

Who is the girl? asks Noor-Aftab.

An Afghan like you and me, answers the girl-woman.

What has she got on her head? asks Noor-Aftab.

However much Shirin-Gol concentrates, she cannot guess what the little girl is carrying on her head.

I don't know what she's carrying, says Shirin-Gol, whatever it is, it's incredibly heavy.

It's pretty, says Noor-Aftab. And then she says, I know what it is. She's carrying the crescent moon.

Shirin-Gol smiles, strokes her child's head and says, yes, maybe it is the crescent moon.

Shirin-Gol's mother says, she's a thin, little girl, with a thin, colourful, floating dress. She's carrying an enormous heavy monster on her head, and she comes from Afghanistan like us and she's going to Pakistan like us.

That's a lovely story, cries Noor-Aftab, tell some more.

It isn't a story, says her grandmother, and it isn't lovely either.

Go on anyway, pleads Noor-Aftab.

Shirin-Gol pulls her daughter on to her lap, smiles and tells the story. Fine, I think you're right. It is a crescent moon. It was daytime, the moon had nothing to do. He was getting bored. So he reached the edge of the great and infinite sky. He only really wanted to bend over the edge of the sky and look at us humans on the earth, when he slipped and fell down to earth. The girl found him, felt sorry for him, picked him up and put him on her head and now she is bringing him back to the edge of the sky, so that he can climb back in, rise back to the top and shine for us humans tonight. For you and for Nasser, for the twins, for grandma, for our new friend and her daughters, for her son and her husband and all the good people and the believers and the non-believers on God's earth.

The next time the moon falls from the sky I will find him, Noor-Aftab cries, and bring him back to the edge of the sky.

Noor-Aftab climbs down from her mother's lap, picks up one of the bundles they have brought with them from Afghanistan and puts it on her head, swaying back and forth in front of her family, the girl-woman and her daughters.

A heavily laden truck roars and crashes noisily past and coats Shirin-Gol's head and body with its black, stinking smoke. When the truck with its great black tyres, as big as a human being, drives past Shirin-Gol, she realises that the crescent moon on the girl's head is a mudguard, the iron mudguard of a truck.

The truck is laden with blankets, chairs, tables, huge sacks, chickens, children, women, men going back to their homeland, Afghanistan.

One woman with a canister on her cloth-covered head, stops in front of Shirin-Gol and holds out her hand. Shirin-Gol looks at the cloth and smiles.

Can you help me? asks the woman, do you have any money?

Shirin-Gol shakes her head.

Would you have a piece of bread?

Shirin-Gol shakes her head.

The girl-woman takes a note out of her pocket and gives it to the woman.

The woman walks on.

Are you rich? asks Shirin-Gol.

The girl-woman does not laugh, says, no one here is rich, everyone helps everyone else, today I will help her, tomorrow someone else will help me.

God protect you, says Shirin-Gol.

That was a lovely story you told, says the girl-woman, can you tell us another one?

Shirin-Gol closes her eyes, thinks for a moment, opens her eyes and says, you see the women in their blue, white, orange and green *burqas*? You see the way they are all striding past us, proud and upright, with their heavy weights on their heads?

Yes, yes, yes, cries Noor-Aftab, skipping up and down.

Quiet, you'll frighten them, sit down and listen, says Shirin-Gol, pulling her daughter back on to her lap. Do you see them? They are queens and princesses. They are of noble blood and proud and well-to-do. And they are on their way from one of their palaces to the next.

What are they carrying on their heads? whispers Noor-Aftab.

Don't you know? asks Shirin-Gol.

Noor-Aftab shakes her head and looks at her mother expectantly.

That's their treasure.

Why don't they have their servants carry their treasure? asks Noor-Aftab.

Shirin-Gol thinks for a moment and says, they are kind

queens and princesses, they want to carry their weights themselves, so that their servants can rest. Also because of the weight they carry they have to keep their heads good and upright, and that means that they keep their proud way of walking.

And the old man there, calls Noor-Aftab, the one carrying a huge, heavy bag that's making his back bent. Is he the king?

I don't know, says Shirin-Gol.

And the boys with the glittering caps on their heads, and the boxes on their backs, says Noor-Aftab, are they princes?

I don't know, says Shirin-Gol.

Why do men carry their weight on their backs and women carry them on their heads? asks Noor-Aftab.

I don't know, says Shirin-Gol.

So that they have their hands free and can hold on to their children, says Shirin-Gol's mother.

Shirin-Gol is about to say something when there is a sudden commotion at the gate. A crowd of ragged children are screeching and crying and trying to escape the fury, sticks and blows of the border guards. They keep their hands protectively over their louse-ridden heads, they run and fall. The children look like tired little skeletons when they drop with exhaustion by the gate, among the rubbish they are carrying.

Without knowing why, the girl-woman starts crying. Without knowing why, Shirin-Gol, her mother and the children suddenly fall silent and watch the women, children and men carrying their loads. They see the girl half the size of Noor-Aftab, with a twisted iron pipe on her head. They see the heavy, greasy iron engine-part on the back of the tiny boy, who is covered in grease from head to foot. They see him wobbling with the last of his strength, walking with knees bent, constantly putting his load back down again so that the weight doesn't break his bones. They see the children with no name, no age, no desires, no past, no future. They see the children for whom life means only getting over the border unscathed and coming back. For a piece of bread the size of their hands they carry a new, greasy, heavy part, whatever it might be, on their bent backs, on their little heads, drag it on sacks across the ground. At the border gate they wait until the guard is looking away, hope that he isn't only playing a game with them and off they run. They see the boy with the crutches, the cripple, who has, like hundreds of thousands of other Afghans, stepped on a mine that has blown his leg to pieces and torn off his arm. The one-armed, one-legged boy on the crutches has tied a rope around his waist, and is carrying two canisters full of oil or petrol or whatever behind him. They see the cripple being beaten by the border guards because he isn't fast enough and is holding up the traffic.

They aren't queens and kings, princesses and princes, says Shirin-Gol's mother.

I know, says Noor-Aftab, pushing her lower lip over her upper, looks at her grandmother and repeats, I know, but it's nicer if I think they are.

You and your children smell of hunger, says the girl-woman. Shirin-Gol says nothing.

Once again the girl-woman leaps to her feet and disappears.

We should go, says Shirin-Gol's mother, this isn't good company for us.

She is a good person, says Shirin-Gol.

I would rather be dead and I would rather know my

children dead than to sell my . . . Her mother does not go on, pulls her veil over her face and stares, cloth-headed, towards the border gate.

When the girl-woman comes back she has two pots of tea, a flat loaf for each of them, a bowl of yoghurt and even sugar for the tea.

You have a long journey ahead of you, she says, please help yourselves, eat as much as you can and then you will have to be off or you will be going through the Tribal Areas in the dark. Along the road the Pakistani soldiers have their sentry posts everywhere, they won't let you through. It is better for you to take off into the mountains, into the areas of the Free Tribes, the Pakistanis have no authority there.

Shirin-Gol and the girl-woman embrace and kiss each other goodbye, and each wishes the other a long, healthy and peaceful life.

As soon as Shirin-Gol and her family leave the border area they do as the girl-woman has advised, and leave the asphalt road. It is just as the girl-woman said. It is easy to find the path, there are other Afghanis everywhere, ahead of them, behind them, as far as the eye can see. From a distance they look like tiny, colourful ants, walking behind one another in a long line. Some overtake them, others stay behind. Some are carrying heavy loads, others are empty-handed and dressed in rags. Some are carrying children, others are alone.

Below the paths, in the hills and mountains, the asphalt road snakes up to the Khyber Pass.

In the Tribal Areas not far from the Pakistani border city of Peshawar, Shirin-Gol, her children, her mother and the twins walk by long, high walls with wealthy houses, real palaces behind them, where healthy, rich people live who always have enough to eat and do not know the smell of hunger. They are drug-dealers, the people say. Men who deal in opium, who have so much money that they can't even count it all. One of them is supposed to have offered the Pakistani President to take on the Pakistani national debt if the President granted him and his family asylum. The people say the Pakistani President was delighted by the wealthy drug-dealer's offer, but couldn't accept it because his friend, the American President, was opposed to the idea. So the drug-dealer built his palace in the Tribal Areas, an area that did not really belong either to Pakistan or to Afghanistan, where no president, government or king had any authority. The wealthy man can do as he pleases, or get anybody else to do it for him. Here either everyone is his own master or is paid by a master to work as a guard, as a smuggler or whatever. Each man carries one, two or more weapons. In the shops in the bazaar all kinds of weapons are manufactured and sold. In other shops opium and heroin are weighed and portioned out for sale. And everywhere both opium and hashish are smoked.

Shirin-Gol likes the smell coming from the shops and stalls, mixing with the smell of freshly grilled mutton from the kebab stalls and creeping under her veil.

Let's have a rest, she says, and crouches down at the side of the road in front of a shop, shuts her eyes and breathes the fragrance deep into her empty stomach.

What do you think you're doing? Be off with you, calls a boy from the shop behind her. The boy is hardly older than the twins. He crouches on the floor at his little workbench, working away with a screwdriver on a pistol with a wonderful mother-of-pearl handle.

Please, brother, I am tired, my children are tired, my mother is ill and my brothers are exhausted, we are thirsty.

Are you hungry as well? asks the boy from the shop.

Shirin-Gol sees the boy through the thin net in front of her eyes and nods her cloth-covered head.

The boy leaves the pistol with the mother-of-pearl handle on the floor, picks up the crutch lying beside him, puts it under his arm and comes out of the shop. His stump dangles like a piece of dead flesh from his body. The one-legged boy crouches beside Shirin-Gol and says, come into the shop, you won't be disturbed there, you can take your cloth from your face and rest. It is time for prayer anyway, and I was going to get something to eat, be my guest.

We won't be any trouble, you are too kind, says Shirin-Gol, let us rest here for a moment and we will be on our way.

You are no trouble at all, I would be delighted. Please come in, says the boy. Please. It is far too dangerous for you out here. You should have stayed in the mountains. It will be dark soon. Please come in.

Please, *Madar*, let us go in, pleads Noor-Aftab, standing up and walking, without waiting for her mother's answer, ahead of her into the shop and crouches on the floor, next to the pistol with the mother-of-pearl handle.

The boy stands up, pushes the twins into the shop, takes Nasser on his arm, carries him in and sets him down beside his sister on the floor. Then he hobbles over to the kebab stand on the other side of the street, buys grilled meat, rice and bread, spreads out a plastic cloth on the floor of his shop, distributes the food, squats down and says, may God always be merciful to us, please eat, there is enough there for everyone.

You were sent by God, says Shirin-Gol, sitting with her back to the street, with her veil pushed back.

The boy says nothing, looks at Shirin-Gol for a long time

and says, my own sister has fled with her two children, the age of your children, with my mother and my younger brothers and sisters. No one knows where they are. May God will that they meet another kind soul who will feel sorry for them and help them.

The boy squats on the ground, on his healthy leg, with the stump of his other leg lying in front of him like a little cushion. He looks at Shirin-Gol, kneads rice with his fingers, tears off a small piece of meat, puts both in his mouth, chews, goes on looking at Shirin-Gol and says, they must still be alive, I can feel it.

Of course they are still alive, says Shirin-Gol.

Will you make me a pistol too? asks Nasser.

No, pistols are not good, says the one-legged boy, pistols kill people.

Did a pistol kill your leg? asks Nasser, putting a big piece of meat in his mouth.

No, a rocket, says the one-legged boy, a rocket killed my leg. We were fleeing, we were in the desert, it was night, a rocket went off, everybody screamed and ran in all directions, and then there were Mujahedin all over the place. They took my sister, her children and my mother, locked them in their jeeps and drove off with them. I called and shouted, I wanted to go with them, but they didn't hear me.

What did you do then? asks Shy-twin.

Then I got up, but I fell over again straight away, and then I saw I had fallen over because my leg was torn off and I only had one leg. Then I quickly bound the stump with my shirt, I had learned to do that in school. The teacher said, if you step on a mine or get hit by a rocket and your arm or your leg is torn off, you must immediately bind the stump so that you do not bleed to death. So, I did that and then I fainted.

And then? asks Cheeky-twin.

I was lucky, says the one-legged boy. A man found me and carried me for many days and nights on his back and he kept washing my wounds until finally we arrived in Pakistan and found a doctor. The doctor sawed off another piece of my leg, he said it had to go because it was rotten. He sewed up what was left.

Did it hurt? asks Shy-twin.

I can't remember, says the one-legged boy.

And then? What happened then? asks Cheeky-twin.

The man who found me and carried me for days was very kind. He said his son died in a rocket attack and if I wanted I could live at his place and work for him and he paid for the doctor and gave me something to eat every day. And since then I have been at his place making pistols for him.

How long did you go to school for? asks Shirin-Gol.

Two years.

I was at school as well. Russian school.

Once the war is over I'm going back to school.

So am I, says Shirin-Gol, I'm going back to school too, I want to be a doctor.

Insh'allah, says the one-legged boy.

Insh'allah, says Shirin-Gol.

Torkham, Shirin-Gol reads from a sign on the left of the gate at the Pakistan border with the Tribal Areas the next morning.

Can you read? asks an Afghan woman watching Shirin-Gol.

Bale, says Shirin-Gol.

What does it say there? asks the woman.

Shirin-Gol reads loudly and clearly.

ATTENTION
Entry of foreigners is prohibited beyond this point
By order of government
Welcome to the Khyber Agency
Keep to the left

And what else does it say? asks the woman.

Nothing, that is all, says Shirin-Gol.

Oh, says the woman, takes two of the six or eight children with whom she has just crossed the border, and goes on.

Shirin-Gol wonders what Torkham might mean and cannot guess. It sounds like *gham*, the Persian word for grief, suffering.

Don't stand around here, yells a policeman, swishing his stick through the air.

Salaam, we are visitors, says Shirin-Gol.

You are refugees, says the policeman, clear off.

Where is your father, asks a fellow Afghan as they register for the Pakistani refugee camp.

At home, answers Shirin-Gol.

I wasn't asking you, replies the man, you are probably another of the ones who fell into the hands of the godless Russians and lost your shame and decency in one of their schools. Disgrace, disgrace, a thousand times disgrace, curses the Afghan and spits greenish-yellow stuff into the sand at Shirin-Gol's feet, where it settles and dries.

Shirin-Gol is about to say something. Her mother claps her on the back of the head with the flat of her hand. Shirin-Gol says nothing.

My father is at home, Cheeky-twin hurries to say.

What is he doing there?

Fighting.

On whose side?

The side of the Mujahedin.

Which Mujahedin?

I don't know.

Allahu-akbar, says the Afghan, getting furious again.

He is fighting on the right side, Cheeky-twin says quickly, he is in the mountains fighting with my brothers.

And my sisters, says Shirin-Gol, they are fighting too, they are fighting side by side with my brothers and my father.

Cheeky-twin casts a furious look at Shirin-Gol and says, my father and my brothers are fighting for the fatherland, the Prophet, the Koran and Islam.

Off you go, yells the Afghan. Off you go, off you go. Get moving. Take this piece of paper, bring the *sia-sar* down to the back there and you will get a tent assigned to you. And remember, the Russians are gone. *Tamam*. And remember one other thing, this piece of land may be called Pakistan, but that's irrelevant, because the English betrayed us, stole it off us and gave it to the Pakistanis, but it is Afghan soil, it belongs to us, we will conquer it back, it is our country and the laws of Islam and the Prophet pertain here. We are Afghans, faithful Afghans, who honour and respect their religion, merciful Islam and the wise Prophet, and love our homeland. The only laws that are valid here are our laws and no others.

The Afghan looks at Cheeky-twin and says, from now on you are responsible and no one else, you understand? Make sure that the *sia-sar* in your family do not raise their voice in public, it's unseemly. Do you understand me?

Yes, sir, I will do that. I understand.

Really? You understand? So explain to me, urchin boy, what are you supposed to do?

Bring the black-headed ones, the ones with the black heads, the *sia-sar* somewhere or other.

And who are the *sia-sar*?

I don't know, sir, I don't understand that bit, sir, says Cheeky-twin.

Allah-hu-akbar, snorts the Afghan. You see, your head is full of godless Russian nonsense as well, you will have to get rid of that, we'll make sure of that. Your brother and you will go to Koran school. Here, take this. Go to the *madrassa* with this piece of paper tomorrow and report to the mullah. You little idiot, what do you think *sia-sar* could mean?

I don't know, Cheeky-twin replies in a whisper, shrugging his shoulders.

It means women whose hair hasn't turned white yet, snorts the Afghan, the ones that have all their beautiful, black curls to turn your head and my head and the head of everyone like us and stop us thinking clearly. So that we grow weak and the enemy and the devil can defeat us. You see? That is devil's work. You understand?

I understand, sir.

Cheeky-twin turns around to his sister and snorts at her in the same tone as his compatriot. *Sia-sar*. Black-heads. That's what you are. And now I am in charge.

His compatriot smiles contentedly, spits and ruffles Cheeky-twin's head.

On the way to the tent Shirin-Gol pulls Cheeky-twin's ear and hisses at him, don't get notions about yourself. That nonsense from that stinking, uneducated mullah doesn't apply to you, not now and not in a hundred years. You understand? *Sia-sar*, that means me, but I can see, I can speak, I can answer, I can ask questions and I'll beat you if I have to. And I'll do it when I feel like it. You understand?

I understand, Cheeky-twin says politely and grins at the cloth with his sister underneath it.

The tent in which Shirin-Gol, her daughter, her son, the twins and her mother are living is made of plastic the same blue as the domes of the loveliest mosques.

Shut the door, orders Cheeky-twin.

That isn't a door, you brat. And if we don't leave the tent open we will die in the heat.

But the strange men can see you.

What men? I can't see any men. I can only see cowards who have fled their homeland so they don't have to fight.

Whack, and for the first time Cheeky-twin has dared to give his older, beloved sister a clip around the ear.

Shirin-Gol hurls herself at him, presses his arms against his back, thumps him on the back of the head, beats him on the backside, shoves him into the corner and says, you try that one more time and . . .

And what? hisses Cheeky-twin. I am in charge here.

All the blood from her body has rushed to her head, Shirin-Gol pulls down her head-cloth, stands in front of her brother and shouts, oh yes? You are in charge? Then off you go and get us something to eat. We are hungry.

Fine, says Cheeky-twin, and vanishes.

The minute he is gone Shirin-Gol pulls her head-cloth back over her and goes out as well.

Outside among the tents it smells of piss and shit. Everywhere there is dirty, stinking water, everywhere children are running about, with rags hanging on their bodies instead of trousers, shirts and clothes. Children with runny noses, screaming, sitting apathetically around.

Their mothers squat beside them with their thin arms on their knees, their heads propped on their hands, staring into space.

Your pride will go as well, says a woman sitting on the ground outside her tent, when Shirin-Gol walks past her.

They have lost their pride and their dignity, thinks Shirin-Gol, lowering her head and walking on.

What do you want here? a hysterical voice cries suddenly from a tent.

Shirin-Gol gives a start and turns around, a young woman her own age comes running out of the tent, grabs her by the arm and pulls her away from there. Please forgive me, says the girl, it's my father, he's gone mad, he's only normal now when he's got opium or morphine, but I have no money, I don't know how I'm going to get him any.

Opium? Morphine? What's that? Shirin-Gol wonders to herself and walks on as quickly as she can. On the way back to her own tent she suddenly hears shouts and a general commotion. Men, women and children are running in every direction, pushing and shoving each other, quarrelling. A man the people describe as a steward is swinging a stick around, yelling and chasing the people away. Apparently someone has stolen money from someone else, and a fight has broken out. Shirin-Gol asks a woman where she can get something to eat. The woman looks at Shirin-Gol, nods in a particular direction and says, you need a card or you won't get anything. Shirin-Gol is about to ask the woman where she will get a card, but the woman has moved on.

At the soup kitchen hundreds of people stand with pots and bowls, jostling, pushing each other, men with sticks are yelling, delivering blows. Shirin-Gol pushes her way forward, pushes with the rest of them, is shoved and pulled and knocked over until she finally forces her way through the door where the food is supposed to be.

On a kind of pedestal stand three enormous pots, so big that three people could crouch in each one. Behind each pot stands a man stirring the broth with a huge ladle. The first in line holds up his bowl, the men scoop the red broth from the pot, tip it into the bowl, the bucket or whatever the people hold out to them.

Where is your bowl? yells the man, or do you want me to pour it into your skirt?

Where is your food card? bellows another man.

Shirin-Gol is about to say something, but cannot get her mouth open, and the next moment someone has pushed her on the other side of the narrow corridor with the raised pedestal and the three pots and back out through another door. The woman who was ahead of Shirin-Gol in the food distribution area and heard what had happened says, you need food cards, ask your neighbours who have been here longer, they will explain everything to you.

Shirin-Gol can't remember what she thought a refugee camp would be like. Maybe she thought a refugee camp would be a friendly place where there were people who looked after the refugees, welcomed them and comforted them and told them everything would be fine. Maybe she thought a refugee camp was a clean place where every family had a hut or a room, where there were streets that were regularly cleaned, where there were schools, doctors, nurses. Maybe she thought that in the refugee camp you would get everything you had lost in the war, clothes, beds, blankets, pots, shoes, combs, exercise books, books and all the other things that people need when they have fled their home. At any rate Shirin-Gol had not imagined that a refugee camp was a place where they scream and spit, a place where she had to live in a tent with holes and tears in it, which stank, which had no floor so that you had to sit and sleep on God's bare earth. At any rate Shirin-Gol had not thought that in a refugee camp there would be no food, no water, no groceries, no pots and nothing else unless you paid for it, unless an aid organisation registered you and gave you a food card, a blanket card, a mattress card, a pot card, a doctor card, a whatever-else-you-can-think-of card.

Shirin-Gol is lucky, the twins are allowed to go to Koran class, so they get blankets, mattresses, and cards for a sack of potatoes.

Somewhere in the camp there is supposed to be a woman who looks after new arrivals, the people say. Shirin-Gol is lucky and finds the woman, she gives Shirin-Gol a pot, a cup and some fat.

Why are you doing this? Shirin-Gol asks, you've hardly got anything yourself.

Everyone helps everyone else and one day if you've got so much that you can help others, I might need your help, says the woman. And if you like, come to see me tomorrow. I am always walking around. Many women have problems with their husbands or problems in the family, it takes its toll on their nerves. The men are sitting around unemployed and unoccupied. Before you know it you've got frustration and arguments.

How could I help? asks Shirin-Gol.

Very simple, says the woman, very simple, we listen to them, that is all we do. And by doing that we help the other women, but we help ourselves as well. You will see. As soon as you help other people you have the feeling that your own life isn't wasted, that it is still some use.

Maybe I will come, says Shirin-Gol, thanking her for the pot, the cup and the fat.

Haven't you got a man in your tent? hisses a fellow Afghan when Shirin-Gol sticks her food card through the slit into the little cabin.

Go home and send your brother, says another, when Shirin-Gol stands in the queue to fetch water. Pull your veil over the face, says another compatriot, when Shirin-Gol is sitting in the blazing sun outside her tent, drawing words in the sand.

I'm thirsty, complains her daughter, Noor-Aftab.

I'm hot, weeps her son, Nasser.

Where is our food, we're hungry, howl the twins when they come back to the tent from the Pakistani and Arab teachers who have been teaching them the Koran.

I want to die, says her mother.

Shirin-Gol puts her hands over her ears, sits in her corner in the hot plastic tent, with her eyes shut, only listening and only seeing when someone addresses her directly. Shirin-Gol, do this, do that, go here, go there.

During the night Shirin-Gol has a dream. She dreams that Afghanistan is ruled by a kind man. He is neither a king nor a Russian, neither a Mujahed nor a Taleb. He is simply a good man who wants to do good for people. The good ruler sends his emissaries throughout the whole country, telling all the women and girls that they don't have to cover their faces with veils from now on, and can go about the world without a *hejab*. And then he gives each of them so much to eat that it lasts them until the end of their days, for themselves, for their children and husbands and their brothers and fathers who are fighting in the mountains and who now do not have to fight any more.

A shame it was only a dream, thinks Shirin-Gol when she wakes up.

When Shirin-Gol stops blocking her ears and keeping her eyes shut she doesn't know whether days, weeks or months have passed. A man is standing outside the tent talking to Cheeky-twin. Shirin-Gol, come here, he calls. Come on, hurry up. Your husband, Morad, is here.

Chapter Six

AN ACCIDENT AND A GENEROUS
SMUGGLER CHIEF

Morad finds work as a smuggler. Every day he crosses the
border into Afghanistan, into the Tribal Areas, where the
governments of Pakistan and Afghanistan have no authority.

Whether Afghan kings, the English, the Russians or the
Communist government are in power in Afghanistan,
whether the Pakistani government is headed by a despot or
an elected president who stays in power through
corruption, the Tribal Areas have always been ruled by
independent tribal lords.

Morad smuggles medicines, drugs, weapons into the
Tribal Areas. And out of the Tribal Areas he smuggles
refrigerators, bicycles, televisions, carpets, computers,
blank and pre-recorded video tapes, video recorders and
other useful products, products bearing the promise of
happiness that the West has to offer the poor of the world.
The goods are unloaded at the harbour in Karachi and
elsewhere, transferred to lorries, driven across Pakistan
and into the Tribal Areas of Afghanistan, unloaded, packed
on the backs of Morad and hundreds and thousands of
other smugglers, lashed down so that none of the valuable
freight is lost in transit, because the paths on which the

goods are brought back into Pakistan on foot are narrow, steep and stony.

From the distance Morad and the others look like a thousand tiny, colourful ants, climbing up and down the mountain carrying their heavy loads all day long.

Because the goods do not stay in Pakistan, the dealer does not have to pay duty on them. According to a law from the days of the British, no duty is paid on goods that reach Pakistan along paths and roads that haven't been re-inforced, that have not been asphalted. The goods come from Japan, England, France, Korea, Bulgaria, Germany, the USA, the whole world. The Pakistanis do not object to the Afghans doing this business for them. On the contrary, they are grateful to them for it. The Pakistanis like to be able to buy cheap articles from all around the world, they themselves would never go into the free Tribal Areas, clamber around in the mountains and risk their lives. And anyway, the Pakistanis charge high rents for the shops and cabins where the Afghans sell their contraband.

The worst thing for Morad is when he has to smuggle refrigerators, he is happiest smuggling cigarettes. They are light, and no one notices if he loses a couple of packets along the way, smokes them himself, swaps them or sells them.

Meanwhile Shirin-Gol is spending the whole day in the refugee camp, along with her daughter Noor-Aftab and her son Nasser, the ones she loves above all else. Every day that God grants her she gives her children a thousand kisses, a thousand and one loving glances, and every time she looks at them both she gives them a smile. She wants them to have a good life, to know neither hunger nor fear, their eyes should not have to see war, their ears should not hear explosions, they should not have to sit by the corner of the house looking after their brothers and sisters, she would like them to learn and one day serve their homeland, rebuild the country, guide it into a happy future and make their mother and father proud.

At night, when Morad is asleep, Shirin-Gol secretly creeps over to his jacket, takes out a few notes and hides them.

By day, when Morad is travelling in the mountains and smuggling refrigerators, bicycles or cigarettes, the children from the neighbouring tents gather in Shirin-Gol's tent, where she teaches them and her own children how to read and write, do sums and paint, sings and plays with them, tells them what Fawzi had told her when she was a little girl, when she had come out of the mountains, afraid of turning into a naked woman.

The parents of the children pay Shirin-Gol as much as they can for this. A little money, fat, tea, rice and whatever else they can spare.

Things do not go well for long for the secret school, because the stinking mullah, the self-appointed camp leader, his lackeys and his Kalashnikov which officially he is not allowed to own, but which in reality he keeps constantly at the ready, do not want girls to walk in public or go to school, or women to work.

They shout at Shirin-Gol, swing the stick, hitting her accidentally on purpose. They scold Morad, insult him, deliberately thump him with the stick on his shoulders and his head, spit at his feet and accuse him of not paying enough attention to his wife.

She does what she wants, the men shout at Morad, she consorts with people, she has no decency and no dignity. Your wife is dishonouring the *rish-sefid*, the white-beards, the eldest and other men in the camp. Tame her and keep a closer eye on her, or people will end up thinking you are not a real man.

Shirin-Gol really wants to sink into the ground, she is ashamed, appalled, she blames herself, her conscience torments her, she should have known better. What does her poor Morad look like, standing there? Like a little boy. The stinking mullah and the self-appointed camp leader have treated him like a little boy. Morad stands before them with his head pulled in, staring at his bare feet. The sight of him turns Shirin-Gol's heart to paper and with a great rip tears it into two pieces. Under her cloth Shirin-Gol claws her hand into her thigh, sobs quietly and would rather be dead than see her Morad like that and know how ashamed he is at this moment. Ashamed before the men, the neighbours, his son, his daughter and even herself. Why didn't she tell him? Why didn't she let him know she wanted to teach the children?

It would only be fair if he were to yell at or even hit her, she knew it wasn't all right, she should have asked him, he would have said no and that would have been that. Or he would have said no, they would have talked about it, she would have won him over, as she had always won him over about everything, then at least he would have known what was going on. She is paying for that now. Morad is profoundly hurt, insulted, humiliated. And it is her fault. The stinking mullah and the self-appointed camp leader have been gone for ages, but Morad is still sitting in the corner in his blue plastic tent, sitting in complete silence. He sits there all day, all afternoon and all evening smoking that stuff.

Shirin-Gol asks, what is that?

He doesn't look at her. Medicine, he murmurs, falls silent again and goes on smoking. The tent is full of the smoke and smell of the medicine, a sweet, heavy smoke that dulls Shirin-Gol's senses, and even her daughter and her son are woozy with it.

A few days pass. The stinking mullah and the self-appointed camp leader come back to see Morad, bringing a letter for his wife to read. And from that point on and into the future, Shirin-Gol, now that she can read and write and there is nothing to be done about it, is to read and write letters for them.

It may not bring in any money, but every now and again they take her some wheat, a tin of fat, rice, a box of tea. And she is to say nothing about it. She is not to tell a single soul that she has become the reader and writer of the mullah and the camp leader.

That is God's mercy, thinks Shirin-Gol, and she gets used to thanking God for every day he grants her. She thanks him. For his mercy, for his goodness, for her own health, that of her children, that of her husband. For the fact that her children, she herself, Morad, have not stepped on mines, that they have not lost arms or legs. She thanks God for the fat, for the rice, for the tea, for the wheat, for the little mud walls that she is building slowly but surely with Morad around the blue plastic tent. For the fact that the little wall will get bigger, will have a door, a window and a roof, and Shirin-Gol will finally remove the tent from underneath and have a proper room, a real home.

She will sell the tent and with the money buy wool and dye. She will spin yarns, boil up dyes, dye the wool, make a little carpet, sell it, buy food, fat, tea, rice, wheat. Shirin-Gol thanks God for the healthy, skilful, rapid, powerful hands he has given her, with which she cooks, brings her children into the world, sews her clothes, washes, works in the field, weaves wool into carpets, calms her Morad's tired body, carries her children, pats them on the back as she rocks them to sleep. Shirin-Gol thanks God for the buyer she finds in the city for her carpet, for the letter she gets from one of her brothers in the mountains, in which he has a scribe write that he and the rest of the family are, thank God, well, that they are still fighting. Sometimes don't know themselves who is shooting at them and who they are shooting back at, but they go on shooting, for the Prophet, the Koran and Islam.

Shirin-Gol thanks the Lord God for everything, everything she owns and everyone who is still alive.

At one point, one day like every other, when everything is the same as always and yet everything is different, there is a pulling and jerking, burning and tearing sensation in Shirin-Gol's stomach. She feels wretched, she is hot, then she shivers again, her head is spinning, the children are howling, there is no water in the camp, the fire will not light, and when it finally flickers into life it stinks, the air is heavy and damp and stinks as well, cockroaches with shiny backs climb up her children's legs, mice gnaw at her pathetic stores, her neighbour whines and complains, her neighbour's children are howling and shouting and crying, her neighbour's wife is screaming like a mad person, tearing her clothes off, slicing her thigh with a knife.

For that day and everything else it brings, Shirin-Gol doesn't thank the Lord God. She curses and damns the day, her life, her fate, her birth, the war still raging in her homeland, Pakistan, still strange to her, the stinking camp and everything else that occurs and doesn't occur in her wretched life. Then it happens.

Morad is brought to the mud hut by two men, one

carrying him by his arms, the other by his legs.

Morad is barely alive. He is wailing, he is in pain, not fully conscious, his leg has been crushed, his arm is bleeding, his chest is bleeding, his head is bleeding. Blood-Morad. He has slipped down the mountain with a contraband refrigerator lashed to his back, he has somer-saulted, rolled over and over, again and again, with first him on top, then the refrigerator, until he landed in the valley, himself on top, the dented refrigerator beneath him. And all because on that one day Shirin-Gol would not thank her God.

A doctor is called, Blood-Morad needs medication, he has to go to hospital, his arm, his chest, his back, it is all shattered, it all has to be sewn up and covered in plaster.

Shirin-Gol asks everyone she knows for money, her mother, the neighbours, the stinking mullah, the self-appointed camp leader. Anyone who is able and willing gives her something. She will have to pay it back. How? She doesn't know yet. She takes the money to the hospital, it is not enough. What is she going to live on? How is she going to feed the children? Pay for the medication, the doctor, the hospital, the taxi, food for Blood-Morad?

During the night Shirin-Gol has a dream. She dreams the plastic tents are not tents and are not made of plastic. They are mud huts. And she dreams the shit and piss are not piss and shit. Instead, at every corner of the camp there are little stands with opulent displays of fruit, meat and rice, anyone can help themselves, as often and as much as they like. And the whole camp smells of rose water, sweet spices and freshly baked bread.

A shame it was only a dream, thinks Shirin-Gol when she wakes.

The last beans, full of holes where the worms have been

at them, the last rice, the last wheat have all been used up. Her son's stomach, and her daughter's, are rumbling with hunger. Shirin-Gol herself is dizzy, she sees stars when she gets up. Hunger is boring a hole in her stomach. The children are starting to lick their fingers and gnaw away at them. Shirin-Gol begs from her neighbours, stands around in front of the camp and stretches a hand out from underneath her cloth, gets a few coins that are not even enough for bread.

A man stops and asks her if she is hungry.

Yes, sir, may God protect your goodness if you can help me.

What is in it for me? asks the man.

Shirin-Gol doesn't know what the man means.

Is that your daughter? asks the man, reaching his hand out towards the little one.

Horrified, Shirin-Gol pulls her child to her, curses and swears at the man. Godless creature, she hisses at him, you should be ashamed of yourself. Have you no mother, no father, no shame, no decency?

The man laughs, spits greenish-yellow stuff, rubs his crotch and says, your arrogance will pass, as it has passed for all of you, it will pass for you too.

The next morning, Shirin-Gol, trembling with hunger, takes her hungry daughter and her hungry son by the hand. For a moment it feels as though they were the twins and she the little girl. The big sister of the old days.

She spends all morning looking in the bazaar in Peshawar, before she finds the smuggler chief Morad is working for. Shirin-Gol is lucky. The Pakistani takes pity on her. He too has children, he too is a father. He is polite, kind, forthcoming, he offers Shirin-Gol and her children a glass of tea and a bite to eat, gives her money, wishes her

Morad a good recovery, even pays for a taxi for Shirin-Gol and her two little children to take them back to the camp.

Two weeks pass. The same taxi driver comes to the camp, bringing a bundle of rice, fat, wheat, a piece of silk, more beautiful and noble than Shirin-Gol has ever seen or even touched. All a present from the kind and generous smuggler chief. Shirin-Gol and her children eat the rice, the fat, the wheat, and she cooks food that she takes to the hospital for Morad. She sells the silk for good money, buys medication and pays the doctor.

Another week passes. The taxi driver comes back again, empty-handed this time. The *sahib* would like to speak to Shirin-Gol in person. Shirin-Gol takes her children by the hand, walks behind the man, past the blue plastic tents, past mud huts half-finished and completed mud huts, past screaming children, stinking waterholes, little stalls, apathetic mothers, mad women under cloths, opium-fogged fathers, dirty children with louse-ridden heads, smeared mouths, piss-drenched trousers, filth-encrusted feet, sun-dried skin, pus-filled wounds.

At the entrance to the refugee camp Shirin-Gol climbs into the waiting taxi, is driven through the noisy, stinking city to the noisy, stinking bazaar. Past spitting men, greasy men, lecherous-looking men, men with fat stomachs. Past men spitting greenish-yellow stuff, kneading and scratching their cocks when Shirin-Gol drives past them with her children on her lap. Past all that and much more besides, to the home of the generous smuggler-chief.

Shirin-Gol gets out, is led to a fan-cooled room the like of which she has never seen before and will never see again. Shirin-Gol sits down on the little clean, soft cushions and mats scattered around the bright-green distempered room, tells her children to sit still and not to eat too many of the sweets on offer. The peace, the cool air, the soft cushions, the smell of rose water in the clay bowl, the quiet, regular fluttering of the fan, the ice-cooled lemonade calm Shirin-Gol and her children, too.

Slowly the children doze off. Shirin-Gol lays a hand on each, strokes them, pats her hand gently on their little fragile backs with their parchment skin, in a low quiet voice she sings a melody that comes from her heart, and smiles, is happy, thanks her God for this moment of peace and tranquillity. Quietly, not to disturb the peace, the generous smuggler-chief comes into the room, gestures to Shirin-Gol to stay where she is, to go on singing, not wake the children, not disturb the moment. He takes off his shoes, creeps in, sits down on the cushion next to Shirin-Gol, looks at the singing cloth for a long time, listens, enjoys, becomes a child himself, smiles, clicks his prayer-beads along with Shirin-Gol's tune.

The servant brings more ice-cooled lemonade, biscuits, juicy, red watermelons and a box.

For you, says the generous smuggler-chief, laying the box in Shirin-Gol's lap, opening the lid and gently touching her stomach as he does so. Shirin-Gol thinks it is an accident and twitches, but says nothing and does not move away from the strange man. The children are lying in her lap, she doesn't want to disturb their sleep, the man is nice, there's a lot of money in the box, she doesn't want to annoy him and who knows, she probably only imagined his hand on her stomach.

And what happens next? Maybe she imagined that as well. Maybe the man's intentions are not dishonourable. Shirin-Gol says nothing. Maybe it is best that way. For Shirin-Gol, for her children. And for Morad, too.

Carefully, very carefully, gently, with two fingers, the

generous smuggler-chief takes the tip of Shirin-Gol's veil, lifts it slowly up, frees her face from the cloth, looks at her, dries Shirin-Gol's tears with his dark hands, kisses her on the forehead, kisses the weeping eyes, the tear-wet mouth, pushes his tongue past her beautiful white, pearly teeth, into her ice-cooled-lemonade-tasting mouth, sucks, licks, breathes heavily, lays the box aside, rises to his feet, walks to the door, pulls the bolt, comes back, gently, carefully lifts the girl from Shirin-Gol's lap, Shirin-Gol utters a quiet, choking sound, the man smiles lovingly, lays her daughter down on cushions on the other side of the room, then the boy, comes back to Shirin-Gol, kneels down by her, holds the box out to her and asks, do you want the money?

Have I got a choice? asks Shirin-Gol.

Yes, replies the generous smuggler-chief in a kind, gentle voice. You can try your luck out there like many of your female compatriots. There are plenty of my fellow countrymen in the bazaar who would take you in a flash.

I know, says Shirin-Gol.

Your husband cannot work. He earns no money. You have debts. Many debts. If you do not take my money today, tomorrow you will have to take money from lots of men. For you and sooner or later for your daughter's body as well, your son's body.

I know, says Shirin-Gol.

But then I won't want you any more, says the man, running his finger gently over Shirin-Gol's lips.

I know, says Shirin-Gol, wiping the tears from her face.

You are even more beautiful than I thought, says the generous smuggler-chief.

Shirin-Gol says nothing.

The man places a hand on Shirin-Gol's breast, presses

and rubs it, with his other hand he opens the first button of her dress, the second and all the others, takes her naked, soft, white, firm maternal breasts in his hands, presses them, rubs them, strokes them, licks them, kisses them, bites them gently, pushes a hand into Shirin-Gol's lap and into her, pulls down her long *tonban*, her long, white pants, lifts her skirts, plunges his hard cock into her body, moves up and down until he pulses, groans, quietly lest the children wake, pushes hard, claws his dark fingers into Shirin-Gol's hips, holds her, rocks, relaxes, lays his sated body on Shirin-Gol's mother-body, lies there sated on her, comes to rest, hums contentedly. Sing, he orders, closes his eyes and listens to her sobbing, low voice.

Shirin-Gol let it happen.

She squats on the floor in her hut, rocking her body back and forth as though music was playing somewhere, she looks at her sleeping children without seeing them.

For you, my daughter, she whispers. I did it for you. For you, my son. For you, my Morad. For myself, so that we can all stay alive.

The years turn into birds, flock together and fly away. Winter and summer come and go. But the images recalling that shame are as clear, as distinct as they were on the first day.

Green distempered wall. The taste of ice-cooled lemonade in her mouth. God does not help Shirin-Gol. He will not take these images of shame and disgrace out of her head. He has etched them into her memory and does not make them go away.

And even the knowledge that many hundreds and thousands of Afghan women have done the same is of no comfort to Shirin-Gol.

And even the knowledge that there is a market in Pakistan where Afghan women are offered and sold like cattle is of no comfort to her. Some of the girls are thirteen, eleven or as little as five years old. They are groped, men grab their sprouting breasts, clutch their buttocks, reach between their legs, laugh, slobber, men look in their mouths, push in a finger. Prices are negotiated. Money is pushed back and forth. Human beings are bought and sold.

Shirin-Gol knows all that. She knows she is not alone with her shame. Shirin-Gol knows all that. And she knows the only way out of this shame is her death. She knows that. She simply does not know what to do with her children.

Chapter Seven

ANOTHER CHILD AND ANOTHER FLIGHT

Since the birth of her third child, her second daughter, who Shirin-Gol calls Nafass, Breath, every single day that God gives her Shirin-Gol is reminded of the generous-smuggler-chief.

Green distempered wall. The taste of ice-cooled lemonade in her mouth.

Nafass has more delicate bones than her brother and sister, darker, smoother, softer hair, darker skin, she is like her father, the generous smuggler-chief.

Your Pakistani daughter is pretty, people say, looking at Shirin-Gol provocatively, waiting for an explanation, whisper behind her back, point at her, swear at her. Policemen, soldiers, officials, men like Malek, ask her pointedly if the little girl is hers as well.

Morad sees the child and knows she is not his, but never, not once, has he wasted so much as a word on the subject. Other men whose wives had given birth to Pakistani children knocked their wives' teeth out, stabbed them and their children, threw them out into the street, killed them. Morad comes out of hospital, drags his sick and wounded body into the corner of the mud hut, sits down, stares at the canister of fat, watches his wife opening the sack of rice, heating water in a real brass pot, lighting a fire with proper firewood, cooking beans and potatoes that are free of worms and holes. Morad looks at Shirin-Gol's big, pregnant stomach, sighs, says, thanks be to Allah, there are still God-fearing people who do not forget the poor and the needy. Thank God, says Shirin-Gol, puts her hand on her pregnant stomach, puts salt in the boiling water, takes a pack of American contraband cigarettes out of a bundle, tears off the wrapping, throws it into the fire, hands the pack to her Morad, goes back to her fire, scoops water from the tub, washes her hands with proper soap, squats on the floor by the cooking-pot and stirs the simmering water until it starts to boil and spit.

Shirin-Gol stirs the rice with a proper spoon so that it doesn't stick to the bottom of the pot, scoops off the foam, knocks it off on the stone the pot is resting on. The fire responds furiously when the rice-water foam falls in. Shirin-Gol pulls back her head so that the smoke and steam do not burn her eyes. She peels a proper onion, gets tears in her eyes, cuts open a proper, fresh, fat aubergine, gets black fingers from its skin and says, without looking at Morad, your boss, may God preserve him and his goodness for us, sends for me once a week. I go to the city and come back each time laden with presents. He has even given us clothes for the children. He sends you his greetings and his best wishes and says you can start working again when you are better. And he says not to think about it and not to worry because as long as he is there he will take care of us. And you are to say if you need something and if it is in his power, he will get hold of it for you.

The fire responds furiously. Shirin-Gol pulls her head back.

Morad says nothing.

The wife of our neighbour, *hadji** Nabi, has disappeared, says Shirin-Gol. She went to the city to beg three weeks ago. She didn't come back in the evening.

Morad says nothing.

The *hadji* and the other men looked for her for three weeks until they found her body. She had a noose around her neck. People say a stranger raped the poor innocent creature. Instead of paying her, he strangled her and left her lying in the gutter.

Morad says nothing.

Now her poor husband, the *hadji*, doesn't know how he is going to feed his motherless children.

When are you going back into the city? asks Morad.

Today, says Shirin-Gol, snorting back her tears.

Tell him I'm in pain. I have a pain that needs numbing. Tell him I need opium.

Yes, says Shirin-Gol, in a voice neither quiet nor loud, and stirs the rice in the pot to stop it sticking to the bottom.

Days, weeks, months, a year and more pass, Morad hardly ever leaves the mud hut, he sits all day in his corner, dozing, enduring his pain, watching his Shirin-Gol, his daughter, his son and his second, dark-skinned daughter, who is taking her first steps and saying her first words. And he smokes. Opium. Every day, twice, three times, so many times that it isn't long before neither he himself nor Shirin-Gol knows how many times it is.

Morad's head goes limp, his eyes are watery. Opium tongue. Opium face. Morad hardly ever speaks, soon he doesn't even think. Doesn't know if he is alone in the hut,

*A Moslem who has done his pilgrimage to Mecca.

if Shirin-Gol is with him, if his children are talking to him or talking to each other or if anybody is talking at all.

Only when Shirin-Gol hums a song in her low, soft voice does he understand, smiles, shuts his eyes and disappears into a world more beautiful than the one in the corner of his mud hut in the Pakistani refugee camp. A world even more beautiful than his opium world.

It seems as though no one and nothing can wean him off his opium, until one day the neighbours come running into his hut, shouting Morad, Morad, and calling, pull yourself together, your wife has been arrested by the Pakistani police.

The men support Morad, bring him to the police station, guide his hand when he has to sign the piece of paper to get his wife back, support him on his way back to the camp, set him down in his corner, where the mud wall has worn smooth from him leaning against it for so long. The men shake their heads, feel sorry for him and leave.

Shirin-Gol they put in the other corner of the hut, where she cowers, wraps her arms around her legs, makes herself small, rocks her desecrated, humiliated, injured, beaten body, abused now by strange men, back and forth, stares crazily at the bare mud wall and says nothing. Insane.

Noor-Aftab, Nasser and Nafass howl, they are hungry, they want something to eat, her little dark-skinned daughter wants the breast, the children pee in their skirts, in their trousers, snot runs from their noses, flies feed on the corner of their eyes, dust is encrusted on their skin, but Shirin-Gol cannot see any of that, and she does not even come out of her corner when the man with the taxi comes to take her to the generous smuggler-chief.

Morad gets cold, he trembles, foam runs from his mouth, his head hums, hammers, knocks, spins, presses down on him so much that he cuts his thigh and his arms. His bones are nearly bursting, his skin threatens to tear apart, he screams, roars, whimpers, weeps, but Shirin-Gol stays crouched in her corner, not whimpering, not weeping, soon not making any sound, not moving, she crouches and crouches, tips over. Just like that. Cowering as she is, she tips over and lies where she is.

Bahara, another Afghan, a neighbour, a friend, a kind soul, herself someone who needs help, herself someone who bears so much suffering in her breast that it threatens to burst on her, worthy of pity herself, has mercy, sits Shirin-Gol up, moistens her lips, drips water into her mouth, washes her face, her hands, her feet, cooks a pot of broth, cooks rice, feeds the children, puts a plate of food in front of Morad. Bahara sends Shirin-Gol's children out, shoos Morad out, takes Shirin-Gol in her arms, holds her, rubs her stiffened back, hums her a song, talks to her.

Carefully, as though she were made of glass, Bahara takes Shirin-Gol's dress off her, washes it, undoes Shirin-Gol's hair, washes it, combs it, weaves two new plaits, washes her body, rubs it, kisses Shirin-Gol's forehead, talks to her in a soft voice, tells her of her own suffering, drips sweet tea into her mouth, puts rice in her mouth, stays with Shirin-Gol until a tear moistens Shirin-Gol's dry eyes and runs down her cheek, past her lips and down her neck, and falls into her washed skirt where it disappears.

As though she had spent all those past days waiting for that one tear, Shirin-Gol suddenly starts talking and will not stop talking until she has told Bahara all the things that happened that day, the day she went mad.

Shirin-Gol is in the bazaar buying opium for Morad, when a Pakistani policeman hits her on the veiled head with his truncheon, so violently that she is sent reeling, that she cannot see, falls over and cannot get up again. Immediately Shirin-Gol's fellow Afghans gather, roaring and shouting, abusing the policemen as Afghan-haters, as woman-haters, only willing to touch the weak and defenceless.

Shirin-Gol tries to get up, she wants to get away, she is ashamed, she does not want any excitement on her account and the people gather, but her head is spinning, she slips, totters, hears voices from all directions, stands up, falls back to the ground, hits her head on the kerbstone, her hand lands in the rotting gutter by the side of the road.

Her compatriots talk to her, tell her to come to, they want to help, they want to get her on her feet, but there are only men there, strange men, it is not done to touch a strange woman.

The Pakistani policemen lay into the men and drive them away, two policemen lift Shirin-Gol up by her arms and legs, the third beats a path through the people, they throw Shirin-Gol into their car, drive with her through the city, and are going to drop her on the other side of the city when one of the three men lifts her cloth and looks at her face.

Shirin-Gol comes to, holds her hands in front of her face, the policeman pulls them away, touches her lips, lifts her skirts, opens his trousers, forces his way into her and laughs contentedly.

All Shirin-Gol can see is his gold tooth, all the time she smells his rancid breath. The other two policemen do not pay any attention to the first to begin with, then, one after the other, they too let their trousers down and force their way into Shirin-Gol. After they have all satisfied their stinking lust, they throw Shirin-Gol at the side of the road, leave her lying there and drive off.

A Pakistani teacher who lives nearby finds Shirin-Gol, calls his wife, they help Shirin-Gol to stand up and take her to the police, to make a deposition. Instead she is arrested. No one believes her. Instead they swear at her, laugh at her and humiliate her.

Shirin-Gol and Bahara have heard many such stories, both women have often wept at the unjust fate that befalls their sisters, women who have been abandoned by God and the world, forgotten, alone and abandoned to the injustice of war, of hunger, the whims of men. Shirin-Gol and Bahara hold each other tight, weeping together, and they know these will not be the last tears that they weep.

As on all other recent nights, since being raped by the Pakistani police, Shirin-Gol cannot get to sleep. Terrible images, noises, pain, infinite shame, the feeling that her skirts are being hoisted up, the feeling of strange men's hands on her skin, the gold tooth, the rancid breath wake her with a start. Quiet, choking cries emerge from her throat. Shirin-Gol holds her hands in front of her mouth so that the scream does not jump out of her mouth, opens her eyes wide, stares into the darkness of the hut, trembles and weeps.

Four days pass, or is it six or eight? There are sparks in the air, the voices of the people are hard and as sharp as knives, each word cuts, makes a little explosion. Shirin-Gol keeps her hand on her heart so that it doesn't jump from her body, her breath is short, it only reaches her throat and then immediately leaves.

Where is Morad? she asks.

Noor-Aftab shrugs.

Ask the neighbours, says Shirin-Gol.

Noor-Aftab runs out, comes back into the house, shrugs.

Cat got your tongue? What's up? Talk to me, you cheeky thing.

Noor-Aftab looks at her mother, pushes her top lip over her bottom lip, lowers her eyes and whispers shyly, no one knows where he is.

Shirin-Gol pulls her daughter down to her on the floor, kisses her, looks her in the eyes, says, my little ray of sunshine, I'm sorry your mother went mad.

I know, says her daughter, and brushes a strand of her black hair, gleaming like pitch, out of her face. I know, she repeats, you went mad.

In the evening Morad comes back and has something to hide. He doesn't look at his children or at Shirin-Gol. He neither speaks nor hears when others speak to him.

Shirin-Gol, Shirin-Gol, come out, cries Bahara, everyone is talking about it.

Shirin-Gol lowers her eyes. About what? she asks, only to gain some time.

The three policemen, says Bahara, throwing her hand over her mouth and choking the rest of the words in her throat.

The three policemen? asks Shirin-Gol, what about the sons of bitches?

Dead. They are dead, says Bahara, closing her eyes as though the dead had just appeared before her eyes.

Dead? Who . . .?

No one knows who killed them, says Bahara. They say everything is in chaos at the bazaar, everyone is being questioned, lots of Afghans have shut down their stands and stalls.

Shirin-Gol and Morad say nothing until evening. Shirin-Gol spreads out the mats and blankets, lays the children down to sleep, crouches down in front of the hut as she does every evening, looks out over all the tents, the half-finished and completed huts of the refugee camp. Shirin-Gol hears the voices of the people in the camp getting quieter and fewer until everything is in silence. The clattering of the pots and bowls subsides and finally stops. Shirin-Gol hears the nearby city getting quieter and quieter until it too falls almost silent. Every now and again a baby howls into the night-time peace, someone coughs quietly, very close by someone pees, someone else groans.

The air becomes thin and light, dust and stench vanish and take the smell of cooked fat and rancid oil with them, the stench of rubbish swollen by the sun, of stale piss heated by the sun. Shirin-Gol opens the little bottle that the generous smuggler-chief gave her, drips a drop of the rose water into her hand, rubs her hands, holds them up to her nose, breathes in the fragrance, leans her head against the post of the opening that is not yet a door, closes her eyes and finally drifts off.

When she opens her eyes again she doesn't know if she is waking or dreaming. Further down, where the city is, the sky is on fire. Huge flames, as though half the city were ablaze, jump and leap yellow and red.

The wind brings the stench of burnt plastic, burnt wood, burnt other things to the camp. Shirin-Gol gets up, a few neighbours come out, whisper, utter horrified cries. More and more people stand outside their huts and tents, look over towards the fire, whisper, pray to God, fall silent.

The next day, a Saturday, everyone knows that the Afghan bazaar of Peshawar has been burnt out. Completely and utterly burnt out. Nothing, absolutely nothing remains of it. All the stalls, all the stands, all the shops, socks, shirts, trousers, cigarettes, paper, pens, hair-clips, spices, rice, clothes, veils, cloths, shoes, caps, belts, toys, everything,

everything, even the great tree that stood at the edge of the bazaar, has burnt down. The people take buckets and pots to its remains and select bits of the wood that has burnt to charcoal, to take home for firewood.

It was a short circuit, some say, it was an act of revenge, say others. Revenge for the three dead policemen.

Whatever it was, it was a black Friday, when hundreds of Afghans once more lost the livelihoods they had put such effort into building up.

We have got to go, says Morad hoarsely, when Shirin-Gol comes back to the mud hut from the water wagon and at long last she doesn't look mad any more.

I know, says Shirin-Gol, looking into the eyes of her Morad, who has finally awoken from his opium twilight that lasted so long, so terribly long.

Opium-Morad isn't Opium-Morad any more.

You aren't trembling any more, she says.

I'm not trembling any more, he says.

You're not foaming at the mouth any more, says Shirin-Gol.

I'm not foaming at the mouth any more, he says, looks at Shirin-Gol, takes her hand and says, I thought you were mad and did not see the foam and the trembling and the fear.

I was mad, says Shirin-Gol, but I still saw your trembling, your fear, your foaming at the mouth. I heard your cries, your weeping, I saw your pain, but I was mad and could not help.

It would have been my duty to help, says Morad, lowering his eyes. He cannot go on, his throat seizes up with tears and takes his voice away.

You have always helped me, and you have helped me now, says Shirin-Gol, running her hand over her Morad's hair, and it feels as though she were stroking one of the twins on the head.

Morad lifts his head, takes his wife's hand, kisses it, for the first time since getting out of hospital he looks Shirin-Gol in the eyes, which are full of pain, and says, I did what I had to do and what I could do, and will always do what I have to do and what I can do.

I know, says Shirin-Gol, gently touches his lips and says, whoever killed the three policemen, may God's forgiveness be upon him, and may He take the burden of guilt from his shoulders.

Chapter Eight

A Mountain and a Woman
of the Rocks

Shirin-Gol gives her mother and the twins everything she can't carry with her, kisses them goodbye, and goes back to Afghanistan. Along with her daughter Noor-Aftab and her son, Nasser, whose father is Morad, her Pakistani daughter whose father is the generous smuggler-chief, the Pakistani child in her belly, whose father is one of the three Pakistani rapists and Morad, who treats all the children Shirin-Gol has given birth to, and has yet to give birth to, as though they were his own children.

They cannot go back to the mountains, where Shirin-Gol was born and where Morad fought for years by the side of her brother until he did not want to fight any more, played cards, won and instead of the money got Shirin-Gol as his wife. There, one lot of Mujahedin are fighting another lot of Mujahedin. And in the cities of the country, in Kabul, Mazar, Kandahar, Herat and Jalalabad, war is still raging.

Let's go to the white mountain of light, says Shirin-Gol.

Where's that? asks Morad.

How should I know, answers Shirin-Gol.

*

When their children can hardly bear to walk any more, when they don't know where they are and how long they have been walking for, how often they have climbed up and down, when they have not seen a village for days, have not met a soul, when Morad thinks Shirin-Gol has lost her senses again, she still wants to go on.

If we cannot find somewhere to stay tomorrow, says Morad, we will be dead in less than four days.

The night is the coldest since they've been in the mountains. It is as though the air is full of tiny splinters of glass. The fire does not warm them. Their faded, thin fabric shirts, trousers and dresses flutter in the wind, whip against their thin bodies. The children pull their heads down between their shoulders. They blow warm air into their hands, red and blue with cold. Their fingers grow moist, a layer of ice forms. Six little icy hands. Three little icy noses. Three little icy mouths.

Shirin-Gol dies a thousand deaths at the sight of her children, who barely have life in their bodies. They have stopped whimpering, the only sound from them is the chattering of their teeth. They squint their eyes to tiny slits against the cold, knife-sharp wind. Sometimes they fade away, then they open their eyes wide again, looking helplessly for their mother.

Shirin-Gol and Morad spread out the plastic sheets and their thin blankets close by the fire, lay the children between the blankets. Noor-Aftab, Nasser and Nafass press their tiny parchment-skin-and-bones bodies tightly together. Rigid with fear they cling to one another, hold each other tight. They become a three-headed knot. Shirin-Gol presses her pregnant body to them. Morad pulls the blankets and sheets together, wraps them around his family and ties the ends. Once again he goes off into the icy darkness, pulls up bushes and thorny shrubs, tears them from the earth, makes a second fire, watches over both fires and keeps the fires, himself and his family alive.

The biting wind becomes a storm. The stars disappear behind clouds. Snow falls. Everything turns white. The rocks, the mountain, the knot of people under the plastic and also Morad and the two fires. When the first light of the sun creeps over the high peak, Morad sees clouds of smoke rising on the other side of the mountain. Eight clouds of smoke from eight chimneys. A little village.

It is four or more days' march from such-and-such a city in northern Afghanistan, somewhere in the middle of the nowhere of the endless Hindu Kush, so far from everything and everyone that it has been too much effort even for the war to find its way here.

The village has eight huts that cling to the mountain and all look the same. The huts are on stilts rather than the ground, each one has a door, two windows and a long chimney with three small openings and one big one. Except when snow is on the ground, the people constantly gather wood and anything combustible, and stack it under the huts. In the winter, they bring it up through openings in the floor and keep themselves and their fires alive.

Eight and more people live in each of the eight huts with the long legs and chimneys. All the inhabitants of the village belong to the ethnic group of the Hazara, who are considered strong and tenacious, industrious and clean. Because of their broad, Asiatic faces, almost beardless, their slanted eyes and broad noses some people say the Hazara are descended from the Chinese, others that they are the descendants of the Mongols.

The inhabitants of the eight huts do not know why their

forefathers came to the mountain, built their huts and stayed here.

Why do you live here in the middle of the mountains? Alone? Abandoned by everyone and everything? asks Shirin-Gol. Why don't you go down to the valley, where there are other people, where you don't get so much snow in the winter?

Why did you come here? the people ask in reply.

The people are nice, but sceptical. They are frightened, shy and reticent. Until they realise that Shirin-Gol, her children and Morad have no evil intentions, that they are exhausted, they need help, need somewhere to stay.

Until two, three, four or who knows or cares how many years ago, a mullah lived in the hut that Shirin-Gol and her family now move into. The mullah prayed for people when their mothers gave birth to them or God took them back. He made *ta-vis*, amulets, for the people and hung them around their necks. He married men and women. He blessed sheep, horses, goats when they were born or slaughtered, when they were ill and when they got better again.

Like all other mullahs he became a mullah because he had supposedly learned the Koran and even knew how to read and write. At least that was what he claimed, no one was able to check one way or the other, because none of the villagers had ever learned to read and write. How could they have done? Their village is several days' journey from other villages, from the city, from other people who can't read or write either.

No one knows where the mullah had come from, for how many years he lived there, who his teachers were. Why he had come alone and stayed alone. No one knows whether he had a mother who missed him, a father who needed him in the fields, brothers, sisters. No one knows why he did not take a wife, although many a father would have liked to give him his daughter, why he had left no son behind, why this and why that. The main thing was that he was there. The main thing was that he offered his services. The main thing was that the villagers did not treat him badly and have a clear conscience before their God. *Al-hamn-dul-allah*. Everyone liked him and everyone mourned him when he died. For that reason they are all glad that there is someone in the village again who can read and write and has more intelligence than all the villagers together. It is good that the mullah's hut is empty and Shirin-Gol and her family can stay there. A shame she is only a woman. Good that the village is so small and everyone is related by blood and everyone understands and knows everyone else so that it does not matter whether she is a man or a woman. Good that she is a woman, because who knows, if she were a man perhaps she would have tried to win power for herself in the village. A shame she is already married and with children because otherwise one of the men from the village could marry her so that she would have to stay for ever and never leave again, unless God brought her back. Good that she is married, because then there are no arguments about her. A shame that she is poor and has no possessions, because now the villagers have to feed her, her children and her husband. Good that she has no possessions, because that way she and her husband and her children have to muck in with everyone else. A shame that the mullah threw his books in the fire before he died and Shirin-Gol has no books she can read to find out what herbs and medicines cure pains and illnesses. Good that at least once a year someone goes into the city and will be able to bring a book back next time.

*

It is spring. The air no longer consists of breath-thin, fragile glass. The meadows are full of juicy, bright-green life, tender and strong, stubbly, squeaking and scratching, cracking and breaking under the feet. The sun is thin and its light watery. The snow on the mountain peaks is dull and heavy. The water from the streams is clear, cool, alive. The cows, sheep, goats, donkeys and horses give birth to their young. Little white, pink, yellow flowers grow between the rocks. The trees grow blossoms, leaves, fruits. The people lay aside their heavy furs and blankets, roll up their sleeves, squat, while the sun shines, more outside under God's heaven than inside in the dark mud huts, lean against the walls and long legs of the huts, hold their hands in front of their eyes to shield themselves from the sun that gets stronger by the day, press fresh mud on to the sooty walls of their huts, laugh, gossip, go to the fields, sow seeds in the fields, milk the cattle, air the stables, clear the storerooms, lay blankets, sleeping-mats, cushions in the sun, hum little songs, sleep at night under the clear sky, filled with an infinite number of stars. In short, people do everything their mothers and fathers did before them, every year when winter left the village, the mountain, the fields and the bones and hearts of the people.

Shirin-Gol stretches her body, hidden and protected beneath cloths and veils, but still humiliated and abused, stretches her raped and pregnant body to the sky as far as she can. As though she were pulling apart painful knots that the years had tied in her soul, her body, until they tore. She stretches herself out long until she stands on the tips of her toes and her fingers play *houri*, angels, in the air, which only she and no one else can see.

Shirin-Gol hoists her *tonban*, steps in to the stream, the

water plays around her feet, she is as happy as – as when? Happier than ever before.

For the first time in her life Shirin-Gol's shoulders are unburdened, her body is not leaden, it is no threat to her own life. Put your legs together, girls do not sit around with their legs apart, or the wolf will come and bite everything you've got, Mole-sister had told Shirin-Gol when she was a little girl. A hundred times, a thousand times, again and again, put your legs together, she would scold, biting her lower lip and casting a menacing look at Shirin-Gol.

Shirin-Gol kept her legs together. Always. She was raped anyway.

Be quiet, her mother had said, nice girls stay silent, otherwise the bird will come, fly into your mouth and choke you. Tell the child to lower her eyes, or she'll get used to it and later she'll look strange men in the eyes, her father had said to her mother. Pull your headscarf down your forehead, put on your veil, pull your feet in, lower your eyes, don't speak when your brothers are speaking, make way, get out of the way, do this and don't do that, because you are a girl. Or do you want people to think you are *kharab* and want them to look at you and destroy our family's reputation? The girl is too wild, people said and Shirin-Gol's mother smacked her with the palm of her hand on the back of her head. The girl talks too much, people said, and her brother hit her in the mouth.

Shirin-Gol sits with the other women in the shade under the huts, drinks tea, gossips, cards wool, weaves skeins, weaves away at the women's carpets, sings a song, drumming out a little rhythm on a metal plate, sews a little shirt for the child in her belly, kneads whey, carves a comb, combs her children's hair and the hair of all the other children in the village, who crouch in a long row like little frogs, come to her one after the other, wanting auntie to comb their hair smooth, weave plaits, pull out knots, felt, a flea or a louse.

A little higher up, where the little stream springs from the rocks, Shirin-Gol lies down on her back, stretches her big stomach with the rapist's child in it to the sky, stretches out her arms and legs, shuts her eyes, dozes and dreams of a time free of fear, of a place that has seen no war, a life like the one she is living now.

Come quickly, calls Noor-Aftab, Abina, Abina, the daughter of what's-his-name, our neighbour, she is dying, she is trying to get the baby out of her stomach, but it won't come.

Shirin-Gol puts on her headscarf, takes the sharp sickle that she uses for cutting wheat and grass, for cutting back bushes, the one she cut the chicken's throat with, and runs after her daughter to her neighbour's house, to his daughter Abina, who cannot get the baby out of her stomach and is about to die.

Help us, pleads Abina's mother.

I am not a midwife, I am not a doctor, says Shirin-Gol, looking at the women and realising that none of them knows what a midwife or a doctor is. I am not a healer, not a mullah.

You come from the city, you can read the Koran, you have seen the world, help my child or she will die.

What has reading the Koran got to do with anything? You have given birth to your children on your own before, Shirin-Gol tries to excuse herself. She is afraid to get involved, because if anything happens to Abina or her child, Shirin-Gol will be held responsible. Delicate Abina is lying on her mattress on the floor, she is twelve, maybe thirteen years old. Beside her crouches her first child, with its hand in its mouth, crying and sobbing.

The colour in Abina's face is white, cold pearls of sweat sit on her forehead. Her eyes have slipped upwards, only the whites are visible. Her lids tremble. Her arms lie like two little branches limply on the floor as though they do not belong to her. Her legs lie limply on the floor as though they do not belong to her. Her stomach is a sphere staring at the ceiling. Her skirts are wet with the water that has run from her body. Abina is silent, like a corpse.

She is going to die, says Shirin-Gol quietly.

Abina's mother screams, cries, tears out her white hair, hurls herself on the floor, kisses the half-dead hands of her pregnant child. The door springs open, Abina's husband and her father come into the hut. If God is to fetch her back and she must die, then she will die, says her father, but Shirin-Gol-jan, dear sister, you yourself are carrying a little life beneath your heart, please don't shoulder any blame, please try at least to save the life of my child and the baby in her stomach.

Bismi-allah, on your own head be it, says Shirin-Gol, rolls up her sleeves, picks Abina's first child up from the floor, presses it into the arms of Abina's father and sends him out of the hut. When Abina's husband is about to go too, she holds on to him, looks him in the eyes and says, you are staying. The poor boy opens his mouth, he looks for words that he cannot find, walks backwards, tries to free himself from Shirin-Gol's solid grip.

She shoves the young husband over beside the half-dead girl and says, press her stomach.

Shirin-Gol slaps the pregnant girl in the face, puts damp cloths under the nape of her neck, on her forehead, pushes blankets and pillows under her legs, calls for more water, clean cloths. She tells the women to open the door and the window, let in some fresh air, knead Abina's feet, rub her hands. Somehow – she does not know herself – Shirin-Gol manages to get Abina back to life.

Hoist up her skirts, says Shirin-Gol to the women. Draw in your legs, little Abina. No, it is not a sin if I see your naked body. No, it is not a sin for your husband to be here. That's good. No, you do not need to have *sharm*, you do not need to be ashamed. The child in your stomach is his child as well. No, your blood is not impure, blood is sacred, blood keeps us alive.

Fetch water, she says to the women. No, not this water, it is dirty. Make a fire. Fetch fresh water from the spring and boil it, we need hot, clean water. Boil the cloths, put the sickle in the fire, heat it up, no, not with your dirty hands, wash your hands.

Abina pushes and pushes. Her young husband presses her stomach, holds her leg. Abina's mother utters one prayer after another. Shirin-Gol puts her fingers into Abina's mother-opening to get the child out, but its head is too big.

Until now, Shirin-Gol has only helped her own children into the world. She took off her *tonban*, hoisted up her skirts, crept into a corner and squatted down, if there were stones nearby she stuck them under her feet. And she did what all the mothers in the world do when their children are coming into the world. She suffered, waited, hoped, prayed, cursed, wept, clenched her teeth until the new life was out of her body and underneath her, severed the umbilical with the sickle and tied it with a thread. She waited for the afterbirth, meanwhile cleaning the child of blood and mother-fluid, kissed it, wrapped it in her skirt or in cloths and wished it a long life.

At Nasser's birth Morad had brought her two proper bricks, equal in size to put under her feet so she could sit higher. At the birth of Noor-Aftab she had scrabbled a hole in the sandy floor to have more room underneath herself. She left the afterbirth in the hole, scooped earth over it and put a stone on top. That was it. *Khalass* and *tamam*.

But Shirin-Gol does not have a clue what to do in a situation like this.

The women squat around her, waiting for her to perform a miracle. They study her every move, follow her every breath, hear her every word, obey each of her instructions.

Bibi-Deljan, the oldest woman in the village, sits quietly by Abina's head, mutely moves her lips and sends the beads of her prayer-chain first in one direction, then in the other. Bibi-Deljan doesn't have a single smooth area of skin, everything about her is arranged in little wrinkles and creases. Wrinkles and creases that look like the sharp edges and rocks of the mountains she lives in. Bibi-Deljan, the human rock. Rock woman. Woman rock. Woman made of rock. Upright, solid, motionless. Rock head. Rock back. Rock legs. Rock arms.

Apart from her mute lips and the bony fingers with which she sends the beads of her prayer-chain first in one direction, then in the other, Bibi-Deljan does not move at all. She sits there and does not take her eyes off Shirin-Gol. It is as though she wanted to stretch an invisible thread between herself and Shirin-Gol. As though she wanted to creep along that thread and go inside Shirin-Gol, into her head, into her soul, into her blood, her arms, her legs, each one of her hairs. It is as though she wants to place everything her eyes have ever seen, every thought she has ever thought, on the thin thread and give it to Shirin-Gol. It is as though the voices and sounds in the hut were vanishing. As though the colours were vanishing. First Abina's mother's face loses its eyes, its nose, its ears, its mouth becomes a black hole. Then all the other faces lose their eyes, noses, ears, all the mouths become black holes. Only the rock woman's face has eyes, a nose, ears, a mouth. Mute murmuring mouth. Everything is silent. Shirin-Gol closes her eyes, tries to stop the spinning in her head. Shirin-Gol loses all her words, all her thoughts. Only one remains. She can find one thought and one alone in her spinning head. No eyes, no ears, where there were mouths there are only black holes. I could go, leave the hut, thinks Shirin-Gol. No one will notice. I mustn't spoil God's handiwork.

It is God's will that you are here helping us, says Bibi-Deljan in a gentle, calm voice.

Abina's mother gets her eyes back, her nose, her ears, her mouth. She utters a quiet, choking cry as though she has seen a ghost. She throws her hand to her mouth, her other hand claws in her skirts. *La-elah-ha-el-allah*, she says, for two winters and two summers Bibi-Deljan hasn't spoken. Now that my child is dying she has found her tongue again.

Bibi-Deljan, the mute rock-woman, has found her tongue again. Abina's mother has found her mouth and her shrill voice again. The rock woman doesn't take her eyes off Shirin-Gol, goes on pushing the beads of her prayer-chain one by one, first in one direction, then the other.

A thousand little beads of sweat run down Shirin-Gol's body. She trembles, can hardly catch her breath, her hands are helpless. She stares at the opening between Abina's girl-woman legs, sees the child's head, shoves her fingers into the opening, feels the child's soft nose, its ears, its mouth. She tries to hold on to the head, slips off, can't get the baby out. Rock woman. Rock woman. Click. Click. Pushing the beads of her chain.

Give me the sickle, says Shirin-Gol.

The sickle? cries Abina's mother. You use the sickle for cutting the umbilical cord, the child is not even out yet, what in God's name do you want with the sickle?

I don't know, groans Shirin-Gol. But we have got to get the child out of her body somehow.

Abina's mother falls silent.

Shirin-Gol carefully inserts the tip of the sickle past the slippery child's head into the vagina, whispers *bismi-allah* and cuts the vagina open two fingers wide. Blood. Thick, red blood runs over the blade, over Shirin-Gol's fingers. The rock woman doesn't stir, goes on pushing one bead after the other first in one direction, then the other. Click. Click. The rock woman doesn't take her eyes off Shirin-Gol. Abina's mother screams shrilly. Shirin-Gol is choking. She feels dizzy. Her knees go soft. She pulls herself together, puts a hand on Abina's big stomach, pushes, presses, pulls the child out with the other, lays the umbilical cord over the sickle, whispers *bismi-allah* again, pulls the sickle through, ties the clean thread around the severed cord, smacks the child on the back, so that it spits and takes its first breath.

Shirin-Gol lays the child in the young father's arms, tries to thread the needle, trembles, gives the needle and thread to Abina's mother, who appears to have lost her mind and understands nothing. The young father takes the needle and thread, threads the needle, mumbling that this is a woman's job. He pushes a cloth between Abina's teeth, looks at Shirin-Gol, it is neither a smile nor a threat, it is an understanding, gratitude. Do it, he says, God is with you.

God is with me, thinks Shirin-Gol, sticks the needle into one side of the wound, pulls the thread through, makes a knot and does not know how she knows what she must do.

It is as though she were sewing leather, as though she were mending a hole in a shoe. Sticks it in, pulls it out, sticks it in, pulls it out, makes another knot, a third and fourth.

Abina is no longer sentient, no one knows if she will wake up again.

Shirin-Gol stays with her all night. The rock woman stays too. She goes on pushing the beads of her prayer-chain first in one direction, then the other. The young husband does not move from the side of his girl bride.

The sun is just casting its first light over the peak of the mountain to which the eight mud huts cling, the little foal who fell to earth from his mother's stomach two days ago is just whinnying for the first time, the first cock is just crowing, the baby with the thin parchment skin is just crying, the young man is just putting his washed finger in the mouth of the baby, his second child, so that it can suckle on it, when Abina opens her eyes, smiles quietly, sees her young husband, sees her new-born daughter, sees Shirin-Gol and whispers in a faint girl-woman voice, kind sister, may God grant you a long and healthy life.

Weeks pass before Abina gets her strength back, is able to get up and do everything she used to. A long time passes after that before Abina is really alive again, and the person she was before the birth of her second child.

But even when everything is as it has always been, after the birth of her second child everything is different from what it has always been. And everyone knows it has nothing to do with the birth and the second child, it has all to do with Shirin-Gol.

Although Abina has not seen many women over the years, she knows all the women and girls in her village and she knows very well that none of them is like Shirin-Gol.

Shirin-Gol is clever. Shirin-Gol has an answer to every question from everyone, women and men. Even questions that make the men shrug their shoulders. It is clear to Abina that Shirin-Gol is consecrated, a saint, sent by God.

Abina spends every minute she can spare with Shirin-Gol, watching her, listening to her every word, memorising everything, copying her every movement, asking a thousand and one questions. Shirin-Gol does not want her to, or even notice she's doing it, but Abina copies everything Shirin-Gol does, goes to the well when Shirin-Gol goes to the well, cooks dinner the way she does, bakes bread the way she makes it. Like Shirin-Gol Abina always washes her hands before kneading the dough, before feeding her child, before preparing food. Like Shirin-Gol, Abina makes sure that the flies don't settle on her food. As she has learned from Shirin-Gol, says Abina, when the fly settles on shit the shit sticks to its feet, and then if it settles on our food, the shit sticks to our food. But shit is not good for us and makes us ill. As Shirin-Gol used to do, Abina starts drawing words in the sand. Like Shirin-Gol, she starts to say no.

At first her young husband laughs and is happy that his little Abina is alive. Later he gets annoyed with her and wants to beat her when she contradicts him. But instead of drawing her head between her shoulders, Abina catches his hand in the air, looks into his eyes and says, if you love someone you do not hit them. Tell me what you want, if I can give it to you I'll give it to you and if I cannot give it to you I will not be able to give it to you, even if you hit me.

The young husband lowers his eyes and says, I am afraid of you.

Why? asks Abina.

Because you do not obey me any more.

Shirin-Gol said it says in the Koran the husband should honour and respect his wife.

I do that, says the young husband, but you should obey me anyway. You are my wife. Your father passed on to me his responsibility over you and his God-given right to determine you and your fate. If you won't obey me any more, I will take you back to him.

Abina says nothing and lowers her eyes.

Spring is gone, summer has come and has left again, autumn arrives, the leaves on the trees turn yellow, then brown, lose their life and fall. Abina's child grows, gets bigger, cries, eats, suckles at its mother's breast. Abina says nothing. Another woman in the village gives birth to a child. The rock woman puts into Shirin-Gol's hands the string of prayer beads that Shirin-Gol now wears around her neck, says goodbye, goes into the mountains to her rock. Dies, becomes rock. Goes to her God. Shirin-Gol has given birth to her fourth child, whose father is one of the three Pakistani rapists. It is small and delicate, with thin, powerful little arms and legs, with small feet and tiny toes, lively fingers, dark skin like brown parchment. The child has soft, velvety hair, pitch-black. Its eyes are like coals, gleaming. Its lips are soft and full. My Pakistani boy, Shirin-Gol whispers into the child's tiny ear so that it tickles, the little boy pulls his arms in and trembles like aspen leaves. May your innocent eyes see only the good, not the bad in the world. I will call you Nabi. Shirin-Gol washes the blood and fluid from his little body, kisses him on the forehead, on the stomach, on his eyes and his hands, on his feet and his arms and she prays to God to give her the strength and courage to love Nabi no less and no more than her other three children.

Up on the peaks, new snow falls unnoticed, lays its fresh fragrance, its coldness in the arms of the wind that comes down to the village and whispers to the people in the eight mud huts that winter is on its way to them.

A few village boys grow serious, narrow their eyes to slits, look up into the sky and the highest peak, and say there will be so much snow that our huts will be completely covered.

Nasser looks up at the chimney of his hut and calls, there isn't that much snow in the world.

There is, say the other boys.

Cheeky Nasser throws a stone and tries to hit the peak of the mountain with it. Then we'll just dig holes in the snow, he says, and open up the paths.

You can't shovel away that much snow, say the other boys.

My father can, says Nasser, inflating his chest.

No, he can't.

Yes he can. He has seen the world, so he is going to know how to dig a hole in the snow.

The other boys know better. The first snow falls, lies solid and heavy on the paths and won't be shovelled away.

Why don't we build roofs over the paths? asks Shirin-Gol. If we connect the entrances to the huts, snow cannot fall on the paths.

The men look at Shirin-Gol, exchange glances and shrug.

When the snow comes, it covers everything and everybody. Every bush, every tree, every rock is covered.

Everything, everything, everything turns white. The people can't leave their huts. The snow blocks every crack and every fissure, the wind and the cold stay outside, and inside the hut it is warm and cosy.

Every day Morad climbs up the wooden ladder under the chimney vent and pokes holes in the snow with a long wooden pole so that fresh air comes into the hut and the smoke from the fire can escape. The children enjoy the stick-thin rays of sunshine that fall like spears into the hut. They enjoy opening the gap in the floor, bringing up new wood for the fire, climbing down and feeding the goat and the chickens.

For a day, two, three, four days, but then they want to go outside to join the other children, to go to the stream, climb on the rocks or wherever.

Why can't we? Has the sun gone away? For ever? Are the other children and people buried in their huts too? When is the snow going away? Are we dead? *Shahid*? Snow martyrs? Why aren't we in a different village? One where there's no snow.

After so-and-so many days, Shirin-Gol says, let's play a game, the names game. She writes her name on the wall in charcoal. My name tells of sweet flowers, butterflies and bees that sip at them, draw in the pollen with their little tongues, feed their children with it and make honey that we humans are then able to eat.

Me next, calls Cheeky-Nasser, writing his name under that of his mother and beaming around, big-eyed.

You have to say what your name means, says Noor-Aftab.

Nasser sticks out his lower lip, looks at his mother and demands, you say it.

Nasser means friend, the one who is always there for you, who helps and is kind. Shirin-Gol picks up Nasser, pulls him on to her lap and tickles him to make him laugh.

Dost. I'm the friend. Everyone's friend, he cries.

And now Noor-Aftab, says Shirin-Gol, smiling at her daughter.

My name is an easy one, every child knows what it means and I'm bored, complains Noor-Aftab.

No, that won't do, calls Nasser, you've got to write it, and you have to say what it means.

Bored, Noor-Aftab writes her name on the mud wall, bored, she says my name means Light of the Sun, and that is why I get sick and miserable when I cannot see the sun.

No, you don't, says Shirin-Gol. Morad, your turn.

I'm not a child.

Neither am I, says Shirin-Gol.

M-o-r-a-t, Morad scrawls slowly on the mud wall.

Wrong, wrong, wrong, calls Cheeky-Nasser, rubs out the -t- with his hand and writes a -d- in its place.

Noor-Aftab says nothing, ashamed on behalf of her stupid father, and looks at the flap of wood that closes the window, as though it were open, as though she can see the mountain behind it, the chamois that find their food among the rocks.

Go on, says Nasser, what story does your name tell?

Leave me alone, murmurs Morad.

No, says Shirin-Gol.

Morad says nothing. His daughter's shame becomes a spear that pierces his breast like the long pole that he pushes into the snow through the chimney.

During the night Shirin-Gol cannot get to sleep. She turns to Morad and says, I can't even tell whether it is day or night any more. How many more stories am I going to have to make up? How many songs are we going to sing? All the walls of the hut are full of words and pictures already.

When spring comes, I'll work some fresh mud and put it on the walls.

I can't bear the darkness anymore, whispers Shirin-Gol. I don't want to go on, I have no strength left.

Morad's finger finds Shirin-Gol's lips, he strokes them gently. Her breath quickens. Blood rushes to her body. Her heart grows warm. Morad strokes her neck, her shoulders, her arm, her breast, her stomach. And for the first time since – Shirin-Gol doesn't know since when, then she remembers – since he had the refrigerator-accident, Morad pushes his pleasure into her body. Shirin-Gol throws back her head, strokes Morad's arms, his back, feels his breath on her throat, hears his groaning, his contentment, his pride and the hissing in the hot embers of the fire.

The snow is melting, calls wide-awake, Cheeky-Nasser into the darkness, to wake Noor-Aftab, Nafass and even little Nabi with his loud voice.

What have you been doing in the dark winter days? asks Abina.

Sleeping, sleeping, sleeping, laughs Shirin-Gol, showing her white pearly teeth. And when we weren't sleeping we were singing, cooking, eating, playing, writing, writing and writing. All the walls are full of words and little pictures.

Kissing, kissing, kissing, calls Cheeky-Nasser, pointing at his mother and then his father and saying, this one kissed that one.

We should build a roof over our door, says their neighbour, Abina's father, then we could visit each other next winter and we wouldn't be so lonely.

That's a good decision, says Shirin-Gol.

The children slap clumps of mud against the pillars that

the men build for the roofs, leaving the impressions of their hands and fingers. Abina and Noor-Aftab draw names in the moist mud, and they build little shoe-huts, as big as four chickens, beside the entrances to the huts. Nasser and Nafass knead little people and put them on the shoe-huts so that the shoes won't be lonely.

Before spring is over all the paths have pillars and roofs.

Shirin-Gol-jan, the men say, drink some tea with us and tell us who the Russians are. Why did they come to our country? What guest-gift did their leader give to our leader? Why did they wage war against our brothers? Why did they go again? When did they go? How long is ten years? Did they get what they were looking for? Who is fighting who? Aren't they all Afghans? Aren't they all Moslems? Brothers and sisters?

Summer comes, the fruits on the trees are ripe and big, the grapes on the vines are juicy, the cherries are red and ripe and almost want to bust, the tomatoes are fleshy and fragrant. The women spread a cloth between the branches of the mulberry trees, spread blankets out on the ground, bring out basketfuls of tomatoes, beans, peas, herbs, slice them, pod them, top and tail them, lay the fruits, the vegetables, the herbs out to dry.

Stores for the winter. Winter stores.

That is beautiful, says Shirin-Gol.

What? What is beautiful? ask the women.

You are. You are beautiful. The fruits. The cloths. The podding. The peeling. The drying.

It is our life, say the women.

Wherever I've lived, says Shirin-Gol, the Afghans don't know anything about this life any more. It is knowledge that the wars have destroyed. The fields are mined, the peasants have gone to war, people are always in flight. They have forgotten how to prepare fields, to raise sheep and cows, lay in stores.

The women laugh and say, then they should all come here, we will show them and remind them. We haven't forgotten anything. We do everything as we have learned it from our mothers and our mothers' mothers. How do the other women in our homeland live, tell us.

There isn't much to tell, says Shirin-Gol. Women in Afghanistan have never had much. But since the Russians came to our country, since the Mujahedin have been fighting their wars, since the Taleban seized power in parts of the country, women have lost even their last rights and their last freedom. They have lost everything. Their honour, their dignity, their knowledge.

The women stop laughing, stop topping and tailing.

We haven't lost anything, but we haven't gained anything either, says Abina. Our life is always the same.

But we are alive, says another woman. In peace. And quiet.

Fine quiet that is, says a third woman. The quiet of fear. We are afraid. Even our husbands are afraid. Of everything and everybody. Of strangers. Of the people in the city.

Go on, says Abina, tell us about the rest of the world.

I don't know the rest of the world either, says Shirin-Gol.

Tell us about the places you know, say the women.

Some time ago, before the war destroyed everything, Shirin-Gol tells them, many people in the city had electricity. If you have electricity, with a ball so small it fits in my hand you can make more light than you can with four oil lamps.

That's sorcery, whispers a woman.

Be quiet, says Abina, let Shirin-Gol tell her story.

In the city women do not die when they're bringing children into the world. Children do not die because they have diarrhoea, fever or consumption. They say there are even places where severed arms can be sewn back on again.

La-elaha-el-allah, the women cry in disbelief.

People make cars and aeroplanes.

What are cars and aeroplanes? ask the women. What do they need them for? Have these people a prophet? A God? Does our Allah know their God?

We are all God's creations, says Shirin-Gol, and he loves us all. Women and men to the same degree. *Al-hamn-do-allah*.

Shirin-Gol remembers her teacher, Fawzi, the half-naked woman with the lovely smile in the Russian school, and a story she told. A bird needs two wings to fly. The world is like a bird. It too needs both wings. It needs women and men so that it doesn't come to a standstill.

But we are not birds and we cannot fly, one woman says.

I am a bird, whispers Abina. A bird with two wings. One for women. One for men.

Shirin-Gol-jan, the men say, you are making our women *kharab*, bad, rotten.

Kharab. Like a rotting fruit.

Kharab. Like a broken window.

The men say, the mullah, may God have mercy on his soul, never said any of this.

The mullah was a man, says Shirin-Gol.

Summer goes, winter comes. Children are born. God takes a few people back. A ninth hut that clings to the mountain is built, for Abina, her husband and their children. Abina's stomach grows big again, this and that happens again. Sometimes the people argue, sometimes they agree. Sometimes they want to take away the cloth between the mulberry trees so that the women don't congregate under it, sometimes they don't. Sometimes the women obey their husbands, sometimes they don't. Sometimes they want to hear what Shirin-Gol has to say about this or that. Sometimes they don't want the stranger to poke her nose into their affairs. Sometimes Shirin-Gol says, I have had no news from a soul, I don't want to stay here any more. Sometimes she says, at least it is peaceful here, and my children have enough to eat and a roof over their heads.

Shirin-Gol's Pakistani son Nabi can already stand on his own feet, he can walk and say his first words. Nabi. I want. Nabi is tired. Nabi wants a wee-wee. Hungry. *Madar*. *Pedar*. Give. Leave me alone.

Shirin-Gol is at the stream washing Nabi, Noor-Aftab has just come to see her mother when there is a loud rumbling in the sky. A wind, strong as a storm, rises up and throws everything into confusion, clothes flap, chickens flee for the safety of the shoe-huts, donkeys bray loudly, the people run in all directions, women screech, girls hold their arms over their heads, children drop to the ground, gaze into the sky and see a bird, bigger, more monstrous, noisier, blacker, louder, more evil than they have ever seen before.

The enormous black monster-bird flies once over the village. Then once again. Slowly. Thoughtfully. Flies lower. Hovers in the air. Looks at them with its terrible eyes that sparkle and glitter in the sun as though about to spew fire on the huts and the people running back and forth. The monster slowly, very slowly raises its head, turns away, shows the people its tail and vanishes again behind the peak of the mountain.

God is punishing us for our sins, the girls screech.

The day of reckoning is near, call the women.

What should we do? ask the men.

We'll get our slingshots and defend ourselves, say the boys.

That was a helicopter, you fool, cries Cheeky-Nasser, getting a scowl from his mother. He puts his hand on the shoulder of the boy he called a fool and says rather more quietly, no, not a fool, and then in a loud voice again, that was not a bird though, it was a helicopter.

They will come again, says Shirin-Gol. They will come again with their iron birds and with rockets spewing fire, they will shoot at us and destroy everything.

Even our shoe-huts?

Even our shoe-huts.

And our words in the mud?

Our words, our huts, our path-roofs, our stream, our fields, our stores, our mulberry trees. Everything. And then they will come and stab, shoot and kill everything with any life in it.

Who sends the iron bird?

The war.

Why? What have we done?

Nothing, cries Shirin-Gol. You do not have to do anything to war to make it come. When war wants to come it comes. Regardless of who you are and what you have done. Stop asking questions, grab your things, we have got to hurry, we have got to get away.

Shirin-Gol-jan, the men say, you have told us about the world, you have helped our children into the world, you have been a sister to us, whom we have honoured and respected, you have brought us words and the path-roofs. But you will not get us away from here. Our life is here. We were born on this patch of ground. We are a part of these mountains, these rocks. We are like these stones. You cannot take them away, either. We would be lost anywhere else in the world. If God wills it to put our lives to an end, then it is his will, and we will accept our fate. And who knows, maybe war will think things over, see that there is nothing worth having here, and that we are doing no harm to anyone. God is merciful. Maybe war will leave us in peace.

War in peace. Peace-war. War-peace.

However much Shirin-Gol begs and pleads, the people absolutely refuse to go. They want to stay, even if it is the final day that God grants them beneath his sky.

Shirin-Gol grabs together everything she can carry. Morad, Noor-Aftab, Nasser, Nafass, Nabi and she shake hands with everyone, embrace and kiss everyone they are allowed to embrace and kiss, and hurry to leave the village.

The sun has not yet disappeared behind the peak. Shirin-Gol, Morad and the children have reached the mountain across the valley, where they spent their last night in the mountains before they reached the village with the eight huts.

The people aren't yet so small that Shirin-Gol cannot see them. Their voices aren't so far away that Shirin-Gol cannot hear them. Abina is carrying her child in her arms and walking over to the last hut. Abina is putting her hand to her mouth and calling, Shirin-Gol, God be with you. Shirin-Gol is about to reply, when the black iron bird comes hovering over the mountain. Silently at first. Then another bird appears. They both hover, whirring quietly, then loudly screaming and screeching, circle above the village once, lower their heads, fly lower and lower, fire rockets, one, two, three, four.

Shirin-Gol stops counting.

Morad and she hide the children behind a rock, cover their ears, close their eyes, press their fearful bodies close together and wait, until the mountains fall silent once more.

Shirin-Gol doesn't have to look to know what is happening. Whoever the men are who are sitting in the helicopters – why are they always men – whoever they are, in whoever's name they are fighting – fighting? That is not what they're doing. They are just firing. On defenceless people. On unsuspecting people.

In whoever's name they are fighting, they land their helicopters on the ground, storm through the village with their Kalashnikovs and knifes. Set fire to everything that burns. Lay mines, so that no one can ever live in the huts again.

Everyone who is left alive, everyone, everyone, everyone, even Abina and her child, they shoot. They stab. They slit open.

Chapter Nine

AZADINE AND A SMALL RESISTANCE

I don't want to go anywhere, Noor-Aftab screams at her mother. What sort of life is that? You drag us from the city to the country, then back to the city, then we are travelling day and night through some deserts and mountains or other. Sometimes we almost dry up and burn, then we almost turn to ice and freeze. You drag us to Pakistan, to a stinking, filthy refugee camp, where first our father goes mad and then you do. Then you drag us into the mountains, to some village and even today you do not know exactly where it was. A village where we make friends and they all get killed. We are forever going from right to left, top to bottom until I'll soon have had every patch of ground in the country under my feet. Now I'm here in a village that even the spirits of the dead, may God protect their souls, are fleeing. *Madar*, please. *Madar-jan*. I cannot go on. I don't want to go on. I have no strength left. I don't want to get used to new people only to have to leave them again, only to have to watch someone coming and killing them. I have seen enough in my small life for seven big lives. Come what may, I'm staying here.

Here? Where's here? asks Shirin-Gol. Here is nowhere.

There is nothing and nobody here. No one we know.

Noor-Aftab's face is white like the little cloud in the sky. White. Colourless. Colour gone. Daughter-with-no-colour-in-her-face is crying. Crying tears that lie like light spring rain on her skin. Her voice is hoarse, as though a little thunder had wandered into her throat.

Where is there anyone we know, anyone we trust? she shouts, stamping her bare foot on the hard, dry floor and banging her fist against the skeleton of the former hut. That anyone isn't anywhere.

Look around you. We are in the middle of the desert. In the middle of nothing. No tree, no bushes, only burst, yellow earth, with cracks so big you have to be careful not to fall in. No people, no fields, no village. Nothing to eat. We are running out of water. We have no roof over our heads. The sun will fry us and leave only so much of us that we'll only be food for vultures and flies. You see the red painted stones everywhere? It's all mined around here. Not even a dog wants to live here, let alone people.

I'm staying, shouts Noor-Aftab. And if it has to be, I will die here. So what? Then call me a dog.

Shirin-Gol crouches on her feet, her arms on her knees, a deep, lovely laugh slips from her throat, lies down on the faint breeze and flies across to her daughter. Noor-Aftab has folded her arms over her chest, stuck out her lower lip, she stands with her back in the frame of the hut, looking at her bare feet.

Come here, says Shirin-Gol, stands up, embraces her daughter, who is more than a head smaller than she is herself. Shirin-Gol crouches on the floor, pulls her daughter into her lap, kisses her, strokes her hair and says, my pretty ray of sunshine. That is all she says. Just, my pretty ray of sunshine.

Where do you want to go? asks Noor-Aftab.

Shirin-Gol doesn't know, tries not to lose her smile and her composure, thinks for a moment, strokes her daughter's back as though rubbing in ointment.

To Iran, says Shirin-Gol, not knowing where the idea comes from. To Iran.

To Iran? whines Noor-Aftab. That is another country. Once again, another country. We'll have to cross a border again. I don't want to go back to a refugee camp.

We're not going anywhere yet, says Shirin-Gol, we haven't got the money for the journey and we don't know the way. Don't you worry. First of all we'll go to the nearest village, your father and I will try to earn money, that will take time, weeks, maybe months. Only then will we set off for Iran, and you'll see, everything will be fine then. You will be able to go to school. You will learn a lot of things. You will have a job.

Noor-Aftab looks sceptically at her mother. A job?

Yes, says Shirin-Gol, in Iran even girls and women can have jobs. They can be absolutely anything they want.

I want to fly, says Noor-Aftab. Aeroplanes. I want to fly people back and forth. Not bombs. People.

That's a nice job, says Shirin-Gol.

Shirin-Gol crouches on the ground among the skeleton of a hut, in some former village, on the way from somewhere or other to somewhere else, and knows that for the first time she has given her child a promise that she will probably never be able to keep.

Everything is going to be fine.

Shirin-Gol, Morad and their four children are lucky. They do not have to walk longer than the evening of the fourth day before they reach a village where they can stay. It isn't too small and it isn't too big. Strangers aren't immediately conspicuous, and the rest of the inhabitants do not see them as a threat. Not so many people live here that new arrivals are left to their own fates.

On the very first evening, the owner of the tea-house sends Morad a pot of freshly brewed tea and offers him a little room behind the tea-house, where he and his family can live.

We have no money, says Morad.

That doesn't matter, says the tea-house owner. At this time of year there is enough work for everyone who's prepared to get up early and put his back into it. You can work, earn money and pay the rent for the room later.

War is raging everywhere. There is no work to be had anywhere in the country. In all the cities and villages where they have been, life is paralysed. And here is a man standing in front of them, pouring his tea-house guests freshly brewed tea in little glasses, filling them with hot water and ensuring they are all supplied with fresh tea, saying there is work.

Morad is about to thank him, about to ask him what kind of work it is, he is smiling and about to open his mouth, when Cheeky-Nasser, who has been hiding behind his father until now and keeping his mouth shut, calls out, my father can do all kinds of work. He's been a Mujahed. He's fought in the mountains. Then he was a smuggler.

Really? A smuggler. That's good, the tea-house owner says, unconcerned, we've got work for smugglers as well.

Cheeky Nasser is so pleased with the tea-house owner's reply that he plucks up courage, comes out from behind his father's protecting body, inflates his chest and says, I want to be a smuggler, too.

Really? So you want to be a smuggler as well?

Yes, says Nasser firmly. When I'm as big as him, pointing at his father.

Morad closes his half-opened mouth, loses his half-smile, puts his hand on his son's head and pulls him to him.

And until then? Will you start working in my tea-house? You could serve the men tea, wash the glasses and saucers, shoo away the flies, break sugar into little pieces, sweep the carpets on the plank beds and whatever. You could do everything the other boy who was my helper used to do, before he decided to go into the fields and work there.

Nasser looks at the tea-house owner, his eyes wide, looks down at himself, as though to examine whether he is big enough and suitable for such responsible employment, looks at his father, sees Morad's severe expression, says nothing and vanishes again behind his protecting father.

All right then, says the tea-house owner, laughing, you've just arrived, if you like come back tomorrow and then we'll talk. And to Morad he says, here, brother, take the pot, and I've got some bread too, and some rice. The room isn't big, but it is better than sleeping in the street. Walk around the tea-house, you can't miss it.

What difference does it make what kind of work it is? asks Morad.

A big difference, says Shirin-Gol, covering up her children, who are finally sleeping on mattresses again after who knows how long, putting their heads on pillows and covering themselves with blankets. They might want you to kill people for them, or go to war, and then it won't be long before you are killed yourself.

Let's go to sleep first, says Morad. I'll talk to him tomorrow, and then we'll see how things are.

Fine, says Shirin-Gol. Let's see tomorrow how things are.

By daylight the village is smaller, much prettier and friendlier than it seemed in the darkness of the previous night. Basically it consists only of a single sandy street. At one end is the way in and out of the village. At the other end you run into a big iron gate. The light-blue paint of the gate is pocked here and there with little bullet-holes or whatever, that look like little, painful wounds and pimples. The door hides a shadowy, big, almost circular garden, where old trees give cool shade. To the right and left of the biggest tree, which stands in the middle of the garden, stand two identical, plain houses. In one of the houses lives the governor of the village, in the other is the village jail.

The only other jail that Shirin-Gol has seen before is in Kabul. In the time of the Russians the enemies of the Russians were locked up in it, tortured and murdered. When the Mujahedin came to power, the friends of the Russians were locked up, tortured and murdered. But whoever was locked up, tortured and murdered in it, Kabul is still the capital, and as far as Shirin-Gol knows, a proper capital also needs a proper jail. But what does a little village, where everyone knows everyone else, need with a jail?

We need it, the people say.

What for?

Because that is how it is.

A long time passes before Shirin-Gol learns from Bahadur, the fourth wife of the second-most-important Mujahedin commander, the reason why a little village like this one has to have a jail.

The reason is the Americans, says Bahadur. One day a

young American with a pretty white four-by-four came, and two more pretty white four-by-fours came to the village shortly afterwards. The American, his colleagues and his translator, marched through the village with a lot of fanfare and noise and all their colourful clothes, spoke to all the men they could find, drank tea everywhere, looked at the opium fields, watched the men scraping and collecting the opium from the capsules, asked how much the owners of the fields earned, how much the workers earned. The Americans went from shop to shop and asked what this and that cost, and at some point they drove off again. After a few days the American came back. And he brought with him a message from his government. We were to plant so-and-so many fewer poppies, and harvest so-and-so much less opium. The American said his government would even give us money for it, but only when we had built a prison to lock up the men who went on producing too many poppies or manufacturing too much opium. And because he offered us quite a large sum of money for that, we quickly declared the second house in the governor's garden, where the mullah had lived until then, to be a prison. The mullah moved to another house in the village. *Khalass* and *tamam*.

So much for the prison, says Bahadur, but as to why the American, whose name was Dan or Dun or Don, and his government were interested in us planting so-and-so many fewer poppies and manufacturing less opium, that was something we never really understood. He told us that in his country and other countries in the world many people grew ill with opium and died. We asked again and again why he had come all that way to see us and give us money instead of forbidding people in his own country to buy opium. We told the American, who, by the way, was very nice and very handsome, that our fields were mined, and that we could not plant them with cotton, rice and wheat as we had before. That we could only survive by planting poppies. We told him that it took an awful lot of time, money and lives to remove the mines from fields. We could only transport wheat by truck. You can stick opium in your pocket, set off on foot and sell it. We explained to him that we would like to take his money, and set up a jail in which we could lock up some man from our village every now and again. We explained all that to Don, or whatever his name was. But I'm not sure, says Bahadur thoughtfully, whether the American understood. At any rate we kept the jail, it turned out to be useful enough. Because sometimes our governor receives visits from relations or other governors or important people. They get put up in the second house. Of course we don't tell them it is really our jail. But even if we don't have important guests in the village, the men sometimes use the second house. It may sometimes happen that a man doesn't want to sleep in his own house because he has had a row with his wife or because he just wants a bit of peace and to be on his own. Then he spends a few nights in the jail.

At first Shirin-Gol thinks Bahadur is just making up the whole story to boost her own importance, but then she and Morad hear the same story from other people in the village and begin to believe it. And before long Shirin-Gol, her children and Morad are telling the story to visitors and new arrivals, as though they themselves had been there when Don or Dun or Dan came to the village with all his fanfares.

On the side of the road with the governor's prison house on it, just before you get to the light-blue gate, two narrower sandy streets turn off the main sandy street. If you were a bird and you could see the village from above, the streets would look like a person lying on the ground, with their legs pressed firmly together and their arms stretched out. Where the person's feet would be is the way in and out of the village. Where the arms would be are the two narrower streets leading off the big one. Where the person's head would be is the round garden with the governor's house and the prison. The room behind the tea-house where Shirin-Gol, Morad, Noor-Aftab, Nasser, Nafass and Nabi live is to the right of the person's navel.

The room is neither small nor big. At the front it has knee-high windows with a wide window-seat. On the other three walls mattresses, mats and blankets lie on the floor, for sitting on by day and sleeping on by night. In the middle, plastic mats lie on the floor. Brilliant, greenish-yellow, friendly mats that look as though they spend all day laughing. Shirin-Gol knocks a nail into the wall with a big stone and hangs her veil on it. In a niche in the wall are a mirror, a colourful picture of a man on a horse, stabbing a dragon with his lance, and an old, empty metal tin. Nothing else.

The loveliest thing about the room is the area in front of it. It is big enough to drink tea in in the morning and to sleep out on warm nights. Shirin-Gol, the children and Morad get used to calling this area, with some exaggeration but a lot of love, a veranda. Each morning Shirin-Gol sweeps the dust from the mud floor of the veranda, every few days the children drag the mattresses, blankets, cushions and laughing plastic mats into the sun. With a lot of shouting and jumping around they beat them with sticks so that they cough up their dust, and Nasser sprays the room down with water from a hose. Nasser loves his plastic hose, it is the first hose in his life.

*

After the Mujahedin had chased the Russians from their village, various commanders who had until then been fighting side by side, began a merciless brother-war for power in the village. The present governor and his men were the strongest, and had driven out or killed all the others. Even today no other commander has dared even to come close to the village. That is good for the people. They have cleared the village of mines. They have rebuilt their homes. They have rebuilt their shops and their stalls. They have started to clear their fields of mines.

Shirin-Gol's veranda abuts a poppy field. So Shirin-Gol, Morad and the children have the prettiest view that anyone could imagine under God's heaven. Not far from the glass door and the windows of their hut grow fragrant, white, mauve and pink blossoming poppy flowers. These colourful flowers grow all around the village. Little squares or triangles, or long, narrow fields, each belonging to a different owner, are surrounded by low walls of stone or mud, themselves overgrown with plants and flowers.

In the afternoon the women sit on the little walls in the shade of the trees, gossiping and enjoying the colours, the scent and the magnificence of the fields of flowers.

Meanwhile the men sit in the tea-house, negotiating, making deals, agreeing on important and unimportant matters, smoking water pipes, slurping down one tea after another, happy that their brave commander, who, by the way, they pay handsomely for, is waging war on their behalf, and other commanders of the Mujahedin cannot advance as far as their village. All the people learn of the war is distant shots and explosions.

The tea-house owner has set his samovar up on a table

at the front. Beside the tea-house, the brother of the kind tea-house owner has set up a street stall under a raffia roof that looks like the raffia roof of his tea-house brother. He prepares meat for kebabs in a grill, and boils rice in a pot over an open flame. He sells them together in portions to the men who squat all day in his brother's tea-house, sending their prayer-beads first one way, then the other, and doing whatever else they do, before the day is over and they go back to their huts to their wives and children.

All in all the hundred, or perhaps hundred and fifty people in the village seem to be content with their lot.

The people look as though they are never in a hurry to go anywhere. Most of them have buried and hidden their images of the war with the Russians so deeply in their memory that hardly anyone talks about it. Most of them thank God for each day he gives them. No one is an enemy of anyone else, and only rarely does anyone cheat anyone. It appears that no one suffers from hunger, and everyone earns enough to survive. Not too much, not too little.

The wealthier men own fields in which they plant poppies. In their shops the less wealthy sell everything the wealthy and half-wealthy are able to afford. Pots, plates, pans, yarn, needles, clothes, radios, batteries for the radios, rice, fat, tea, wheat, nuts, shiny material for wedding-dresses, non-shiny material for other clothes, shoes from Pakistan, colourful blankets, pillows, sleeping mats that they make from the wool from the sheep. In their stalls the less wealthy repair the radios from Pakistan, the clocks and guns of the wealthier men. They mend shoes, sew clothes, waistcoats, trousers and caps, shave the younger men's hair and beards. They work in the wealthy men's poppy fields, or in the shops, stalls and workshops of the half-wealthy men.

There are also a few people who have nothing to sell but who are still not poor. They include the mullah, the governor, the teacher at the boys' school and the traders who come to the village now and again to collect the opium to take to Pakistan or Iran and sell it.

And then there is Azadine. In the days of the king, Azadine went to school in Kabul, and in the days of the Russian war she studied in Kabul. She had to interrupt her studies when the Mujahedin started their brother-war and the universities were closed. Azadine fled first to Pakistan and then to Iran, finished her studies and returned to Kabul. Because of the war, but also because her brother no longer lived there and she could not live in the city as a woman alone, Azadine came back to the village where her father was born and grew up, and where an aunt and an uncle live today.

Everyone is very happy that she has come back, and most people honour and respect her, despite the fact that she is a woman. Not only because Azadine is a good doctor, but also because she is a good and generous person. She doesn't only treat those who can pay, she treats everyone who finds his way to her. God is great, says Azadine, he will ensure that I always have enough to eat and live.

Apart from the inhabitants of her own village, Azadine treats people from many other villages and mountains and valleys from the surrounding area. Some travel for three or four days. They come on foot, on donkeys or horses. Most patients who come from the remote valleys, mountains and villages can only afford to pay a little or nothing at all. Most of them do not even have enough to go to the nearest larger town and buy the medicines that Azadine prescribes for them. If she herself has any money to spare, she gives it to her poorest patients and helps them with their groceries, with clothes or anything else. At any rate, Azadine is one of the biggest-hearted people in the whole region, so people are willing to put up even with the fact that she lives alone and has never married.

Every now and again the mullah knocks at her door and urges her finally to get married. After all, God doesn't like to see a woman living without a man, without anyone to protect her. Instead of listening to his speech, Azadine listens to the mullah's heart, knocks on his lungs, feels his pulse and advises him not to smoke too much opium, to take a walk at least once a day, and not to pester the fathers in the village to marry off their half-grown daughters, because they otherwise bring sons and daughters into the world who are weak and sick.

People must make children, the mullah insists, defending his policy of child propaganda, or rather boy propaganda, at some point the children will be of use to their parents, *yek ruz be dardeshoun mikhore*. He nods in agreement with his own words, looks at Azadine and knows she does not believe a single word.

She is a woman of the devil, the mullah tells his wife, annoyed about the special undertone in his voice that is full of respect for the woman doctor. However much contempt he tries to put in his voice, that respect is always there. And the mullah does not have the slightest notion where that unintended, respectful undertone comes from.

Azadine is not concerned about good and bad advice, or about respectful and disrespectful undertones. However those things may be, Azadine likes the village and the people in it. All of them, particularly the women. Particularly if one of them is unlike all the other women in the village.

*

Shirin-Gol is squatting on the veranda, washing clothes in the zinc bowl, when Azadine comes around the corner. Shirin-Gol is so startled at the sight of the strange woman that her heart leaps into her throat and starts thumping. Since she heard that there was a woman doctor in the village, Shirin-Gol has been wondering how she could engineer a meeting with Azadine.

Shirin-Gol rises to her feet, dries her hands on her skirt, sticks out her hand to greet the doctor, and sees that it is trembling with excitement. Only slightly, but trembling nevertheless. Azadine smiles, and her large, white teeth shine in the sun like the white blossoms of the poppies. She takes Shirin-Gol's hand, shakes it firmly, pulls Shirin-Gol to her and embraces her like a friend. The two women don't say a word. They just hold each other in their arms. They both swallow back their tears. Like two sisters embracing.

Peace be with you, says Shirin-Gol.

And peace with you, says Azadine.

They both squat down on the ground, and are in no hurry to talk to one another.

Azadine looks different from most of the women, thinks Shirin-Gol. Her skin is smoother, her eyebrows narrower, her nose finer, her eyes livelier than those of many other women, her body seems to be lighter, calmer, more secure. Only after a long time does Azadine say, people are saying you lived in Kabul and in Pakistan. They say you are teaching your children to read and write. Is it true, can you read and write?

Shirin-Gol says it is true.

At long last, a woman I can have a decent conversation with, says Azadine.

Shirin-Gol chokes on her own saliva in her excitement, and says, you are the first woman I've seen who is a doctor.

I came, says Azadine, because I wanted to see you, to meet you and welcome you to our village. And I came because I would like to ask you to help me.

Me? Help you? How can I help you?

I don't know, says Azadine. I just don't want to be on my own any more. You can write out my lists of patients, do the filing, write prescriptions. The main thing is that you come to my surgery and spend time with me.

Lists of patients? Filing? Prescriptions? I don't know anything about any of that.

You can learn.

I used to want to be a doctor, says Shirin-Gol.

Come to my surgery, says Azadine. I will teach you everything I know.

What will people say if I leave the house without my husband, work and earn money? I know no one and no one knows me. They will talk about me. They will say I'm a . . . a – what can I say?

A bad woman? asks Azadine. That is nonsense. We have got to stop living our lives according to what other people say.

You are talking like my teacher in the Russian school.

Come to my surgery. I'll invite a few women along. I will tell them you're working for me. They will tell their husbands, and soon the whole village will know that you only leave the house to work for me.

The women in the village are curious about the newcomer. They tell Shirin-Gol a thousand and one stories and ask a thousand and one questions. Where do you come from? Where were you born? Who is your father? Where is your father now? Do you have brothers? Did you know that Azadine has magic medicine? You have to swallow it every day at a particular time, you must never forget, and as long as you swallow them you don't get pregnant. Did you know Azadine never had a husband? Has she told you why she hasn't married?

Tell her, say the women.

But I've told the story so many times. Do you never get tired of it?

No, no, no. Never. The women sound like little girls. Tell us, tell us, tell us.

Azadine laughs, and her eyes look like pretty almonds.

Because I do not need a man, she says. Because I earn my own money. Because I walk alone in the street. Because I do not want anyone who thinks he owns me. Because I do my own shopping. Because I alone decide when I go to sleep, when I work, whether I work or sleep at all. Because I can decide myself when I eat or whether I want to eat at all. And because I am happier on my own.

But what will you do if one day – may God protect you from such a fate – if one day a man or two or three men jump over the wall into your courtyard, rob you of all you own and lay their hands on you as well?

Let them come, says Azadine. I will take my father's gun and shoot them all. Every single one. One after the other.

What will you do if your father's gun isn't to hand and you can't shoot the men? ask the women.

Azadine says, I would ask the first one to come into my surgery so that we can be alone and undisturbed. Then I would give him an injection that would make him faint.

Why not give him an injection that would kill him? ask the women.

Maybe I'd kill him too, says Azadine.

What will you do with the second one?

I'll tell the second one I've hidden my gold and my treasures in the bucket that hangs over the well, and when he bends over the well to get at the bucket, I will push him into the well with a great kick up his backside.

And the third? The third? ask the women, wide-eyed.

The third? The third is the handsomest. The youngest. The strongest of all. He has eyes that glow like coals. His hair is like silk. He has muscles like a panther. He is as gentle as a pussy cat. That's why I'm saving him for last. The third? I think – no, I know – I would spare that one his life. I will keep him for myself.

The women giggle contentedly.

Shirin-Gol doesn't know what to make of the doctor's story.

I will get the handsome one to do all the heavy work and maybe . . .

At this point Azadine makes a long pause, the women giggle and laugh and put their hands in front of their mouths. Azadine looks around and says, maybe I'll let him come into my room every now and again.

All the women talk at once, laugh, giggle, slap each other on the thigh, bend and bow with laughter, their arms wrapped around themselves and each other.

What will you do with him there? they want to know. Go on, tell us, tell us. What will you do with the handsomest, the youngest and the strongest? What will you do with him?

I'll do whatever I like with him, replies Azadine, making the women laugh even more. Shirin-Gol laughs too. And she thinks, this is the first time in my life that I have laughed out loud. And without knowing why, Shirin-Gol says, mostly to herself, this is resistance.

What was that?

Shirin-Gol says nothing.

Say that again, says Azadine.

Shirin-Gol lowers her eyes, doesn't want to, until the women call, encourage her and Shirin-Gol dares to repeat what she said.

This is resistance, she murmurs.

The women fall silent, look at each other, look at Shirin-Gol, look at Azadine. Laugh.

Shirin-Gol is right, says Azadine. Everything we do here is actually resistance. What would your husbands and fathers say if they saw you here, hot and red in the face, with your hair down, laughing, giggling about stories involving strange, handsome men?

The women say nothing.

Finally the kind tea-house owner's second wife, who only speaks if the tea-house owner's first wife isn't there, says in a loud, brave voice, my husband would say I'm a bad woman.

So would mine, say the other women, and talk all together.

Shirin-Gol says nothing, and doesn't know why she said what she said.

Azadine has an assistant, say the people in the village. It is the wife of that new man, Morad. Azadine's assistant has good hands, say the women.

Some people don't like seeing another woman walking in the streets of the village all of a sudden. Without her husband. Walking back and forth. Soon she knows everybody. Talks to everybody. Doesn't lower her eyes. Works. As if she were a man. They don't like to see that. But all in all most of them don't object to Azadine having an assistant. Shirin-Gol is a hard-working woman with a lot of sympathy for her fellow human beings. And since she has been helping Azadine, the doctor can see and treat far more patients every day than she could before.

Shirin-Gol spends most of her time listening to the women and girls telling her about their lives. The women ask questions that they themselves can answer better than anyone. They talk only in order to have talked to somebody. The women talk about men who beat them. They talk about their husbands' first, second, third secondary wife, who treats them badly. They say that for weeks and months they haven't been outside or even had any fresh air. The women say that their visit to the doctor, to which, on top of everything, they are accompanied by their husband, son, father, brother or uncle is their only chance of getting out of the house. The women squat in front of Shirin-Gol, start talking and then can't stop. At first many of them say they would rather be dead than alive. By the end, when they have to go back to their lives, they say, thank God he sent us a sister like you, now my heart is lighter.

The more stories and dreams Shirin-Gol hears from the women, the more she notices how unfree her own life is as well. Shirin-Gol dreams of a more beautiful life. Of a free life. Of life in another country, Iran. Shirin-Gol believes that in Iran people treat their daughters and sons the same way. She believes that her children could go to school in Iran, and learn a profession. She believes that Morad could find work there. She believes that Iranians like Afghans and treat them well. Shirin-Gol believes she could have a proper life in Iran. She believes and dreams. Dreams and believes.

There is peace in Iran, thinks Shirin-Gol. There is

neither war nor mines, neither hunger nor ruined houses. There are gardens with fruit-trees, bakers and green-grocers, schools and streets.

But this is your homeland, says Azadine. Here you are with your own people. Here you have work, here your children have peace and quiet. You have a life here too. What are you missing? What are you looking for? What do you need?

Shirin-Gol looks at the doctor, sighs heavily. As though chains were pressing on her chest. As though her body were made of lead.

I don't know, she says. I lack nothing. I lack everything. My people are here. But they are still all strangers. My children and I have everything we need to stay alive. But still we have none of the things you need for a proper life. I have work, my husband doesn't. That makes him sick, he becomes irritable. A man needs a job. My children have peace and quiet, but what will become of them? Tomorrow they'll be grown and they'll have to start a life of their own. What will they do? What will they live on? My daughters cannot go to school or learn a profession. My sons go to school, but every other day the teacher doesn't turn up because he has to work somewhere else to earn money. I don't know, says Shirin-Gol.

You're ungrateful, says Morad, we have got everything we need. We have a hut. Our hut has doors and windows. We even have a little veranda in front of our hut. People are kind to us. Our son goes to school and has a job in the tea-house. You have work. And I've found work too.

What?

Yes, says Morad, I've found work. From tomorrow morning I'm going to be working in the poppy field.

Thank God, says Shirin-Gol, stirring the rice that is boiling away on the fire and slurping and blowing big bubbles that burst loudly and react when they leap from the pot and fall into the fire. Thank God, says Shirin-Gol, waiting for the chain around her chest to burst, lighten, vanish, for the lead to disappear from her body. Thank God, says Shirin-Gol, amazed that the chains are still there, the lead is still there, and she stirs the rice and watches the bubbles jumping out and landing in the fire.

Morad crouches down by Shirin-Gol beside the fire and the rice-pot, watches the hot, leaping bubbles for a while, and says, now we haven't got any money for the journey to Iran anyway. And if we are going to start a new life there, we are going to need some money. Let's stay here for the time being, live our life as best we can, and see what happens.

Fine, says Shirin-Gol, let's stay and see what happens.

The fragrant, vivid white, mauve and pink poppies lose their delicate flowers, leave bare, yellowish-brown round heads, a little bigger than big hen's eggs, which look as though they've been sliced off at the top and are wearing a crown. Like a queen with a crown.

The long leaves of the poppy hang dry and sandy like slack, dead arms on the powerful, hairy, chest-high stems that stand in rows with their woody crowned heads like thin, ugly, dead soldiers.

Early in the morning, before the sun appears in the sky, Morad throws back his blankets, climbs over Shirin-Gol and the knot of his sleeping children, splashes cold water in his face from the plastic hose, doesn't dry the water, just shakes it off, shivers with cold, takes his jacket off the nail in the wall, swallows the taste and smell of sleep in his mouth, goes over to the other end of the field, where his new employer is already waiting for him. It is the kind man who owns the tea-house, and the room where Shirin-Gol and her family live, and the little field in front of it, where the poppies stand in rows like dead soldiers.

Morad's work is neither hard nor easy. He goes from plant to plant with three tiny blades, fixed in a hand-sized piece of wood and fastened tightly with a thread. He makes cuts, neither too shallow nor too deep, three, four or five incisions in the pot-bellied poppy-pod, and white milk swells out of them like blood from a wound. As soon as the cut stops exuding milk, Morad scrapes off the dark brown, sticky mass and collects it in a leaf. Over a period of days he slices each pod around the outside again, and again fresh white milk swells out of it and turns brown. Morad scrapes it off and smears it on a leaf. The clump gets bigger and bigger until the capsules are dry and there is nothing left of their precious juice.

Every evening Morad has a handful of the stuff smeared on leaves. After a few weeks he has one or two kilos altogether. It is pure, clean opium, for which the Pakistani trader will pay the kind tea-house owner 500 dollars and more per kilo. One or more kilos. Pure, clear opium. The trader will get 1200 dollars and more for it in Pakistan. Opium that will be turned into heroin, and sold in America and Europe.

We are planting opium, say the people in the village, because it is the only way we can earn just enough to feed our families. What other people do with the opium is no concern of ours.

After the poppies have lost their fragrant, white, mauve and pink blossoming beauty and yielded up all their valuable milk, the women cut off the dry capsules, stick holes in them and let the tiny, round, black poppy seeds trickle out. Some they and their children eat immediately, another portion they put in their food, and the largest portion they store.

The children, or more precisely, the boys, can hardly wait for that time of year. The tea-house boys, the shoe-repair boys, shepherds, salesmen, apprentice tailors, petrol-sellers come back to the field time and again to see whether the men and the older boys are still getting milk out of the poppies, or whether the capsules have finally dried up and they can steal a few of them unnoticed, before they are used as firewood.

The boys break the capsules and make a little hole in them. They let the tiny black balls trickle into their mouths and crunch them with their teeth. Their tongues look as though they had a thousand black pimples.

The boys put two poppy capsules on the ends of a stick to make an axle with rolling wheels. In the middle of the axle they put a long stick to drive their vehicle. They have races, and run through the whole village with their cars.

Their sisters and the other girls stand at the doors of their huts and at the edge of the fields, where now only the dry stems of the poppies stand in orderly rows. Like dead soldiers with their heads chopped off. The girls hold their hands to their mouths with shame, giggling as they yearningly watch the boys at play.

The girls' eyes gleam mysteriously, sending the blood rushing to the hearts of the young men in the village, and the mothers clap their daughters on the back of the head with the palms of their hands and send them to the huts with a shrill voice.

*

Why do you let the traders pocket the profits from the opium? Morad asks the kind tea-house owner. Why don't you take the opium to Pakistan yourselves? You could make much more money.

We are small, insignificant peasants, we know no one, and no one knows us, answers the kind tea-house-owner. We keep our word. The traders come all that long way to buy our opium. They rely on us to deliver it. They trust us, and we trust them. We have our agreement, and things aren't too bad for us.

They're not too bad, says Morad, that's true. But they could be better. If you sold the opium yourselves.

You know best, says the kind tea-house owner. In your homeland and mine people turn up every few weeks and months to tell us we have to change things. That it would be better if things were not the way they are. We had a king, who was deposed by his own brother-in-law who wanted to make things better. The British wanted to make things better in our country. The Russians came and wanted to save us from who knows what. The Americans armed and trained the Mujahedin, to change who knows what yet again, so that everything would be better. The Mujahedin wage war all over the place, for a better Islam. Some commanders shoot at other commanders because they want what's best for us. In Kandahar, in the south of our homeland, a new movement has appeared, calling itself the Taleban and fighting for a better Islam.

The kind tea-house-owner pours Morad a fresh glass of tea and says, no, my dear Morad, I know your intentions are good, but let's leave things as they are, while they're going well.

Fine, says Morad, if things are best for you the way they are, then leave things as they are.

Four days later Morad is sitting in the tea-house again. Four men come in, sit down with Morad, order freshly brewed tea for themselves and for him, lean on the cushions, order water pipes, drink the hot tea, draw the smoke of the water pipes through the long hoses, making the water in the pipe bubble and gurgle, blow out thick smoke, look at Morad for a long time, say nothing, drink, smoke, until one of them says, Morad, what do you think, how much could we get for our packet of opium if we sold it in Pakistan?

Without thinking for too long, without sighing, without even looking significantly around, without pulling on the water pipe, without taking a slug of tea, without knowing how he knows what he is saying, Morad replies, twice as much.

Another four days pass, and one of the four men comes to Morad's hut with a big clump of opium. When can you go to Pakistan? he asks.

Soon, replies Morad. Are you the only one, or do the others want me to sell opium for them as well?

I don't know, says the man.

Let's see how it turns out, says Morad. Whatever I get for it, I will keep a third.

You're a good person, says the man. I trust you, may God go with you and protect you.

May God give you a long life, replies Morad and puts the opium in the niche in the room next to the metal tin that they call the Iran tin, in which Shirin-Gol keeps the money that she and Morad earn.

Another four days pass. In the early morning, before the sun rises in the sky, Morad throws back his blankets, stands up, climbs over Shirin-Gol and the knot of his sleeping children, splashes his face with cold water from the plastic hose outside on the veranda, doesn't dry the water, just shakes it off, trembles with cold, takes the opium and another two kilos of opium that two other field-owners have given, wraps it in a *patu* that he hangs over his shoulders, takes his jacket from the nail in the wall, leaves the room and to the front of the tea-house, swallows the taste and smell of sleep in his mouth.

Morad looks up the sandy main road to the light-blue iron gate, walks to the left as far as the way in and out of the village, leaves it, walks along the sandy country road through the desert over mountains and valleys to Pakistan.

Shirin-Gol has not thought about going to Iran for a long time. All that remains of her dream of going to Iran is the Iran tin. Shirin-Gol's dreams of Iran, the days, weeks and months gather and fly away.

Shirin-Gol is just getting used to Morad's new job, and the fact that again and again he leaves her and the children alone. She is just getting used to not worrying, not constantly thinking of the dangers, the bandits, the mines, the war, when Morad is away selling opium. Shirin-Gol and Azadine have just made an agreement with the governor and the mullah of the village, to set up a school for the girls in the village, so that in times to come there will be women doctors, midwives and women teachers.

Shirin-Gol is happy that her daughters Noor-Aftab and Nafass will soon be going to school. Shirin-Gol has just got used to the fact that her Nasser is first to wake up in the morning, puts on the samovar in the tea-house, sweeps the carpets, beats out the cushions, serves the men. Shirin-Gol is just getting used to the fact that she herself, her children and Morad are no longer strangers in the village. She is telling the story of the American who came to the village with a great deal of fanfare as though she had been there herself. Shirin-Gol is just getting used to being a woman of the resistance. Shirin-Gol is just getting used to all those things and more when four sparkling new four-by-fours with Arab inscriptions and a white flag on the roof come rushing into the village and sweep up the dust from the street. With a lot of fanfare, young, well-fed men jump from the vehicle and say, we are the soldiers of the new Taleban movement. We have come to liberate you and bring you peace. In the name of Islam. In the name of the Prophet, *salallah-ho-aleihe-wa-aalehi-wa-sallam*, praised be he and his forefathers. In the name of the leader of the Taleban, the supreme mullah, Mullah Omar.

Chapter Ten

A VICTIM AND A MARRIAGE

Yes, says Shirin-Gol, and looks at her daughter, the boy has beautiful eyes. Yes, he is handsome. Yes, he is a nice man. He has got power. He has got money. Yes. Yes. Yes. But he is a Taleb.

Noor-Aftab does not look at her mother, does not hear her. The girl is feverish. The skin in her face is so tense as though it might tear at any moment. Her lips are swollen. Breathing is difficult. Talking is difficult. Thinking is difficult. Her eyes are in fever. Her heart is in fever. Hot. Swollen. In fever.

So he's a Taleb, she says. What's wrong with the Taleban?

What's right with them?

They want to bring peace to us and our country. They want to liberate us.

Fine peace that is, snaps Shirin-Gol. May they choke on their peace. I know these would-be Moslems. My own brothers fell into their hands. May God protect them both, and grant that none of them became a Taleb.

Noor-Aftab does not hear. Does not see.

You are a stupid little girl, you have no notion about life

and people, all you can see is how handsome this boy is and nothing else. Open your eyes.

Noor-Aftab does not hear. Does not see.

Since the Taleban came to power, they have taken lots of fields away from their owners. Your father has lost his job because the Taleban have forbidden the growing of opium. Only so they can take over the business themselves.

Noor-Aftab does not hear or see.

No woman is allowed to go into the street on her own and without a blood relative. I'm not, and neither are you. Your fine Taleb has forbidden me to work. What are we going to live on?

Noor-Aftab looks at her mother. Says nothing.

They themselves have found the finest house in the village and moved into the governor's house. The poor governor and his family weren't even allowed to live in the prison. Your fine Taleb and his friends have confiscated the weapons of all the men in the village.

Noor-Aftab says, the Taleban bring peace. In times of peace you do not need weapons.

Whether a king was in power, or the English or the Russians, the men in our country have always had weapons. However badly things went for us, whether in times of war or in times of peace and quiet, in our country there were always a few women who resisted all the traditions, all the pressures of society, their fathers and everyone else that got in their way. Since the Taleban came to power, they have even forbidden Azadine to do her work as before. She cannot go to her patients in their huts now. She cannot go into the mountains and help the people there. She cannot examine men. Only women who come to her accompanied by a *mahram* are allowed to visit her. The women who found their way to us from the remote villages and valleys can no longer set off on their own and come to the village to see us. If they do take the risk, they and their husbands are punished and beaten. What are those people to do? Who is going to go to the bazaar to shop for us? They've even forbidden children to play. Your brothers aren't even allowed to fly their self-made kites. They cannot build their poppy-cars any more. Girls are forbidden to go to school. Televisions are forbidden. Music is forbidden.

So? replies Noor-Aftab defiantly. We didn't have a television or music anyway, we had no time to play and there was no school for girls even before the Taleban. And you and Azadine were the only women who had assumed the right to work. So? Now you're in the same position as the other women.

Noor-Aftab, you've lost your mind. Don't you understand? Back then we didn't have those things because there was a war on, because we were poor, because we have no education and no notion of things. But it wasn't forbidden us. We have just started to build a school for girls because we've fought for it and convinced the governor and the men in the village that it was a good idea. But now it is forbidden to us. Legally forbidden. And we will be punished if we do not obey the laws of the Taleban.

Then let us obey the laws, says Noor-Aftab. And then we will not be punished.

Shirin-Gol looks at her daughter and knows, Noor-Aftab does not see anything, does not hear anything, does not understand anything, there is no point in talking. All she can see is the young Taleb with the long, dark hair that gleams in the sun. The young Taleb with the long, white cloak in which he strides like an angel through the village, light-footed as a prince. The young Taleb with his dark eyes, always in search of his Light-of-the-Sun. In search of Shirin-Gol's daughter, Noor-Aftab.

Noor-Aftab sits in front of Shirin-Gol, stares through her mother, through the wall of the room into the tea-house where the young Taleb is squatting, leaning against the wall, with one hand on his knee, in his other hand a delicate flower that Noor-Aftab has plucked from between the stones and, although forbidden, secretly given to her Taleb.

The young Taleb sits in the tea-house because he is closest to his Sun there, because he leans with his back to the wall behind which she lives, sleeps, sits and thinks of nothing but him. The young Taleb has a smile on his lips, he has closed his eyes because he does not want to see anything. He only wants to see the single image in his own head. The face of the *houri*-like Noor-Aftab, his Sunlight, his devoted one. Mohammed, the Prophet of all devout Moslems, *salallah-ho-aleihe-wa-aalehi-wa-sallam*, praised be He and His ancestors, has said that if a young man's heart is filled with a virgin girl and beats only for her, for the one untouched by the hand of another man, the one who does not belong to another man, then he whose most heartfelt desire it is to possess her, to have her as his wife, should look after her, respect her and protect her from the eyes and attacks of strangers.

Shirin-Gol looks at her daughter and knows she is not half a child any more, she is half a woman. She knows that no power in the world, not even the love, warmth, protection and security of a mother will hold her daughter any longer.

Let him come, says Morad. We'll see what happens.

Fine, says Shirin-Gol, let him come. We'll see what happens.

*

My grandfather fell in the war against the British. My father fell in the war against the Russians. Like my elder brother. My elder sisters were hit by a rocket. The Mujahedin violated one of my other sisters and her daughter. She stabbed herself and her daughter because she could not live with the shame, and regained her honour in that way. *Al-hamn-do-allah*. The only person I have left is my respected teacher, the sheikh who was my master in the *madrassa*. So I am alone in the world and have no one who can speak for me. So I've come on my own to ask you to give me your daughter's hand, says the young Taleb. He squats on the floor by the laughing plastic mats, not speaking or moving.

Shirin-Gol looks at his lovely, full lips, his dark eyes, his delicate skin, his soft features, his quiet manner, his confidence, and asks, where is your mother?

She died of worry, says the Taleb without looking at Shirin-Gol. My uncle took me to Pakistan and I lived in a camp there. I had to go to a *madrassa*, where Arab and Pakistani religious scholars taught me the Koran. At some point they wound this black turban around my head and said, now you're a Taleb.

A Taleb, thinks Shirin-Gol, a seeker. What are you seeking, Taleb? she asks.

What all Taleb seek. I am seeking the right path.

The right path to where?

To God. I am a Taleb. A Taleb.

You are a Taleb. You are actually forbidden to talk to me. I am a woman.

There are exceptions.

Whenever it suits you? Whenever it is useful to you?

The Taleb says nothing.

Can I be a Taleb too?

You can. Anyone can be a Taleb.

I want to be a Taleb of freedom.

The Taleb says nothing.

Freedom, says Shirin-Gol.

In the *madrassa* they said they were sending me back to our revered homeland to bring freedom to my people.

What kind of freedom is it that forbids half the population to leave the house?

They told me I was to free our country along with my brothers in faith. My teachers told me that first the Russians with their war and then the Mujahedin with their brother-war had left our country in ruins and were still fighting today. They said people were prisoners in their own homes, they couldn't work or open their shops. They said the Mujahedin robbed people. They said the Mujahedin raped women. They said people were waiting for the Taleban so that we would save them, bring them peace and the true faith.

Why don't you look at me when you speak to me? asks Shirin-Gol. I could be your mother. You are here wanting to marry my daughter.

You aren't wearing a *hejab*, replies the Taleb. I am forbidden to look at the face of a strange woman.

It is a face that has seen the war you've only heard of.

The one I fled from, says the Taleb.

It is a face that has seen hunger, that has seen the dead and the sick. It is my face, and I will determine who can look at me and who can't, and I will allow you to do it, says Shirin-Gol, unable to conceal the contempt in her voice.

It is not up to us humans to change the laws of God, replies the young Taleb. Quietly, in a controlled voice. Sure of what he is saying. Convinced of the laws in his head.

God's law says I am to cover my hair, not my face. Look at me when you talk to me.

The young Taleb says nothing, thinks for a moment, raises his head, looks steadily at Shirin-Gol, gently, warmly, almost lovingly, breathes peacefully, lowers his eyes again and says, what difference does it make whether I look at you or not?

A big difference, says Shirin-Gol. A very big one. I want to see the eyes of the man who forbids me to walk in the street, who insists that I hide my face in public, who forbids me to work. I want to see the eyes of the man who forbids boys to play, who forbids girls to go to school. I want to look in the eyes of the man who has come for my daughter's hand.

It isn't up to me to permit or forbid you to do anything, says the Taleb. My Moslem brothers and I have come to bring you peace. We have come to bring you true Islam and ensure that God's law is obeyed. All the wars, all the suffering, all the sacrifices, all the dead that you have seen with your own eyes, have been God's punishment, because we Afghans have forgotten what it means to be true Moslems. Because we have lost our true faith. Because we have forgotten what goodness, what riches, what peace true Islam means.

Shirin-Gol has trouble keeping herself under control and not losing her polite tone. What has true Islam to do with whether I work or I don't? What do true Islam and peace in our homeland have to do with the fact that I am condemned to be locked within the four walls of my room? What does that have to do with anything at all? Who benefits, who is harmed whether or not our daughters go to school? What you're forbidding has nothing to do with Islam, or anything else.

That's the Islam I have learned. The Islam my teachers taught me. True Islam as written in the holy Koran. The Islam that neither you nor I are able or permitted to doubt. They are the words of the Prophet that all believers must obey, that no human being may change or doubt.

Shirin-Gol is furious, her breathing is so loud, her rage so intense that it fills the whole room.

Please allow me one question, the young Taleb says into the midst of her fury, her rage, her despair, raises his head and looks Shirin-Gol in the eyes, completely untroubled. His gaze and his voice remain warm, almost loving. He says, in all other places, villages and cities where my brothers in faith find themselves, they are greeted with open arms and made welcome. The people are happy that we are finally bringing them peace, that they can finally travel safely from one city to another again, without being robbed and betrayed by bandits, without having to give some Mujahedin commanders money, sheep, even their daughters and wives, every few kilometres. The people are happy that, wherever we appear, weapons fall silent and they are able to open their shops again. That they can set up their stalls in the bazaars again and finally, after all those years, earn money again. Wherever we appear, the people are relieved, because they can sleep through the night and no rockets are going to fall on their heads. Wherever we appear, the people know what a great good peace and tranquillity are. And finally the people know that after all the years of unbelief we are finally bringing them the true faith. Even the governor and commander of your village has joined our movement. The men in your village have handed over their weapons to us. Our leaders are not opposed to schools, not even schools for girls. Once the war is over and we have brought the whole country under our control, we will build the schools up again. Our leader says we will set up separate schools for girls, so they will be able to go to school as well. The young Taleb lowers his eyes before going on talking. I do not understand why you are opposed to us and our holy movement. The Taleb sounds sad when he says, I do not understand why you are opposed to me.

Shirin-Gol thinks for a long time, trying to find the right answer, finally regains the peace and a little of the gentleness in her voice and says, you grew up in a camp in Pakistan, with no father or mother, and you have my sympathy for that. You only came back to your fatherland not long ago. You do not know Afghanistan, you do not know the capital, and you do not know the people or their stories, or their worries, their suffering, their joys. You do not know the Russians, or the Mujahedin, or the wars. All you know are the words of your teachers.

Without wanting to, without knowing or understanding why he is doing it, the young Taleb looks at Shirin-Gol as she talks. He looks at her. Not because she wants him to. Because he wants to.

She looks at him for a long time before she asks the boy, do you believe your leader? Do you believe that one day he really will build schools for girls? That women will study and go to university and be able to become doctors or whatever? And when do you think you will have conquered the whole country? How long will it take before the whole country is at peace and you do everything you're promising us now? Do you think the Mujahedin, Ahmad Shah Massud, Dostam and all those others will give up so easily? Do you think that Iran, India, France, Uzbekistan and all those other countries who support the Mujahedin and the Rabbani government will give up so easily? Only because you come along and say you want to conquer the whole country?

The boy looks at Shirin-Gol and says, you have so many questions for me, and I haven't a single answer for you.

You and your brothers in faith claim to be our leaders. We lay claim to answers.

You are brave, says the young Taleb, thinks for a moment and says, when the war comes to an end, when the Taleban movement has brought the whole country under our control, when this and when that and when anything – only the almighty knows that, only the omniscient Lord God.

The Taleb is just about to sit up straight, he is just about to go on talking, he is just looking at Shirin-Gol, when sunlight falling into the room breaks and a shadow falls over the young man. Gently, peacefully, for four blinks of an eye. A peaceful, gentle shadow enfolds the young Taleb, embraces him, strokes him, touches him, caresses him.

Shirin-Gol and the young Taleb look outside at the same time, see at the same time that it is the shadow of Noor-Aftab. Light-of-the-Sun stands on the veranda and casts a shadow on the young man with the dark eyes that gleam and sparkle like coals, always in search of his Light-of-the-Sun, his Noor-Aftab. A sad brilliance. Full of melancholy.

Noor-Aftab stands there with her forbidden uncovered head, looks in, she stands there for no longer than four blinks of an eye and looks in before moving on and the sun falls again on the young Taleb. Four brief moments. Long enough. Noor-Aftab's gaze falls into the boy's eye. The boy's gaze enters Noor-Aftab's eyes. And falls, vanishes, is lost. Lost. Heart lost. Two lost hearts, for ever, for eternity.

Shirin-Gol's fury, her questions, her doubt flock together, become birds, lift off, fly through the window. Simurg. Thirty birds. Flying. Away.

The boy quivers. His voice quivers. He says, I will look after her, respect her, honour her, defend and protect her against everything and everyone. With my own life, if need be.

The Taleb says that, looks at the prayer-beads lying peacefully in the hand on his lap. He takes another deep breath, as though it was the last time. Then he says nothing. He says nothing further.

His loneliness, his sadness, his dignity, his honesty, his goodness, his warmth, the love in his words, in his voice, settle on Shirin-Gol's heart.

She is still a child, says Shirin-Gol.

The Taleb doesn't raise his head or look at Shirin-Gol or speak, or, apparently, breathe. He just sits there, head lowered. Motionless, silent.

Everything is as it has been all afternoon, since the young Taleb came to ask for Noor-Aftab's hand. Shirin-Gol and the boy have hardly moved, they are sitting there as they have been sitting the whole time, and yet everything is different from how it was before.

Simurg does not come any more.

The days become Simurg, thirty birds in search of the most beautiful bird of all. They flock together, lift and fly off. Vanish.

Sometimes Shirin-Gol sits in her room, sometimes on the veranda. She cooks, washes the clothes, looks into the distance where she imagines Iran to be. Shirin-Gol sighs, cleans and washes the rice, washes the vegetables that the young Taleb has sent her as a present. Shirin-Gol beats the mattresses and cushions, blankets and mats on the veranda, beats the dust from them, even when all the dust has been gone for a long time. Shirin-Gol washes the floor of the room with water from the plastic hose, even when it has been brilliantly clean for a long time. Shirin-Gol squats there and looks at the poppy capsules standing in rows like soldiers, bleeding white milk. Milk that turns brown.

The sun rises in the sky, goes once around the room and the veranda, sets, makes way for the stars and the moon, comes back the next day, goes again. Morad squats in the corner of the room, smoking and smoking, always silent. Noor-Aftab squats on the little wall surrounding the field, not eating, not drinking, not talking, only sighing and looking dead-eyed at the sandy floor under her feet. Nasser squats on the veranda, throws stones, hits nothing and nobody but goes on throwing anyway. Nasser squats like that until he tips over like a sack, lies there in the dust staring straight ahead. Nafass and Nabi squat on the floor. Happy that all their brothers and sisters, their father, their mother are around them. Happy that the world is not so big any more that everyone disappears every morning and only comes back in the evening. Happy-sad.

We have run out of rice, says Shirin-Gol. And flour. And sugar, tea, fat. We have run out of wood. I can't make a fire.

Morad smokes and stays completely silent. Noor-Aftab sighs and sighs. Nasser stares and stares. The two little ones suck their fingers and smile. No one smiles back.

Simurg is gone. Will not be back.

For God's sake, says Morad, we should let them do it. He should marry her. Let's take the money he'll give us for her and see what happens.

Fine, says Shirin-Gol, then let him marry her. Let's take the money and see what happens. We'll see.

You will have to go to him and tell him of our decision. I'm sick, says Morad, I cannot go.

I know, says Shirin-Gol.

She gets up at the crack of dawn, washes her face with water from the plastic hose, puts on her veil, throws it over her face, walks around their room to the tea-house, turns right up the sandy road to the light-blue iron gate whose paint has been flaked off by bullet-holes and looks pocked with little painful wounds and pimples. Shirin-Gol knocks with a stone on the iron gate, behind which the governor's prison-house used to be, where the Taleban house is now. The grey of early morning, still sunless, echoes and clatters. Shirin-Gol gives a start and drops the stone.

With a loud shuffling noise and the slap, slap of plastic laces a sleepy boy, no older than Nasser, opens the gate and starts back when he sees the blue cloth in front of him, checks that he isn't mistaken and that there really is a woman standing alone in front of him. The boy stretches up as far as he can to the cloth-head and whispers behind a hand, you should not be alone on the street. Go home. If the Taleban see you, you'll get into trouble.

Shirin-Gol knows the boy. Before the Taleban came to the village, like most of the other boys in the village he used to go to school in the morning and work in the afternoon. Sarvar was the men's-tailor's helper.

Sarvar, what are you doing here? asks Shirin-Gol, throwing back her cloth and startling the boy even more.

You must not show your face, the boy whispers with such agitation that white balls of spittle leap from his mouth.

What are you doing here? Shirin-Gol repeats, putting her hand on the boy's chest.

Nothing, says the boy. I work here.

Here? For the Taleban? What sort of work is that?

I open the door when someone knocks, I clear away the tea-glasses, drive away the flies, arrange the shoes when the men take them off and go into the room, I . . .

That's fine, Shirin-Gol interrupts him. And why don't you sleep at home when your work's over.

People have no money now, and they cannot afford any new clothes. I lost my job, and the Taleban told my father I was handsome. They gave him some money and said they wanted me to be here day and night. My father took the money and said I was to stay here and do what the Taleban demanded of me.

A strange heaviness that she cannot explain, a heaviness as though she had drunk liquid lead, falls into Shirin-Gol's stomach. She leans against the light-blue iron gate to keep herself from falling over, slides down it, crouches by it, puts her head on her knees and tries to chase away the terrible thoughts and images that have entered her head from God knows where. Thoughts and images of adult men grabbing the little boy, stroking him, calling him to their rooms at night, lying next to him, pulling him to them, pressing him, caressing him.

Shirin-Gol, Shirin-Gol, what's up with you? asks the boy in a bright, bell-like voice. Do you want a glass of water?

No, my boy, it is nothing, sit down by me. Tell me. How is life among the Taleban?

It is good, says the boy.

Why is it good?

Because I have got enough to eat.

That is good, says Shirin-Gol.

And because the Taleban like me and are very loving and kind to me.

The lump in Shirin-Gol's stomach presses and pushes, gets heavier and heavier, climbs up her throat, wants to choke her, wants to jump out of her mouth. Shirin-Gol rises to her feet, forgets why she has come, runs her hand over the boy's freshly-shorn head and walks back home along the still deserted street, to her room, hangs her veil on the nail on the wall, lies down under her blanket, lies there. Awake.

Man's hand settles on boy's body. A man satisfying his lust.

Man's lust.

The sun is just rising over the hill, the first cock in the village is just crowing, the first donkey is just braying, everything touched by the light of the sun is creaking and cracking, Noor-Aftab is just sitting on the little wall surrounding the field again, looking dead-eyed at the sandy ground beneath her feet, Nasser is just throwing another stone and hitting no one and nobody, Morad is just tossing in his sleep, Shirin-Gol is just throwing the water from the bowl she has just used to wash Nafass' and Nabi's faces, when the young Taleb comes around the corner, sees Noor-Aftab, smiles tenderly, lovingly, so that she almost forgets to breathe, throws her hand to her mouth so that her delight doesn't leap from it.

The Taleb walks past her, crouches down by Shirin-Gol, looks at her, smiles and says, you came to see us this morning. What did you want?

Nothing, Shirin-Gol replies abruptly without looking at the Taleb.

You aren't looking at me, says the Taleb.

Your laws forbid you to be here in my house, my daughter and I are not wearing the *hejab*.

But I'm only going to go when I know why you came to see us.

Whatever the reason might have been, it has ceased to exist, and I have forgotten it.

I bring money, says the young Taleb. These are hard times, no one has enough, everyone should help where he can.

I do not want your money, says Shirin-Gol, because I will not be able to give what you will one day want in return.

What I would like to have, says the Taleb, laying a bundle of money in front of Shirin-Gol and rising to his feet. What I want to have, he repeats, no money can buy.

Before he goes, he steals another shy smile from Noor-Aftab, then disappears again, walks in front of the tea-house, turns right, walks up to the light-blue gate, crouches in front of it and does nothing all day but look down the street to the village.

Why did you send him away? asks Morad. Perhaps that Taleb's a good Taleb. Maybe there are good and bad among the Taleban. Maybe he is honest about his attitude to Islam and his God. He brings us money, he brings us food, he is polite, he isn't forcing us to give him our daughter. He doesn't report you for sitting in front of him without the *hejab*. He obeys when you tell him to look at you, he obeys when you tell him, go, come.

I am not going to give my daughter to a man who lays his hand on little boys, says Shirin-Gol.

Maybe you are wrong, says Morad, maybe it is the best thing for Noor-Aftab if we give her to the boy as his wife. She might have a good life with him.

Maybe the best thing would be for you to come to your senses, for us to pack our things and go somewhere where there is neither war nor the Taleban, who use little boys as their playthings.

What with? asks Morad.

The money we'll earn. We will have to work until we've got enough money together, yells Shirin-Gol, slinging the wet dress she was just washing into the bowl, sending the water flying, drenching her.

Again the days flock together and fly away. Like thirty birds in search of the most beautiful, most splendid bird of all, the Simurg, the days flock together and fly away. Again this and that happen. Again nothing happens, everything happens. The Taleban go among the people more and more often, with ever fewer scruples. Down in the village, where the person's feet would be if you were a bird and could look at the village from above, the Taleban erect a barrier, put the former radio-mechanic and the former women's-tailor next to it, put a Kalashnikov and a radio in their hands and tell them they are to let no one in or out unless authorised by the Taleban. The Taleban close the boy's school and turn it into a mosque and a Koran school. For boys. They order all men to let their beards grow and shave their heads or let their hair grow long. They run through the village with thin rods, hitting boys for flying kites, or just hitting them because they're nearby. They shout at women and girls who dare to leave the house without men to accompany them, and even if there is a man present they want to know whether the woman really needs to leave the house.

None of the Taleban who have come to the village was married. By now each of them has married a girl from the village. Their leader couldn't make his mind up, and has married two girls. They are sisters, and daughters of the mullah, who is happy about the marriage, because after all the Taleb is a believer and an influential, powerful man. His daughters will want for nothing, and they will always be together and never lonely. Apart from the little boy not much older than Nasser, the Taleban have also installed other little boys from the village in their house, as servants, runners, fly-swatters, to look at, to touch, to do whatever.

All the Taleban have brought women and little boys into their houses. Apart from one. The one who fell in love at first sight with Noor-Aftab, and she with him.

Shirin-Gol is just saying, maybe he is a good Taleb, maybe he is not like the other Taleban. Morad is just saying, maybe that is right. Morad is just taking a powerful draw from the water pipe that the young Taleb has given him, when one of the other Taleban comes around the corner and on to the veranda, sees Shirin-Gol's uncovered face, turns his back to her, gives her time to pull the veil over her face, crouches down by Shirin-Gol and Morad, puts a bundle of money by their feet and says, in an impertinent, stinking, ignorant tone, is that enough for your daughter? The wife I have taken is still a child, she cannot give me a son, I have to take a new wife.

Morad squats in the smoke from the water pipe and can't utter a word. Shirin-Gol wants to take the sickle lying on the floor beside her, put it around his throat and slit it. She stands up, is about to open her mouth, is about to say something, when behind the stinking Taleb the young, kind, gentle Taleb appears, puts his hand on the stinking one's shoulder and says, this sister's daughter is already promised to me. You are lucky that we are brothers in faith and I respect you, because otherwise I would have to stab you now, to salvage my honour and that of my bride.

The stinking man stands up, studies his brother in faith in his long, white shirt that makes him look like an angel. His stinking gaze travels once from top to bottom and then from bottom to top, and settles on his eyes. The stinking man spits greenish-yellow stuff that sticks to the hard, muddy floor of the veranda, lies there and leaves an ugly crust there for days and weeks and forever, even though Shirin-Gol sprays it away with water from the hose and washes it into the field, so it looks like a fish lying on the shore and slipping back towards the river because no one has sliced it open and fried it over an open fire.

Did the stinking man know his greenish-yellow spit would leave an ugly crust for ever? He took his money with him, left his greenish-yellow spit and his ugly stain. For ever. And his ugly last words, too. Stinking, final Taleb words, the sheikh will not live for ever, won't always be there to hold his protecting hands over you and your bride.

Neither Noor-Aftab nor the young Taleb have an extended family, so they must both content themselves with celebrating their wedding among strangers. That brings bad luck, people used to say back then. When there were no wars, when people still lived in peace and the families and tribes all stayed together in one farm, in one camp. Back when fathers were still fathers, when they had the final say and determined who would marry who and who would not. Back when mothers were still mothers and their sons' brides served them as though they were queens. Back when fathers still had money and could give their daughters a dowry. Back when the bridegroom had a father who could give him a hut, a room, a tent where he would live with his wife and bring him grandchildren. Back when people had sheep and rams that they could slaughter at their weddings and distribute the meat among the needy so that it brought good fortune. Back when everything was different. Back then. When was that? Had back then really ever existed? Maybe people lie. Maybe there has never been anything like back then.

It is better to celebrate with strangers than not at all, people say, since back then has ceased to exist.

So a day before the wedding night the women come to Noor-Aftab, squeeze into the room and on the veranda, drink tea that the kind tea-house owner brings. Anyone who can brings presents. Some black kajal, with which Noor-Aftab paints her upper and her lower eyelids black. Pollen for the cheeks. Rose water to make her smell good. Brilliant fabrics for the marriage dress, other fabrics for the other, if God wills it, equally happy and joyful days of her life. Wool for the winter blanket. Fabrics for mats and cushions. Noor-Aftab is even given a little gold bracelet. Another woman gives a whole bowl full of sweets that she has made herself. Yet another gives coloured threads which, that evening, she weaves and knots with a lucky *ta-vis* into Noor-Aftab's freshly washed hair. Azadine gives a package that Noor-Aftab is only to open later, when she is alone. It contains hundreds and thousands of contra-ceptive pills. The mullah's wife who brought her daughters to the house of one of the other Taleb a few months previously, gives Noor-Aftab two clay bowls. Everyone brings what she can and what she doesn't urgently need. And because it is a wedding, and the wedding of a Taleb at that, the women are even allowed to sing a few songs and clap their hands. Every now and again one or other of them can't stand it anymore, gets to her feet and even dances.

Behind the light-blue gate at the other end of the street something very similar is happening. The little boys from the village are running around, pouring fresh lemon juice and tea into the empty glasses of the male guests who have come to congratulate the groom and bring him their presents. The tailor gives him a new, long, white outfit. A few men give a few grams of opium. Most of them give the young Taleb money.

When the sun slowly sets and is about to disappear behind the hill, the women trill loudly and drum ever more quickly on their plates and bowls, dance ever more uninhibitedly and sing and call and clap, and Noor-Aftab, sitting on the veranda in the middle of the women and girls and all the hubbub, feels dizzy.

The mullah's wife gets to her feet, stretches out her arms, calms the other women and girls. They all fall silent. Seven girls who, like Noor-Aftab herself, are untouched and still virgins, stir a pot of henna until the powder dissolves. They dip seven thin wooden sticks into the pot of red paste. Back then, they would have been seven happy virgins. There are not seven happy people in the whole village, let alone seven happy virgins.

There is a war on.

The main thing is, they are virgins.

Seven non-happy but not unhappy virgins paint, with seven thin henna sticks, the soles of Noor-Aftab's feet, the palms of her hands, the backs of her hands, her face, the nape of her neck, her arms, her legs, tickling Noor-Aftab, putting her in ecstasy, so that her skin tightens and she gets funny little dots all over it. Making her giggle and laugh and bringing tears to her mother's eyes at the sight of her daughter's happiness. Tears of mother-joy. Tears of joy. Grief-joy.

While the seven non-happy but not unhappy virgins are painting Noor-Aftab's hands and feet, the mullah's wife moves her prayer-beads first in one direction and then in the other, incessantly murmuring words that she claims are Sura something-or-other from the holy Koran. And again and again she says, may the henna cool your blood, because a bride should not go to the house of her husband with her blood aflame, and she should not be turned from girl to woman with her blood aflame. That was how our forefathers did it, and that is how we do it today, and may God protect all his creatures that are and have been and those who are yet to come and grant them long life.

At the same time, behind the light-blue iron gate that looks as though it has painful wounds, seven young men who have presumably never touched a woman, are painting the soles of the young Taleb's feet, the palms of his hands, his forehead and the nape of his neck with red henna. The mullah sends his prayer-beads first one way and then the other, praying so quietly that the Taleban cannot hear him, and claims it is Sura something-or-other from the holy Koran.

I would like my brother, the eldest Taleb, to say a prayer, says the young groom, smiling happily.

The eldest Taleb, the leader of all the Taleban who came to the village so-and-so much time ago, smooths his shirt, his *patu*, his trousers, the long train of his turban and whatever other fabrics he has draped himself with, stands up with a great deal of ceremony, sits down in front of the groom, inflates his chest, makes himself important and murmurs quietly, so that the mullah cannot hear him, into his beard and claims it is Sura something-or-other from the holy Koran, and may the Lord God and the Prophet, *salallah-ho-aleihe-wa-aaleehi-wa-sallam*, praised be he and his forefathers, may they grant our beloved brother in faith a rich life and many strong and healthy sons.

*

During the night Noor-Aftab cannot sleep. For the first time since she can remember she is not lying next to her mother, her sister, her brother, a friend from the refugee camp. She is lying all by herself outside on the veranda under God's heaven, which he has made particularly beautiful that night, all for Noor-Aftab, with thousands of wonderfully beautiful stars and a moon more sweet and beautiful than ever. Noor-Aftab holds her hand in the light of the moon and looks at the henna-red flowers, ornaments and words that the seven virgins and her mother have painted and written on it. Noor-Aftab stretches and knows, without knowing how she knows, but she knows very well, that her beloved, her hero, her *pahlevan*, her idol, who will become her husband tomorrow, as she lies under God's heaven, is also holding his henna-reddened hand into the moonlight and also knows that she is lying not far from him, longing for him and thinking of him.

Noor-Aftab is playing with the *houri*, the angels in the dark night, that only she and no one else can see, she is humming a happy little song when Shirin-Gol rises from her covers, comes to her daughter on the veranda, lies down beside her, takes her girl in her arms and says, you are lucky to be marrying a man you love and who loves you.

I know, whispers Noor-Aftab.

I wish everything had been different. I wish your eyes had never looked on war, and your heart had been light. I wish – I don't know. I wish so much.

I know, says Noor-Aftab.

The next morning, very early, the sun is just casting its first light over the mountain when the seven non-happy, but not unhappy, virgins and a few other happy-unhappy, unhappy and happy women come back. They assemble on the veranda behind Shirin-Gol's room, each of them with a needle, thread and yarn, some have brought pearls, a coin, a shell, glittering sequins. A few of them sew the skirts, lay the fabric in folds and sew them tight. One fold, four folds, a thousand folds. The more folds, the more happiness, health and wealth. The more wealth, the more sons. Two happy-unhappy but giggling virgins sew the right sleeve of Noor-Aftab's wedding dress. Two happy-unhappy virgins with dancing eyes sew the left sleeve of Noor-Aftab's wedding dress.

The little veranda between the room and the poppy field has become a cloud. A cloud of green, yellow, red, orange fabrics glittering and gleaming, billowing and settling around the bodies of the sewing women and virgins.

The young groom paid for the fabrics, the women say. Shirin-Gol's daughter is lucky to get such a good man, they say. She will have a good life with him. He is rich, he has a good position, and his Arab sheikh loves him best of all his students. The mullah's wife even knows that the Taleb's teacher treats him like a son and has made him one of his heirs.

The women sit among the fabrics, sew Noor-Aftab's wedding dress, drink tea, tell each other everything they know or even only think they know, are glad they can finally leave their huts and rooms again, sit together, talk, laugh and simply be together. Because of this great happiness that has been granted them, because of the wonderful fabrics, the wedding dress, the stories about the young, rich Taleb, the women and virgins get more and more enthusiastic. Some women rock their bodies back and forth to the music, time and again some lose control of themselves and lose their decency and start singing and beating a rhythm on saucers, on glasses. One of them starts quietly, a second joins in, and suddenly they are all singing, beating, laughing.

As they do so the girls and women constantly look over their shoulders, afraid that someone might come and yell at them for being bad girls, *kharab*. Because someone might come and see them dancing. Because their reputation would be ruined.

Bad girls. Easy girls. Whorish girls.

Good girls sit quietly. Lower their eyes. If they have to raise their eyes at all they keep them still. Decent girls don't raise their voices. If they cannot help it and have to speak, they do it with a quiet voice, and use as few words as possible. Good girls keep their mouths closed, so that you cannot see into their mouths and see their tongues. Decent girls breathe quietly, move slowly. Decent girls do not skip, jump or run so as not to rupture their maidenheads. Good, decent girls do not make scandals for themselves, their mothers and above all their fathers. Virtuous girls consider their reputations. Good virgins do not dance at weddings. Decent girls are always afraid of being considered indecent whatever they do.

Good girl. Quiet girl.

Respectable virgin. Unhappy virgin.

One stitch and another and another. Do not speak, do not do this, do not do that, one stitch and another and another.

By early afternoon the dress is ready. The women fasten their needles to the fabric of their waistcoats and dresses. The needles at their breasts look like thin badges. Virgin so-and-so gets a badge for her left sleeve. Half a left sleeve. A needle at the breast.

A few women pull the colourful, brilliant wedding cloud-dress over Noor-Aftab's head, and pull and tie it firmly to her body.

If you were a bird and could see the village from above, the village that looks like a human being lying on the ground, with his legs pressed together and his arms spread, to the right of the place where his navel would be, you could see a green-yellow-red-orange cloud of fabric and in the middle of it little Noor-Aftab, looking like a princess.

A little green-yellow-red-orange cloud that has stopped thinking it might one day fly an aeroplane.

She is still a child, whispers Shirin-Gol, clawing her fingers into Azadine's arm.

She is an intelligent child, Azadine replies. With a big, important *intelligent* before child.

Have faith, says Azadine, it will be fine. The boy is full of love. He is not like other men. He is like a young panther that has been shot and wounded. As a little boy, without father and mother, with nothing but hunger in his belly and fear in his heart, he arrived in Pakistan, was taken to the camp where he fell into the hands of fanatical men. Into the hands of men who have washed his brain in the name of religion, and made him what he is. Who knows, says Azadine, perhaps your daughter's love and her wisdom will bring him back to his senses, the senses they took from him in the *madrassa*.

We'll see, says Shirin-Gol, to herself more than to anyone else. We'll see what happens.

The brother of the kind tea-house-owner has put fresh mutton on all the skewers. He has put out two pots of fragrant rice rather than one, so that none of the guests need go hungry. Someone has got hold of some huge, fat, dark-red, juicy pomegranates from somewhere, pomegranates dripping blood-like when cut open, and put in a bowl.

On the other side of the road the girls stand, holding

their hands before their giggling mouths, squinting over at the red fruits and wishing only that their brothers would steal one of the pomegranates, scoop out the red seeds for them, so that they could crunch them between their teeth and let the sweet-sour juice run down their throats. None of them knows who started it, nor do they know whether the rumour of the magical power of the fruit is true. But now that they are standing on the other side of the street in their colourful headscarves and broad skirts, giggling, hiding their mouths behind their hands, squinting over and squealing the moment one of the boys approaches the bowl, they all know that the red, crunchy apple that has found its way here from Kandahar, is the fruit of love. Anyone who manages to eat some before the virgin bride becomes a woman will be granted happiness, a kind, generous, loving and handsome husband, stronger and more handsome than any of the heroes in any myths and fairytales.

Someone has got hold of juicy, fresh pistachios from somewhere and put them in a bowl. Someone else has found flowers somewhere and put them in a bowl with water. The women have stirred henna in a bowl, so that the guests can dip their fingers in and press a red dot on their foreheads, on their cheeks, their chin, the palms of their hands. On a brass tray lie the presents and money for the bridal pair. In the past people played music and danced, clapped, sang and laughed. The women would have trilled behind their hands, so that you could not see their tongues. Today the joy is silent, no one sings, no one dances, no one trills, the faces of the women are covered by cloths. They squat in the sandy road behind a brown sheet, separated from the men and boys, drinking tea, breathing in the scent of meat and rice, which they cannot wait to taste, squinting over to the men squatting in the tea-house, slurping tea, smoking water pipes so that the water bubbles and gurgles, and quietly, so that no one can hear, telling stories of better times, of times back then. Of times when they didn't have to grow compulsory beards. Times when the war with the Russians was just over, their commander was defending the village against other Mujahedin, when they sold opium and hoped for a better future. Back then.

Unlike the men, the women are not agreed about whether their life was better before the Taleban's seizure of power, or if it is better now that the men with the long beards, long shirts, black turbans and many new prohibitions and laws have come to the village.

Since the Taleban came, says the wife of the kind tea-house-owner, we don't need to set up sentries at night in our streets and courtyards, or even in the tea-house. Our sons and husbands can sleep in peace. Since the Taleban came, my husband is with his children every evening, and if you ask me – the wife of the kind tea-house owner takes a pause, looks around, leans forward and says rather quietly, behind her hand – if you ask me, he has been at home a bit too much since then. We have not a moment's peace. Everyone has to jump to it and do this and that and he is always nagging me to lie down with him. If he goes on like that, I am going to insist that he takes another wife, a young one who still has her strength.

The tailor's wife is glad that the Taleban are in the village and providing peace and order, because since then, she says, my husband can put everything he earns in his own pocket. There is no commander holding out his hand, and no one is impounding any of his hard-earned money.

Instead they bled us dry, hisses the wife of the owner of what are still the biggest poppy fields. First they took a tenth and then a fifth of our fields, and the same amount of seed, and my husband says that still won't satisfy them.

But our commander brought peace as well, says Zuhra, the sister of the men's-tailor's wife. Yes, there was shooting. Yes, we had to set up sentries, but we could still walk in the street.

You could not walk in the street even then, the men's-tailor's wife snaps at her sister, looking around to see if all of the other women had heard what they have known all along.

Her sister continues crossly, your husband did not let you walk in the street even before the Taleban came to the village. You were not even allowed to come to my house, your own sister's house.

But that is different, says Zuhra, he was the only man who forbade me to do this and that. Now there are all kinds of other men, strange, dirty, ignorant men, joining in.

That is true, says the wife of the owner of what are still the biggest poppy fields. That is not something we have ever had in our country, men who cannot read or write and who haven't learned anything, being in charge of our country and making decisions about our people.

What do you think about all that? Zuhra asks the doctor, who is sitting in silence next to Shirin-Gol, who is sitting in silence next to Noor-Aftab and holding her hand.

Azadine sighs, thinks for a moment, raises her eyebrows, sighs again and says, some of them are still half children, others are half men. They notice they are different from their own compatriots. Some of them cannot even speak our language properly. They do not know where Kandahar is, nor where the ancient statues of the Buddha are. They do not know that Mohammed Zahir Shah was our last king, and Daoud Khan, his own flesh and blood, deposed him. The Taleban are confused people, confused and lost.

You speak well, says Zuhra, but what do you mean in the end? Are they good for us or are they bad for us?

They have only just assumed power, says Azadine, and they do not really know themselves yet what they want and how to lead the Afghan people. The future will show whether they are good or bad for us.

Zuhra, her sister, the wife of the men's tailor, the wife of the man who still owns the biggest poppy fields, the wife of the kind tea-house owner, the second wife of the kind tea-house owner, who never speaks if his first wife is nearby, and all the other women nod in agreement and look up into the air as though God were sitting above them and would tell them what the future will bring. And one after another they sigh, raise their eyebrows, think for a moment, bite their lower lips and are not as happy as they could and should be on a day like this when a wedding is being celebrated. Even Shirin-Gol, who is after all the mother of the bride, is not laughing, is not happy, does not even have a smile on her face.

When a guest comes, we smile, says the mullah's wife, so that the guest does not have to look upon an ugly, sad or gloomy face. So that he does not think he might be the reason for the gloomy face and the grief. That is why we laugh when a guest comes to our house. And that is also why we laugh when a bride is led to her husband's house. So, women, don't be gloomy. Laugh. Smile. Be cheerful. Do it for the bride.

A little breeze is just rising up. The first birds of night are just waking up and shaking their delicate plumage. The sun is just disappearing behind the hill. Nabi is just standing feet apart in the middle of the sandy road and peeing. Noor-Aftab is just thinking that among the many colourful, brilliant fabrics billowing around her, she looks like a little green-yellow-red-orange cloud. She is just thinking that she doesn't want to sit in silence any more. All this is just happening, when a few boys come running behind the cloth stretched from the tea-house to the nearest hut, behind which the women and girls squat on carpets, drinking tea and chatting. The boys skip up and down and cry out, the groom is coming. The groom is coming.

Noor-Aftab's breathing stops, her heart leaps into her throat, she lowers her veiled head, clenches her hand into her thigh.

On the other side of the cloth the men start moving, one of them ties up the horse decorated with colourful strips of fabric, pearls, flowers and bells. Morad packs up the presents, the money, a few pomegranates, a few pistachios and everything else he wants to give his daughter and the groom for their first night together and the rest of their life together, and loads it all on to the back of a donkey belonging to the kind tea-house owner. The young Taleb rises to his feet, has to hold on to one of the wooden struts that support the airy raffia roof of the tea-house, his knees are trembling so much. He smiles, lowers his shame-filled eyes, takes the reins of the colourful horse, guides it around the cloth, looks at his betrothed, who is sitting next to Shirin-Gol on the carpet on the floor.

Her colourful skirts, the many colourful cloths that cover her face, so that he cannot see her beautiful coal-black, gleaming eyes, cannot prevent the love she feels for him from creeping out from under the cloths, flying through the air, settling on his heart and promising him the tenderness he has known only once before in his life. Out of the darkness of his memories, whose traces have been blurred and erased by the passing years there suddenly appear images, feelings, smells, colours, shapes that he did not know were within him. The young Taleb stands before the mountain of bright and brilliant cloths, and all he can think of is the breast that suckled him as a little boy, and fed him with its milk. He was already able to walk, he already had shoes on his feet, already had teeth, could already speak proper words, when he already knew, without knowing how he knew, that the warmth of his mother's breast would be his only memory of his mother, and it would send him on a quest to find it again for the rest of his life. The young Taleb stands there clutching the reins of the colourful horse, and he knows God is with him, has given him this girl so that he will be reminded of the happiness of his childhood.

It is as though he understands at that moment that his goal is neither faith nor religion, neither the Prophet nor the holy book. This girl that God has given him has been his goal.

Shirin-Gol and Azadine stand up, all the other women stand up, Noor-Aftab remains seated, trembles, totters, almost keels over when the young bridegroom comes over to her, bends down to her, reaches into the bright, gleaming fabrics, finds her arms, finds her waist and helps his bride on to her legs. Noor-Aftab stumbles, supports herself on him, smells through her cloths the rose water on his skin, feels his breath, sees his winter-honey eyes, hears his voice, whispering quietly so that only she can hear, my Sunlight.

The young Taleb leads his colourful bride to the colourful horse, lifts her as though she were a feather on to the stallion's back, knows that he should walk beside her, but does not, he too swings his strong young body on to the horse as though it were weightless, does not see the sceptical, unbelieving eyes of the men, sits behind his bride, presses his breast, which threatens to burst with happiness and fear, to her tender, beautiful, girlish back. He becomes one with her, trembles along with her, grabs the reins, touching her stomach, making her twitch and press even closer to him. He presses his heels into the flanks of the horse, and as he does so he presses his pelvis and his stiff member against Noor-Aftab's girlish hips, and no one sees because of the many fabrics that billow out in front of him like a little bright cloud and veil him from sight. Faint with his excitement and arousal. Arousal that the young Taleb has only known before when sitting or lying close beside another boy in the *madrassa*. Arousal that the boy thought only existed between boys and men. Arousal he now knows was never meant for boys or men, but only for Noor-Aftab, even before he had met her.

The young Taleb guides the horse's head towards the light-blue iron gate that looks as though it bears painful wounds.

Morad, leading the little donkey, Nasser who does not know whether he should be glad that his sister won't be sleeping in the little room any more, and he now has more space for himself, or whether he should be sad because from now on there will be no one to count stars and throw stones with, the two tailors, the kind tea-house owner, who wonders whether his friend's daughter wouldn't have been better off as his third wife rather than belonging to this Taleb, the owner of the poppy fields, the governor, the mullah, the other Taleban follow the horse with the bridal pair. Behind them walk Shirin-Gol, Azadine, the first and second wife of the kind tea-house owner, the four wives of the two tailors, the governor's wife and all the other women whose husbands have allowed them to come to the wedding.

Instead of riding to the light-blue wounded gate, the young Taleb guides his horse into the little road that turns off to the right, and whispers in Noor-Aftab's ear, I have built us a little hut of our own. It isn't as nice as the house I have been living in with my brothers in faith, but we will be alone here and undisturbed.

Noor-Aftab barely grasps what the young Taleb is saying, she is trembling so, she is so aflame, her heart is beating so hard against her breast.

The young groom jumps from the horse, leads it to the door of the new hut, helps his bride down, and she falls into his arms like a little colourful cloud, goes with her into the hut, takes the presents from Morad, goes in, closes the door, just stands there and looks at the colourful cloud that hides his young bride. Tenderly, and without taking his eyes off Noor-Aftab, the young bridegroom lays the presents on the floor. He walks over to his bride, takes the gleaming and glittering cloths from her head and from her face as though peeling away the layers of an onion.

As each cloth is removed, Noor-Aftab sees the face of the young Taleb more clearly and distinctly, feels his breath, the warmth of his skin, his delicate fingers on her face. For the first time they really look one another in the eye, without shyness, without fear of doing something forbidden. For the first time Noor-Aftab is alone, without her mother, her father, her brothers and sisters, with a strange man. For the first time she will be sleeping in a different hut from Shirin-Gol, Morad, Nasser, Nafass and little Nabi.

Do not be afraid, whispers the young Taleb, kissing her gently on her green and blue painted bridal eyes.

I'm not, replies Noor-Aftab in a voice that is tender and warm, firm and loving.

Chapter Eleven

A NEW COUNTRY AND A PAPER HEART

I am worried, says Morad. I am worried about the journey, about the border, about Iranians, about the country and its people.

You cannot be worried this time, says Shirin-Gol, because I am worried this time. I am worried about all the things that worry you. But I am even more worried about staying here. I am worried that we will use up the money the young Taleb gave us for our daughter and then we will have nothing to live on, and nobody to help us.

Shirin-Gol looks at her Morad and remembers the first time he stood before her. Back in the days when she still had shoes. Black plastic shoes with laces, back when she was still going to school, when she was still shouting at her twin brothers not to dawdle. Back then. Back when she bent to tie her shoelaces and blood ran to her head so that she remembered the lake and the boy and the forbidden glances and touches, the unfamiliar, forbidden feeling. Back when she was ashamed, had a bad conscience and hoped her mother wouldn't notice anything. Back when she lifted her blood-red face and stared into the face of a man who looked like the ones who had stayed in the mountains to fight for . . . for what, in fact? Back then, Shirin-Gol could not quite remember what for.

We said we were only giving our daughter to the Taleb because we wanted to go to Iran with the money. Let's try to do it, Morad.

Morad says nothing.

Shirin-Gol sighs and says, let's try, let's see how things turn out.

Morad smooths his Taleban compulsory beard, sighs and says, fine, let's try and see how things turn out.

Shirin-Gol grabs together everything she can carry and takes the rest to her daughter Noor-Aftab.

Shirin-Gol, Morad, Nasser, Nafass and Nabi say goodbye to Noor-Aftab and her young husband, the kind tea-house owner, Azadine, the mullah, the commander, all the other women, children and men in the village that they have made friends with, walk along the street to the way in and out of the village, where the person's feet would be if you were a bird and could look at the village from above, where the Taleban have stretched a rope and sat the former radio-mechanic and the former women's-tailor, put a Kalashnikov and a radio in their hands and ordered them not to allow anyone in or out of the village without their permission.

Where are you going? asks the former women's-tailor, lovingly stroking his beard, so long that it reaches his stomach.

Nasser holds his hand to his mouth and giggles at the sight of the former women's-tailor. Since his sister got married and is not keeping her eye on him every minute of every hour, Nasser has started giggling behind his hand as she used to do. Pulling his head between his shoulders as she used to. No longer holding on to his mother's skirts or his father's trousers, like her. Nasser has developed the habit, like his beloved, much-missed sister, of lowering his eyes and staring at the floor. As if doing so might prevent her vanishing from his life entirely.

Nasser laughs like Noor-Aftab, says Shirin-Gol, chokes back her tears, affectionately running her hand over the boy's head and kissing him.

Nasser is Noor-Aftab, says little Nabi. I want my sister, he says. The sister who has suddenly vanished from his life.

Nasser has lost his sister.

Nasser does things that were Noor-Aftab's tasks and hers alone. Nasser washes little Nabi's bottom when he comes back from the wee-wee hole at the back of the field.

Nasser has become Noor-Aftab, cries little Nabi.

Now Nasser stands there on one leg, half hidden behind his father, giggling behind his hand and actually looking at the ground, but squinting up every now and again at the former women's-tailor, affectionately stroking his beard.

What are you laughing at? asks the man, still stroking his beard.

The endless stroking and the friendly way he asks make Nasser giggle even more. He points at the beard of the former women's tailor and says, the Taleban say your beard has to be so long that it peeps out when you hold it in your fist, and yours is four times as long as that.

The man waggles the end of his long beard as though it were a handkerchief or a flag and says, best to be on the safe side. He hugs Morad and says, we are going to miss you, brother. Where are you going?

Wherever God's paths will take us, replies Morad and runs his hand over Nasser's cap, which sits glittering and gleaming on his close-shorn head.

Where men don't wear beards? asks the former women's-tailor.

There, and where women can move around freely without a veil and work, says Shirin-Gol-cloth and smiles. A smile that no one can see.

The former women's-tailor lowers the rope with which he has been blocking their path, hugs Morad again and says, God be with you, and when you have found that place, the place where men do not have to grow a beard and women can work and do not have to cover their faces, don't forget us, and pray for us to find our way there too.

May God grant you a long and healthy life, says Morad, hugging the former radio-mechanic as well.

Shirin-Gol, the children and Morad have already been on the road for hours when Morad reaches into his pocket and his fingers touch something that one of the men must have secretly slipped it him. It is a lump of opium. Shirin-Gol and he wonder which of the men it might have been, her son-in-law, the young Taleb, the kind tea-house-owner, the former women's-tailor or the former radio-mechanic?

Whoever it was, Shirin-Gol says, may God protect him and his family. The money we get for it will pay for our bread and tea until we get to the border.

You take it, says Morad, my pocket isn't a safe place for it, there might be a hole in it, or it might fall out.

This flight is no different from all the other times Shirin-Gol has fled from somewhere to somewhere else. The sun burns by day, at night it is bitterly cold, the children whinge, forever asking, where are we going, when will we get there, why didn't we stay in our room, until they finally give up, stop asking questions, fall silent and just go on walking.

Shirin-Gol can't remember how many days and nights they have been walking, how long she has been dragging her belongings and the children around. Shirin-Gol can't remember how many times she has lied when the Taleban sentries have asked her questions. No, we are not going to Iran, we are going to see my family in the mountains, no, I cannot read or write, no, I have never worked, no, no, no, yes, yes, yes. Shirin-Gol cannot remember why she is fleeing, where she has come from and where she is going. Forgotten, erased. Go back? Where to? The wind has blown the traces away, the sun has burned the memory, wiped it out, the cold nights have turned her will to ice. Ice that has melted and trickled away in the sunlight of day. Lost.

Onwards? Where to? Why? It does not matter. One bare foot before the other. The road has been hungry, like her children, it has eaten their shoes. Morad has taken back the opium and smoked it. The children have lost their hope, their will, the gleam in their eyes.

Onwards. One bare foot before the other.

Mashad, the first city in Iran, is full. Full of Afghan brothers and sisters, arriving and departing. Full of hunger, unemployment, grief. Thousands, millions of Afghans. Long live Iran.

This is not a good place for us, says Shirin-Gol. Let's go on and see what happens.

Let's go on and see what happens, says Morad.

Still more days, still more paths, lovely houses, no war, proper roads, asphalt, no ruins, road-signs, cars, no mines, buses, lorries, traders, shops, people with more than just rags on their bodies, people with shoes on their feet, people with flesh and fat on their bones, with life in their eyes, women with eyes, with noses, with mouths, with skin. Women without cloths over their faces, a new world, a new hope, a new life – how many times has one wished for this? So-and-so many times.

Isfahan is good. Warm. Peace, an empty hut, nice neighbours, who bring along their old children's clothes and even some for Shirin-Gol and Morad, and let them have them. A kind ice-seller, who gives the children red, green, yellow, watery, sticky ice as a welcome present, and they do not know what to do with it at first, they just hold it in their hands and let it drip on the ground and the new clothes the people have given them. People offering them work, people bringing leftover food and even money. A big, blue royal mosque in a big, beautiful royal garden, many old, ancient, magnificent, splendid palaces, gardens, the glorious covered bazaar, work, schools, school-children, schoolgirls, women teachers, women in the streets, in the shops, in the bazaar, everywhere.

The empty hut is neither big nor small, it used to belong to an Afghan who is going back home. He is leaving behind his mattresses, blankets and cushions, for neither a very large nor a very small amount of money. The rent is not very low, but it is not high, either.

Shirin-Gol is lucky, she can clean the houses of rich Iranians. They like the Afghan woman, because she is clean, honest and forthcoming, because she shows pearl-like teeth when she laughs, because her kohl-rimmed eyes are full of goodness, because she lovingly wraps the foreign children in her arms and comforts them with gentle words. Because she is like an angel sent by God. Afghan angel-woman, sent by God. Nasser sells yellow, green, red ice for the kind ice-seller. Morad works on building sites, but can only do light work because of his refrigerator-accident. The children go to school, and even Morad learns to read and write.

Shirin-Gol dreams of working for a woman doctor again, she cleans and cleans, washes clothes, looks after the children of strangers, darns Iranian clothes and trousers, accepts any work that brings in money, at some point she falls pregnant again, and calls her next two children Navid and Nassim. Shirin-Gol makes a carpet, cooks, sweeps, wipes, washes, goes to the greengrocer without a cloth over her face, just with a headscarf covering her hair, goes to the rice-seller, the baker, sits in the alley in front of the door of her hut, talks to the other women and thanks her God for the new life that may not be easy, but is a hundred times better than life at home. And she thinks, this time everything will be fine. Everything will be fine. God is kind and merciful.

Morad comes back to the hut every day with a smile, kisses his children, gives his wife a smile and sometimes a little caress, a little embrace, if the children aren't nearby, a big embrace and big smile only for her. Morad has stopped trembling, he isn't afraid now, he is regaining his pride, regaining his honour, regaining the man in himself.

During the night he sleeps in the hut with his Shirin-Gol and the children, plays with them, throws them in the air, swings them around, makes a ball out of old newspapers, throws it in the air and catches it, makes his children laugh. On Friday he goes to the mosque with Nasser and Nabi, prays and thanks his God for everything he has given him, thanks him for his children and his Shirin-Gol.

After mosque, Shirin-Gol, the children and Morad take the newspaper ball and a blanket to the river, spread out the blanket, doze, play, eat, just lie there and gaze into the blue Iranian sky and thank their God again.

I have signed up, says Morad.

Signed up? asks Shirin-Gol, smiling and showing her fine, strong, white teeth that gleam like pearls.

Signed up, replies Morad, smiling and showing his teeth, which aren't all that fine any more, all that strong, brown and yellow they are now from all the opium smoking. I have signed up for a literacy course. I am going to learn to read and write so that some day I may get decent work and I won't have to do hard physical labour any more, like a – like a what? A donkey, Morad says, and laughs and laughs, and wipes the tears of laughter from his eyes.

Tears of laughter that often fill the eyes of Shirin-Gol and Morad during the start of their time in Iran.

The start of their time, when everything and everyone in Iran is good to Shirin-Gol and her family.

One day Nasser comes home and says the kind ice-seller isn't going to sell ice any more. He is going to convert his ice-cart, turn the ice-container into a display case, take down the pictures of ice and sell toys. He wants me to help him with his new business, and he is going to pay me more money for it. At first Shirin-Gol is pleased for her son, and the extra money, and then she starts worrying about Nasser.

Nasser is twelve, maybe fourteen years old, he is not half a child any more, he is half a man. From now on, in blazing heat and in icy cold, he travels hundreds of miles across the foreign country, south from Isfahan to Bandar-Abbas on the Persian Gulf. There he buys toys that come in containers from Europe, the USA or the Arab countries, China or wherever. They are actually destined for shops and stores, but sometimes boxes fall off, sometimes they even fall into the water, when they are being unloaded. Sometimes the workers loading the ships steal the goods and sell them. Sometimes the owner of the toys sells all the goods right in the harbour, to avoid paying duty. At any rate, Nasser buys the toys cheaply, carts them, who knows how, to Isfahan, and there the kind former ice-seller, who is still kind but sells toys rather than ice, sells the toys.

Nasser is not like the other boys and men who come to the Gulf and merely seek out a box of this and a box of that, pay for it and disappear with their goods again. Nasser takes his time. He kneels by the goods, carefully lifts the toys out of the box in their clear, plastic packaging, opens it carefully with two fingers so as not to break it, so that he can use the packaging again, studies the toy with love and attention, turns it this way and that, holds it up to the light and tests its weight. He takes a close look at each individual doll, each car, each ball, all the other colourful toys that Nasser has never, ever played with in his own life, and examines them all carefully. He closes his eyes, runs his hands over the cars like a blind man, strokes the little mini-windows, the mini-doors, presses and prods the dolls, feels the fabric of their clothes, smells their hair, shakes the balls and holds them to his ear, takes out the colourful little metal drummers and watches them drumming, examines each individual part before taking his money out of his pocket, paying for the toys and transporting them to Isfahan.

The former ice-seller, now a toy-seller, lovingly decorates his former ice-cart, which is now a toy-cart, hangs out the dolls, cars, balloons, the plastic figures and animals, the girls' necklaces and plastic bracelets to the little roof and the sides of his cart, and calls, in alternation with Nasser, to attract the attention of the children and the parents of the children.

Lovely new toys

Unique in the whole of Iran.

Isfahan is half a world, our toys come from the whole world.

Lovely new toys.

They draw out the *o* and the *y* of toys as far as they will go, and it sounds as though they are singing. A song that recalls the tune of a song that Shirin-Gol hums in the evening so that the little brother and sister and anyone else who happens to be listening can go to sleep without having nightmares.

One day big brother brings a doll home for his Pakistani sister, twice as big as his boyish hand, white, clean skin, beautiful blue eyes, hair like gold and a short pink dress, so short that you can see its panties and its bare legs. Nafass stares at the doll, breathes quietly, for me? Presses the plastic to her breast, closing her eyes, smells the perfumed hair, looks under the short skirt, chokes back her breath and calls out that she needs a *tonban*, so that she won't have to be ashamed of her bare legs and because everyone can see everything. Nafass stoutly refuses to believe that there are women anywhere in the world with golden hair who show off their whole bodies naked like that.

Shirin-Gol laughs at her daughter's astonishment and fury, takes the white doll with the pink panties and says, fine, let's make her a *tonban*.

Shirin-Gol affectionately runs her hand over the hair of her son, no longer half a boy, half a man now, draws him to her, and he resists because after all he isn't a little child any more, pulls him down to sit beside her on the floor where she is squatting, puts her arm around him and says, you are a real Nasser, a companion, a friend for your sister and your mother.

At some point – how long ago was it? Shirin-Gol cannot remember. At some point, at any rate, Shirin-Gol became sure that her Nasser would finish school, study, train for a profession, become an engineer or a doctor or something else important, earn proper money, start a family and be happier than she and Morad had been. Nasser loved writing, doing sums, reading, asking questions, seeking answers. He loved being the first one in his class, even ahead of the Persian boys, he loved jumping to his feet and getting the best mark, a 20, for the correct answer. With a proud and inflated chest, a smile from one ear to the other, Nasser sat down and waited like a cat waiting to pounce on a mouse, for the next question. Sir, sir, me, me, me. The teacher smiles, points at him, Nasser collects himself, swallows down his saliva as he sets his head forward, answers the question, smiles, his eyes gleam.

One morning when Nasser is, as usual, first to get to school, with his second-hand, old but unwrinkled shirt, which, like a good boy, he sticks into his second-hand, old, worn but ironed trousers, the teacher comes over to him, doesn't look at him, seeks his words, speaks, when he finds them, rapidly and without interruption, turns around and goes. Nasser, he says, my dear, good pupil, I have received instructions not to teach Afghan boys from now on.

Khalass and *tamam*. That was that.

Nasser stands there for a long time in his old, ironed trousers, the white shirt, clutching his exercise book and his textbook. He can't move, he can't even move his head, he can neither turn it nor raise it nor lower it, nor jut it forwards to swallow his saliva down. His head stays exactly where it was when the teacher was standing in front of him, not looking at him and speaking without a break or a comma. His legs, his arms, his neck, his stomach, his head, his hands, his feet, his back are hard and solid, rigid and dead like the mud pillars that his father and the other men in the mountain village built for the roofs over the paths. Nasser can only move his eyes. He sees the other boys passing him one by one and going into class. He looks through the window into the classroom. He sees the boys sitting down. He sees the teacher opening his book, looking into it, raising his head, moving his mouth, none of the other boys volunteers an answer, one of the boys looks out into the courtyard where Nasser is rooted to the spot, a second boy looks out, the whole class. He sees the teacher looking out and gesturing him to go, coming to the window, opening it and calling, go home, there's no point.

In the evening, when Nasser has not yet returned home, Shirin-Gol puts on her headscarf, asks her neighbours, the baker, the ice-seller, but no one has seen Nasser. Finally Shirin-Gol goes to the school and finds her son. He is standing there, with his white shirt and ironed trousers, clutching his exercise book and his textbook, and he does not hear when his mother calls him. Shirin-Gol puts her arm around his shoulder, takes his face in her hands, gives him a look full of love, presses his thin body, which feels the way it used to when it was half the size it is today, runs her hand down his dry, rigid back, kneads his arms, rocks him back and forth, hums as though to rock him to sleep, when Nasser suddenly twitches as though waking from a deep, deep sleep.

What has happened, my darling, my great big son, what have they done to you? asks Shirin-Gol, not knowing why her voice is trembling.

Nasser looks at his mother with his beautiful, dark eyes, juts his head forwards, swallows the saliva that has been in his mouth since morning and says, nothing.

Nothing?

Nothing.

That is good, says Shirin-Gol, takes the exercise book and the textbook out of her son's rigid hand, puts her arm around his shoulders and walks home with him. Nasser says not a word all the way home.

Nothing.

All the way home and that evening, the next day and the day after that and all week. He lies in silence under his blanket, sees nothing, hears nothing, barely eats, barely drinks. Is mute. Mute.

Nothing.

When he gets up again and walks about, when he starts sitting up and smiling again, when his younger brothers and sisters hurl themselves at him, laughing, and throw him to the floor, when he is eating and drinking again, Shirin-Gol, as she has done several times every day since her son turned to stone, places her strong hand on Nasser's back and says, tell me about that nothing. Speak and lighten your soul.

Nasser squats on the floor beside his mother, his head laid sideways on his knee, looks at his mother, tries to find words in his head, opens his mouth, but cannot get them out.

Shirin-Gol doesn't stop stroking Nasser's back, just keeps on looking at him, smiles, kisses him, looks at him again. Again Nasser opens his mouth. And finally a sound comes from his throat. He swallows and says, as though he hasn't been silent all week, as though he hasn't been sick all week, as though everything is as it has always been, as though the great Nothing had never been, the boy says, I am not an Afghan.

Not an Afghan.

At first, when Shirin-Gol came to Iran, the Afghans had a good time of it. Very good. So good that there were no great silent Nothings.

At first, when Shirin-Gol came to Iran, their children were allowed to go to school, and they did not have to pay for it. By now Afghans need permits for everything. School permit, university permit, purchasing permit, examination permit, doctor's permit, travel permit, exit permit, work permit, hospital permit, permit permit.

Permits you can only get hold of if you entered the country legally and are able to show legal entry papers.

I do not know what to do, says Shirin-Gol to the Iranian official who is to issue her with a doctor's permit. What is legal entry? I need papers for that. Where can I get them? Should I go to the Russians, the Mujahedin, the Taleban or whoever happens to be in power in my homeland, the ones who are making our life a hell and say, you are torturing me so terribly that I would like to flee to Iran, so could I please have my papers? We hadn't even got shoes on our feet when we came to Iran.

The Iranian official looks at Shirin-Gol, sees the other Afghans in the queue behind her, who also want a permit for something or other from him, lowers his eyes, brings down his permit stamp on the piece of paper that has become damp and floppy by being held in her hand for so long, and murmurs, I will lose my job for you lot.

May God protect you, and may he ensure that you always have good work to feed yourself and your children, and may he grant you a long life.

Fine, fine. May God protect you and your children, too, says the man, waving the next Afghan to his desk.

Shirin-Gol goes happily out into the street, pulls her headscarf, which keeps slipping, further over her face, takes her children by the hand, waits until the noisy traffic on the four-lane road, which still frightens her, becomes thinner, runs to the other side of the road, stops there for a moment to straighten her headscarf again, when she suddenly feels a sharp pain in her back, as though someone had stuck a spear between her shoulder-blade and her spine. For a moment the pain numbs her senses, then she cannot hold back her tears, she clenches her teeth, falls to her knees, turns around and sees four boys standing a little further away. One of them is holding a catapult. All four are shocked and look as though the thirteenth prophet had just appeared to them.

At first Nasser does not understand what is wrong with his mother. Only when she is crouching on the footpath with her hand on her back, looking over towards the four boys, does Nasser grasp that the boys have hit Shirin-Gol with their slingshot. Blood darts into Nasser's eyes. He dashes off, runs up to the boys, bowls two of them over immediately, fists flailing, hits the third and fourth and the other two, who have quickly got to their feet again, and in less time than it would take you to say four *bismi-allahs*, the boys have made off. Nasser is black and blue, his nose is bleeding, his face is scratched and so are his hands and arms.

Shirin-Gol hugs her half-man-son, wipes the blood and tears from his face, tries to stem the blood from his nose, tries to calm her other children, who are all crying now. People gather, give her soft paper handkerchiefs, give her money, comfort her, a woman offers to take her home in her car. A policeman comes, wants Shirin-Gol's address and a description of the boys. They all talk at once, and it all gets very confused. A few people say they were probably just a bunch of cheeky kids whose parents had sent them out into the street and left them to their own devices all day. Obviously they are going to turn into animals and act like idiots if no one pays them a blind bit of attention.

Another woman ties her headscarf tight and says, but do forgive me, my dear sister, what world are you living in? Before she goes on, the woman looks around at everyone. Of course the children in our country live in the street, and of course they're left to their own devices. After all, their fathers and mothers have to work, from dawn till dusk, so that they can give their children a crust in the evening.

One man says, who knows what the Afghans might have done to the children, maybe they were just taking their revenge. A woman who has not uttered a word until now speaks in such a low voice that the others stop talking for a moment so that they can hear what she says.

Probably the woman and her children have done absolutely nothing to anybody, the woman says. Probably they were just walking along the street. But whatever the situation, and whatever happened, whether the woman and her children have done anything or not, they are guests in our country, and you do not solve problems by throwing stones or taking revenge.

The people are silent. Then, as though someone had given them a sign, they all start talking at once again.

Shirin-Gol thanks the woman with the car, the one with the soft paper handkerchiefs and the one who said that Shirin-Gol is a guest in her country and that stone-throwing does not solve problems. Then Shirin-Gol takes her children by the hand and instead of going to the doctor she goes home.

She keeps touching the spot on her back where the stone hit her, she keeps stroking Nasser's scratches and injuries and says, now you look like a Mujahed who has just come from the front.

I am never going to go to war, says Nasser. War is for stupid people. Only people who cannot read and write and do not understand anything think you can solve your problems by going to war.

You are a clever boy, my son, says Shirin-Gol, running her hand over his head time and again, stroking his back, pressing him to her, kissing him.

When Morad comes home and sees his son's injured face, the colour drains from his own face, which turns white, his knees turn to jelly, and he has to crouch down immediately to avoid falling over like a sack of potatoes that isn't quite full and cannot stand on its own. Morad just crouches there with his white face and his jelly-like knees, stares at his boy and says nothing.

Shirin-Gol and Nasser tell him what has happened. They neither complain nor lament, it sounds not as though they are talking about something they have experienced themselves, something that has happened to them, but about something they have seen in passing.

And then one woman gave me a soft paper handkerchief and dripped water on to it from her bottle so that I could clear Nasser's wounds and stem the blood from his nose, says Shirin-Gol.

The woman put a soft paper handkerchief in my hand as well, says Nasser, but I didn't want to get it dirty. I would rather keep it. I put it in my trouser pocket. By way of proof Nasser pats his trouser pocket and looks at his father as though waiting for praise from him for being a hero and not using the valuable paper handkerchief. Because his father remains silent, Nasser says, I am bound to have more urgent need of it at some point, and then I will be happy that I still have it.

For a long time Nasser keeps taking the soft paper handkerchief out of his trouser pocket, looks at it closely, unfolds it and folds it again, lays it over his face and lets it float to the floor like a cloud. None of his younger brothers and sisters are ever allowed even to touch his soft paper handkerchief, let alone play with it.

After the women among their Iranian neighbours hear that Shirin-Gol had been hit by a stone and her eldest son had been beaten up by the same boys who had attacked her with the slingshot, they bring even more second-hand clothes, trousers, shoes they themselves no longer need, even food.

One of the women brings an envelope, and says her husband gave her money so that Morad can repair the hole in the roof of the hut, change the broken window-panes and prepare the hut for the winter.

Even the baker is sorry for Shirin-Gol and particularly for Nasser, who looks for a long time as though he has just come home from battle. And until Nasser's wounds have healed, every day he gives the boy a fresh, hot loaf from the oven. For you, he says, baked specially for you, you see the N? I wrote that specially in the dough.

Nasser loves the fresh, hot loaves from the oven with the N on them, and by now he does not think it was all that terrible to have been beaten up. Because since then his world is lovelier than ever before. Nasser does not have to hurry when he is walking about the place and going shopping or to work, everyone has kind and sympathetic words for him, kind gestures, a present, a warm loaf with an N for him. Sometimes he lies down on the mattress at home, rolls himself up into a ball and just stares straight ahead or dozes. His mother brings him tea, strokes and caresses him. Everyone is nice to him. Everything is soft. Paper-handkerchief soft. Everything is tender and merciful, it feels the way it used to when he was still a little, very little boy and everything was different and much better. Back then.

But Nasser's wounds finally heal. Nasser has to start running and hurrying again when he goes from one place to another, when he is working or going shopping, once more he has to be a big, sensible boy, he is not given fresh, warm loaves with N on them, he does not get warm glances from the neighbours, and Nasser's world returns to the way it was, before that business with the boys with the slingshot and that unjust and cowardly four-against-one beating.

At least that is what he thinks at first. He thinks his world is the old one.

More precisely, though, he notices – and he is not the only one, his brothers and sisters, Morad and Shirin-Gol notice it too – that nothing is as it was before, and everything has changed.

Shirin-Gol knows it has nothing to do with the stones or the slingshot, or with rough boys who are sent out into the street by their parents in the morning and have nothing to do all day and therefore annoy other people and throw stones at them, and it has nothing to do with the fact that four of the boys beat up her Nasser. Shirin-Gol knows that it has nothing to do with any of that. Nothing is as it used to be. Everything is different. It is not as warm. It is not as generous. The Iranians are not as friendly.

At first, when Shirin-Gol, her children and Morad came to Iran, shopkeepers asked for the same amount of money from the Afghans as they did from the Iranians. By now, Afghans have to pay three or four times as much. At first Afghans stood in queues at the baker's or wherever, and when it was their turn they got their bread. By now, some shopkeepers shove the Afghans aside when their turn finally comes, and say, our bread is funded by the state, you are not Iranians, so you have no right to our bread. At first Afghans were not accused of every theft that took place. At first Iranians didn't call ugly, bad words after any Afghan they saw. Later the Iranians get used to saying bad words, and the Afghans get used to hearing them. Soon it is as though it had never been otherwise, as though it had always been so. Soon it is as though Afghans in Iran had always been shouted and sworn at.

Shirin-Gol's neighbours are no longer as helpful as they were at the start. No visits. No presents of hand-me-down clothes and trousers.

Shirin-Gol does not go into the street as often as she used to. The children do not like playing in the alley outside the hut the way they did. Morad cannot find work. We can't, the foremen say, do anything with a cripple.

By now Nasser speaks the Isfahan dialect so well that people believe him when he says, I am an Iranian. They buy everything from him and pay up without complaining. He stands in front of the people with his Persian haircut, his hand-me-down ironed Persian trousers and shirts, looks at them with his deep black eyes, his happy-unhappy eyes and says, my father has died and my mother is old and sick and she will not live much longer. Buy this lovely toy and help a poor compatriot to avoid starvation.

The former ice-seller, now a toy-seller, says, God certainly won't like to see you denying your homeland, your father and your mother.

Nasser nods, does not contradict him and says, it is better this way. With a quiet voice, with his head lowered, without looking at the kind toy-seller, he murmurs, it is better this way.

At first, when they come to Iran, Morad is outside every day. He is either working or looking for work. Later he complains more and more often about pains which, he says, have something to do with his injuries from the refrigerator-accident. I cannot work, he says. He lies there and coughs and groans and sleeps all day and all night and rarely leaves the hut.

Don't you go out to earn money any more? asks Nafass.

I am sick, Morad replies. When I'm healthy again, I'll earn money again.

Why are you sick? asks his daughter.

Morad thinks for a moment and says, because I had an accident.

What kind of accident?

A bad one.

How bad?

Very bad.

Tell us, tell us, calls Nafass, who wasn't born when her father had his refrigerator-accident.

Tell us, calls Nasser, who was too small and cannot remember the time when his father sat in the corner of the hut in the Pakistani refugee camp and stopped seeing or hearing anything.

Tell us, calls Nabi, who had not yet entered the world.

Tell us, calls even little Navid, who was born in Iran and does not know where Pakistan is or know what smugglers are, does not know what a narrow path is, or what a refrigerator is, does not know why men would tie refrigerators to their backs or why they would roll down a hill with them.

The children all sit big-eyed in front of their father, excited to find out what terrible event was responsible for the fact that their father does not leave the hut any more, that he cannot work, that he has stopped earning money, that he has stopped bringing food home. Why everything has changed from before, since they came to Iran. They keenly study every word, every gesture so as not to leave anything out the next day and for all the days after that when they tell each other, and the other children, why things are the way they are.

My father is not a good-for-nothing, say Nasser, Nafass, Nabi, and tell the other children in the alley the story of their father's refrigerator accident. He isn't a good-for-nothing, chatters Navid, copying the others. He is sick, say Nasser, Nafass, Nabi. Sick, chatters Navid. He was walking along a narrow, steep, sandy path with a huge refrigerator strapped to his back, say Nasser, Nafass, Nabi. He slipped and fell, and rolled over and over. First he was on top, then the refrigerator was. Until they both stopped rolling and somersaulting and came to rest in the valley. The refrigerator was still tied to him, like a baby on his mother's back. My father on top, the refrigerator underneath him, say Nasser, Nafass, Nabi, inflating their chests and feeling very important.

Liars, say the children in the alley.

Nafass shouts and screams, wants to beat up the children who call her father a liar and only does not do so because Nasser grabs her by the arm and shoves her into the hut. Nafass, Shirin-Gol's Pakistani daughter, whose father was the kind smuggler-chief, stands in the middle of the hut with tears in her eyes. She does not know what to do with her fury and her desire to swing her fists. She sees her sickly, weak father coughing and groaning, dozing and snoring under his blankets. Nafass clenches her delicate hands into fists, hits at the air and screams, the story about the refrigerator accident is a lie.

It is not a lie, says Shirin-Gol, looking at her daughter and thinks, my poor child. If you knew. You owe your birth and life to the refrigerator accident.

No one is strong and powerful enough to carry a refrigerator on his back, calls Nafass.

Yes they are. Your father was strong enough, says Shirin-Gol, kissing her Pakistani daughter on the forehead.

He is weak, says Nafass, and is sure that she is right. He couldn't even carry me if he wanted to, shouts Nafass, and I am sure I am much lighter than an enormous refrigerator.

Your father used to be a very strong man, says Shirin-Gol. It is true, nowadays he is not so strong, but now he is full of love for Noor-Aftab, your sister who stayed back in our homeland, for your brothers Nasser, Nabi and Navid, and for you.

Why do I look different? asks Nafass.

What do you mean? asks Shirin-Gol. How do you look different?

My skin is dark, and so is brother Nabi's.

Then we will have to wash you and Nabi, says Shirin-Gol, pulling her daughter on to her lap.

Nafass loves this game. That's not dirt, that's not dirt, she cries, spitting on her arm and rubbing her skin as hard as she can. Look, look, it isn't dirt, I'm clean.

So what is it? asks Shirin-Gol.

Nafass giggles, pulls in her head, holds her delicate hands in front of her Pakistani mouth and says, I was born in Pakistan. The sun is so hot there that it darkens the skin of all the people born there.

Morad lies there watching Shirin-Gol and his dark-skinned Pakistani daughter, narrows his eyes to slits, through which everything looks blurred and unfocussed. Shapes and colours blur, become unclear, lose their sharpness. He says, the important thing is how people's hearts are, whether their hearts are big or small, light or dark. The important thing is that their intentions are good.

Nafass points at her father and asks her mother, are his intentions good?

Always, little one. Your father's intentions have always been good, and they still are today.

Morad sleeps until midday, does not wash, does not eat, feels wretched, coughs, sits and walks as crookedly as an old man, keeps narrowing his eyes to slits so that his world loses its sharp outlines. Shapes and colours blur and lose their focus.

It is the opium, says Nasser. The opium is burning holes in his brain.

How do you know he smokes opium? Shirin-Gol asks her son.

I know a lot more than you think.

I know.

Why does he do that to us?

It is nothing he does to us, says Shirin-Gol. He suffers from it more than anyone.

I know.

Morad, you have got to pull yourself together, says Shirin-Gol when the children are asleep. The few *toman* that I earn by doing laundry, looking after children and being a servant are not enough for our food or the rent.

What's wrong with the boy? asks Morad, he earns money too.

The boy? Morad, the boy is a boy, our boy, our child, not our breadwinner. He works twelve or more hours a day, he does what he can. Have you ever asked him how he feels when he travels across the country, all on his own? Have you ever wondered why he has been wearing the same trousers for a year, and doesn't need a new pair?

Morad says nothing.

He hasn't grown for more than a year, that is why he wears the same trousers, that is why he doesn't need new ones, because he has simply stopped growing.

Morad says nothing.

We don't even have enough money for *kefin*, winding-sheets to wrap us up in when we die of hunger and they want to put us under the ground.

What can I do? asks Morad. There is no work.

Shirin-Gol says nothing.

There is no work, Morad repeats. Certainly not for Afghans. What can I do?

Whatever, replies Shirin-Gol. Whatever you can do, do it. I don't care how you do it, just do something so that I can give my children something decent to eat again.

Something to eat, thinks Shirin-Gol. Something decent. Like a decent girl. Decent food, decent girl.

Morad sleeps for another four days and nights, he groans and moans in his sleep, he coughs and spits. When he is awake, he trembles and pulls in his head and crouches in a corner. Another four days pass before he gets up, takes off his stinking trousers and his shirt, drenched in the sweat of fear, immerses it in soapy water himself and washes it with his own hands. Morad spends the next four days shaving his stubbly beard, clogged with white foam from his mouth, cutting and combing his hair, clipping his thick black fingernails and toenails. Clip. Clip. Thick, ugly Morad toenails, with black dirt underneath, fly through the air.

Once again the days flock together and fly off. Like thirty birds in search of the most beautiful, the most splendid bird of all, the Simurg, they flock together and fly away.

And without a word Morad flies away, too. He puts on his pair of trousers that he himself has freshly washed, puts on his shirt, walks to the door, does not turn around, looks up and down the alley, walks down the alley and is gone.

He does not come back till morning, when he takes off his trousers and his shirt, stinking of smoke, hangs them both in the open window so that the air takes away the stench of cigarettes and flies away with it. Like thirty birds, over all the seas, all the mountains, all the valleys.

Morad looks at Shirin-Gol, still does not say anything, puts a bundle of Iranian banknotes on the window-ledge, lies down under his blanket and says, I will bring more tomorrow.

Without a word, over the next four evenings Morad puts on his trousers and his shirt, walks to the door, looks up and down the alley, walks down the alley and is gone. He does not come back until morning. Four times he hangs his trousers and his shirt in the window. Four times he gives the stench of cigarettes to the air.

Four times he lays Iranian banknotes on the window-ledge. Four times he says, I will bring more.

Four times Shirin-Gol asks, where is the money coming from? And does not really want to know.

Four times Morad knows that she does not really want to know, and says nothing.

If people are desperate they do the strangest things, says the grocer from the *baghalli*, weighs the rice, wraps the vegetables in old newspaper, asks more money from Shirin-Gol than the goods are worth and says, God be with you.

Your husband is on his feet again, says her neighbour, that is good, then he can look after his wife and children again. God will that he is careful in everything he does.

When the landlord comes for the arrears and their now-increased rent, he says, if he can earn so much money, why didn't he start doing it before?

The other children run after Nabi and Navid and say, your father is a *gomarbaz*, they are going to throw him in prison.

They mustn't throw my father in prison, says Navid, standing in front of his mother, crying and sobbing, so that Shirin-Gol's heart turns to paper and with a quiet rip tears in two.

A little piece of paper heart and a big piece of paper heart.

Two unequal-sized pieces of paper heart.

Chapter Twelve

SOMETHING DECENT FOR THE CHILDREN TO EAT AND A PRISON

Desperate Morad is looking after his children and his wife again, and is thrown in prison.

A man has betrayed Morad.

What man? Who is the man? Does anyone know this man? How does Morad know him? What has the man revealed? What has Morad done? Why did Morad not say anything? Why did Shirin-Gol not want to know anything? Why does everyone else know everything while Shirin-Gol knows nothing? Why didn't Shirin-Gol know that Morad was playing cards? Why didn't she know that gambling was forbidden in Iran? Particularly for Afghans, who win and are betrayed. Is the man at least ashamed for betraying Morad? For the fact that the father of five children has been thrown in prison and his wife and children have no money again and on top of it have lost their dignity and their good reputation?

Lost.

The man lost a game of cards.

Morad won the game of cards.

Shirin-Gol lost her husband.

Mother-with-no-colour-in-her-face lost the colour in her face. Lost her reputation. Lost her dignity.

Some people never lose once in their lives. Nothing.

Others lose. Always. Everything.

Some people are never thrown in prison once in their lives.

Morad is in prison.

Some people never visit anyone in prison once in their lives.

Shirin-Gol visits Morad in prison.

Nasser, Nafass, Nabi, Navid, Nassim visit Morad in prison.

You said it did not matter how I did it, you said I was to do something so that you could give your children something decent to eat, says Morad.

The *your* in your children, big, heavy, cold.

Shirin-Gol says nothing.

Forty days. Forty nights. It does not matter how, for something decent to eat for your children. *Your*, big, heavy, cold.

Morad comes back, plunges his prison-stench trousers and his prison-stench shirt in soapy water, washes them both with his own hands, hangs them both over the open window so that the air takes away the last of the prison stench and flies off with it, over all the mountains, all the seas and all the valleys.

During the night prison stench rises from Morad's mouth, from his hair, his skin, spreads throughout the room like steam in the public bath, settles on Shirin-Gol's hair, on her blanket, her face, her skin, creeps into her nose, into her mouth, settles on Nasser and Nabi's boyish skin, Nafass' girl-hair, on Navid and Nassim's parchment skin, creeps through all their mouths and noses, settles on all the hearts and turns sticky and greenish yellow. Greenish-yellow stuff on the asphalt of the capital, that won't seep away. Greenish-yellow stuff on the sand by

Shirin-Gol's feet. Greenish-yellow stuff on the veranda. Greenish-yellow stuff on six hearts.

Morad doesn't wait for the sun and the first light it casts through the window into the hut, he puts on the trousers and shirt that he has washed with his own hands, walks to the door, looks up and down into the darkness of the alley, swallows the taste and smell of jail in his mouth, walks down the dark alley and leaves his prison stench and the invisible wings of his cold voice with Shirin-Gol. It doesn't matter how, something decent for your children to eat. With a big *your*.

Maybe our father is dead, says Nasser, when Morad has not come back after forty days and forty nights.

Maybe the prison stench suffocated him, say Nafass and Nabi.

Death-stench, say Navid and Nassim. Stench-death.

Shirin-Gol says nothing.

One night, no one knows how long he has been away, there is a knock at the door, Morad comes in, takes off his trousers and his shirt, hangs them both in the open window and lies down under his blanket.

You smell of home, says Shirin-Gol.

I have been at home, says Morad.

What were you doing there? asks Shirin-Gol and does not really want to know.

Morad says nothing, because he knows she does not really want to know.

Your children have missed you, says Shirin-Gol. *Your* in your children, big, fat and heavy.

Morad says nothing.

And your wife, says Shirin-Gol, with a big *your* in your wife.

*

The bird-days flock together and fly away, over all the seas, all the mountains, all the valleys. Everything is as it was before Morad's prison days, everything is different from before Morad's prison days.

Nasser travels south to the Persian Gulf, buys toys that he himself has never played with, brings them to Isfahan and calls, in alternation with the toy-seller.

Unique in the whole of Iran.

Isfahan is half a world, our toys come from the whole world.

Lovely new toys.

They draw out the *o* and the *y* of toys as far as they will go, and it sounds as though they are singing. A song that recalls the tune of a song that Shirin-Gol hums in the evening so that the little brother and sister and anyone else who happens to be listening can go to sleep without having nightmares.

Nasser no longer hears the tune, because he no longer sleeps in the hut with his mother and his brothers and sisters. In the hut where his prisoner-father sleeps.

As he does each evening, Nasser clears the toys away into the belly of the toy-cart, locks it up, gives the key to the toy-seller, but instead of going home he spreads out a blanket on the cart where the bare-legged dolls with the pink panties lie by day, along with the cars, the drummers and all the other toys that Nasser himself has never played with. He lies down on the blanket, looks into the sky with its infinite numbers of stars, sighs and goes to sleep.

I have no objection to you sleeping on the cart, says the kind toy-seller, on the contrary, that way no one will think of stealing the cart. The kind toy-seller laughs, making his round stomach wobble up and down. And if someone wants to steal the cart, he will have to steal you with it. Stomach up and down. And when the round stomach has stopped laughing, the kind toy-seller says, but it is not good that you are not sleeping in your father's house. No, my boy, that is not good.

I know, says Nasser, nods, does not contradict, says only, it is better this way. In a quiet voice, head lowered, without looking at the kind toy-seller. It is better this way.

Everything is as it was before Morad's prison days, everything is different from before Morad's prison days.

Nafass, Nabi, Navid, Nassim skip happily up and down and cannot wait for their turn for Morad to throw them up in the air and catch them again. Very high, as high as he can. When they have reached the highest point, just before they fall back down into his safe, strong arms, his so-he-actually-is-strong arms, their little stomachs are empty, there is no air, their voices disappear, their eyes close, even when they resolutely decide not to squeak. Nafass, Nabi, Navid, Nassim hurl themselves at Morad, tickle and pinch him and they all shriek and laugh happily. As long as Shirin-Gol is in the hut. Once Shirin-Gol leaves the hut, even if she is only going to the baker, they want to go with her. Nafass, Nabi, Navid, Nassim want to go with her. Nafass, Nabi, Navid, Nassim do not want to be alone with Morad, because no one knows when he comes and goes and goes and comes and how long he stays when he goes and whether he comes back at all or whether the prison stench might not choke him.

Death-stench, say Navid and Nassim. Stench-death.

Everything is as it was before Morad's prison days, everything is different from before Morad's prison days.

Shirin-Gol lies beside her Morad, longs for his hand, his warmth, his protection, his body, not because she is the wife and he is the husband, but because she cannot bear his pain. Because she does not want him to feel excluded. Excluded from *my* children, *your* children, *our* children. Because he loses his strength, his confidence, his faith without his children. The *his* in *his children* big, meaningful, love-filled.

Morad lies beside Shirin-Gol, hears her breath, smells her skin, closes his eyes, stays alone, without strength, without confidence, without his children, without his wife. Morad on his own. Shirin-Gol on her own. They both lie awake. Both silent.

Morad has been to their homeland, has bought some opium, smuggled it to Iran, he sells it, puts fat bundles of Iranian banknotes on the window-ledge. For something decent to eat for your children. *Yours.*

This time the police come to the house for Morad. This time the fellow-gamblers come to Morad's house. This time Morad is put behind bars for six months, is struck, beaten. Blue and green. Greenish-blue in his face, on his skin, his legs. With a quiet, dull crack that only he can hear, his rib breaks. His head bleeds, his fingers break, with a loud crack that even the prison guard hears. His back goes crooked. His soul turns to glass, flies through the bars across all the seas, across all the valleys, falls to the ground, breaks. His heart turns to paper, tears and tears into a thousand little pieces, with a thousand and one little rips. A rip that only he can hear.

The glass soul breaks.

The paper heart tears.

Half a year, six months after the tearing of the paper heart, six months after the breaking of the glass soul, Shirin-Gol buys Morad free. For so-and-so many *toman*. Where his soul used to be, where his heart used to be, everything is gummed up now, with black, green, greenish-black opium.

So-and-so many *toman* for Opium-Morad.

He would not have survived prison sober, with a clear head, say the people. You must thank God for not killing him.

Thank God.

Be grateful for Opium-Morad with gummed-up soul. Gummed-up heart. Gummed up with greenish-black stuff.

Whose fault is it?

The police? The informer? Morad? Shirin-Gol? The *my* in my children? The heart that turned to paper? The card game? *Passur*? *Javvari*? The smuggler? The Pakistani children? The soul that turned to glass? The war? The Russians? The Mujahedin? The Soviet Union? The USA? The Taleban? The hunger? Something decent to eat?

Iran was good for us, says Shirin-Gol, but it is not good any more.

I know, says Morad.

We must go, says Shirin-Gol.

I know, says Morad.

Hundreds of thousands, millions of Afghans fled to Iran like Shirin-Gol, her children and Morad. Fled the troops, tanks, planes, rockets, bombs, mines of the Red Army. Fled the Mujahedin and their brother-war. Fled foetuses landing with a slap in the street, women's breasts severed, women's stomachs slit open. Fled robbers, bandits, rapists. Fled the Taleban, the Pakistanis and the USA who set them up.

The Iranians themselves know war and poverty, know

what it is to have no way out, to have to flee. At first the
Afghans were welcomed heartily as guests into their
country, received like brothers and sisters. The Iranians
helped them, gave them their things, food, a place to live.
The Iranians gave the Afghans more than any other
country in the world, without getting any help themselves,
either from the west or from other countries, or from the
United Nations. The Afghans did not have to live in
camps, they were allowed to work, allowed to come across
the border, allowed to stay as long as they wanted. A year
passes, two years, many years, twenty-two years before the
Iranians do not want their guests any more. Until there are
shortages of everything in Iran itself, money, room, houses,
flats. Bread, schools, universities. Until it gets hard for the
Iranians to share the things they are short of with the
strangers. They could gather the Afghans all together,
transport them to the border and throw them out. But even
now, when they can't and won't share, they support
everyone and help everyone who wants to go back but
hasn't the strength to do it on his own.

Like Shirin-Gol, many Afghans want to go back, but they
don't have the money and they don't want to, they cannot
live under the Taleban. They don't want to live with war,
with mines, with hunger and everything else.

Shirin-Gol is lucky, she is hardworking and clean and
that is why she still has work. Clean, hard work. She cleans
and wipes and washes and scours the house of an Iranian
family, from top to bottom, from right to left, front, back,
between the cracks, the windows, the kitchen, the
bathroom, the toilet. And she sweeps all the carpets. She
likes doing that, because she can have the television on.
Sometimes there are pretty songs, sometimes somebody

says clever things. A man with a serious expression reads words from a piece of paper, forever raising his head and looking at Shirin-Gol as though speaking to her and no one else.

Afghans who want to go back to Afghanistan, says the man. Shirin-Gol stops sweeping and nods. Afghans who want to go back to their homeland are receiving financial support from the Islamic Republic of Iran and the United Nations. To this end, the government has set up centres in the areas and cities where there are particularly large numbers of Afghans. Any Afghan can put his name on a list.

Lists. Financial support. United Nations. The government.

Sweeping the carpet. Krrt, krrt. The broom in her hand is not as new as it was, but it is not old either. That is good. It has adapted to her strength, her pressure, her rhythm, her size. It has finally bent. The broom is still so new that it smells of brushwood. Krrt, krrt.

One hand holds the broom, with the other she leans on her knee. Bent, straight back. Bending. One foot in front of the other. Krrt, krrt. Like life. Sweeping dust from the beginning of the carpet in equal rows, always in the same direction. Starts at the beginning and finishes at the end. Always with the nap so the wool doesn't stick up, and the dust that has crept into the wool comes out. Always one row after the other, right to left and left to right and back and left to right, equal tracks. And at the end of each krrt, krrt, do not swing the broom into the air, keep it level so that the dust does not fly into the air and scatter everywhere. Shirin-Gol likes the last row best. She has swept together all the dust from the whole enormous carpet, grain by grain, flake by flake, crumb by crumb, row by row there has been more and more of it, greyer and greyer, grainier and grainier, flakier and flakier. She has already met some of the grains at the beginning of the enormous carpet and chased them the whole long way from the beginning to here. Like life. It looks lovely, the whole enormous carpet lying there in all its brilliant colours, beaming and waiting for Shirin-Gol to free it from the last row of dust, flakes and crumbs. A moment full of pleasure. Shirin-Gol stands up straight, stretches her back, which has been bent over all the way through the whole enormous carpet, says *bismi-allah*, and krrt, krrt, she sweeps the last row with her back refreshed. More and more dust. Like life. On to the dustpan, into the bucket. *Tamam*. Like life. Like life, that will be *tamam* one day, too. *Khalass* and *tamam*. *Tamam* and freed.

Shirin-Gol writes seven names on the list of those wanting to go back. Shirin-Gol, Morad, Nasser, Nafass, Nabi, Navid, Nassim. She takes her pretty plastic United Nations water container for the journey, signs the piece of paper for the wheat and the money that she will get beyond the border, folds the piece of paper, puts it carefully in her skirt pocket, grabs together everything she can carry, dresses the children in the prettiest clothes they have been given, rolls up the little carpet she has made herself, touches her prayer-beads, given her so-and-so many years ago by the rock woman in the mountains, looks into the sky, calls to her God and asks him to stand by her on the journey and their new life in Afghanistan.

I don't want to go anywhere, says Nasser, and lowers his head. I am staying here, in Iran. I am not an Afghan anymore. I'm an Iranian now.

When is my Nasser-brother coming? calls Navid, smiling.

He isn't, Shirin-Gol answers gently. In a low voice. With smiling eyes, choking back her tears.

God the merciful. Gives and takes away. A brother. A corner in front of the hut. A homeland. A *shahid*. A tent. A village with eight huts on legs and long chimneys clinging to the mountain. A blanket. A poppy field. A veranda. A nail in the wall to hang things on. A plastic hosepipe. Something decent to eat. Prison stench. Opium stench. Greenish-yellow stuff. Blackish-green stuff. A paper heart. A glass soul. A carpet to sweep. Dust, flakes, crumbs. Krrt, krrt, like life. A pretty plastic United Nations water container for the journey. A daughter. A son who is now an Iranian. God gives. God takes away.

Come with us, pleads Shirin-Gol.

You can force me, says Nasser, but the minute you take your eyes off me I will run off and come back here. I am staying, he says, I am not going back to Afghanistan.

Come with us, says Shirin-Gol, you are too young, you are half a child, you cannot stay here on your own, without a father, without a mother.

I can, he says peacefully, looking his mother in the eyes and standing bolt upright in front of her. Straight as a stick.

He is not half a child any more, he is half a man.

Not at all. He will not come. Not-half-child-but-half-man will not come.

Chapter Thirteen

A Flower, Red as Blood, and a Queen

Laden like cattle on the truck, six names and a hundred others return to their homeland. Six names and a hundred others climb down and touch the soil of home.

Morad squats on the dry earth of home and will not get up. The others walk around him, some men try to lift him up. Morad doesn't want to. Fights back with his hands and feet. Other men crouch around him. Morad starts weeping. Weeps, weeps, weeps. Shirin-Gol's heart turns to paper and tears. With a rip. Two pieces of paper heart. A heart made of paper.

Weeps. Weeps. So much so that the other men who have sat down with him start weeping as well.

Shirin-Gol and the wives of the other men and the children of the other men sit down and watch. Some of them weep. Some don't.

Morad squats. Squats and weeps. Weeps until the soil of his homeland that lies around him has ceased to be dry and dusty. Until the sand is fertilised by his tears and little red flowers blossom on it. For every tear, for every drop of blood from his soul a blood-red flower.

Red, blood-red flowers on the dry soil of home.

*

During the night the six names sleep in a transit camp, under a blue plastic tent, the smallest names on the carpet, the others on the bare sand of home.

Shirin-Gol is more awake than asleep, and Morad is not asleep at all, he is reproaching himself, he cannot bear to see the misery of the life he offers his wife and children, after all the years that he has dragged them back and forth, from the south to the north, from Pakistan to the mountains, from their homeland to Iran and back again, all to end up again sleeping on God's bare earth, about the fact that his children have not had fresh water for days, or hot food.

What is the difference between home and abroad? Nafass, Nabi, Navid, Nassim ask time and again, never getting an answer from Shirin-Gol or from Morad. The many countries, cities, mountains, valleys, villages where they have lived, that they have crossed, that they had to leave again, the sand, the desert, the mountains, it is all far too much, far too big for the little souls of the children, which are becoming more fragile, insecure and anxious from one time to the next. What is a country? they ask. What does home mean? Where is my home? What is a border? Where is it? This line? This gate? This flag? Why are we going back? What will we find there? Why don't we just go nowhere? Is home the place where I was born? Where my father was born? Where my sister is? Where my brother is? Is home where I get stones thrown at me, where I am mocked and humiliated? Then home is everywhere. Where I have starved, where I will starve? Then home is everywhere. Where I don't fit in because I am not like the others who have been somewhere else or who never left? Then home is everywhere. But if that is the case I must not go anywhere either.

Shirin-Gol scratches a hole in the ground, lays Nassim in the cool hole, takes off Nabi's warm Persian trousers, the ones given him by their neighbours, and the red pullover given him by their neighbours, and puts on the cool *shalwar-kamiz* she made herself. Nafass puts on the dress she made herself.

Nafass, Nabi, Navid shield their eyes from the merciless sun with their hands, squint, just stand there, look at their cloth-mother. God is angry with people, says Nafass.

How do you know he is angry? asks Shirin-Gol-cloth.

Can't you see? cries Nafass, hitting the air with her little hand. He told the sun to turn the earth into a baker's oven. God is angry and he has told the sun to turn the earth into a baker's oven.

Thoughts stick where they are. The brain is numbed. Muscles are drained of strength. Every movement becomes a power game between the body and the will. All around no trees, no bushes, no shade, nothing but desert, wind and dust. And tents. Blue tents. The colour of mosque domes and the colour of the United Nations. The only shade is in the tents. Glowing, hot, blue plastic shade.

Nafass, Nabi, Navid stand around their father, trying, as they have been trying all morning, at least to keep the merciless sun of home out of their eyes, their other hand outstretched, hardly expecting that they are about to hold the money of home that Morad has just changed at a pathetic exchange rate. Quiet and thoughtful, with trembling fingers, with prayer-like devotion, Morad presses an Afghan banknote into each little hand. They stare at the money, wondering why no miracle occurs, they look suspiciously, quizzically at their father, then they look at the money again, then they look at their cloth-mother, then at their father again, they look at the banknotes again, turn them around, hold them up to the sunlight, fan the heavy air with them as though the miracle they are waiting for is hidden in them, they shake the notes, let them fall to the dusty, hot ground, pick them up again, fold them, unfold them again, hold them close, hold them at a distance, turn them over, test the thickness of the paper.

Is that what happiness looks like? Which of the many signs, which picture, which word on them tells me that everything's going to be fine from now on?

Since leaving Isfahan the children have been waiting impatiently for this very moment. They have looked forward to it time and again. Time and again, in the face of fatigue, hopelessness and exhaustion their parents have got them back on their feet with the promise that everything will be fine.

It looks exactly like the money in Iran, Nafass says in a thin voice, on the point of tears. It isn't at all what you said it would be like.

It is all lies, shouts Navid. Give me the other money, the Iranian money. This doesn't look better than the Iranian money, either. Not at all. Why did we leave Isfahan? I want to go back. I want to go home. I want to go back where my big Nasser-brother is. I want to go where I was born. Come on, there's a truck to take me home. I want to go to the corner, to Agha Mustafa and buy an ice. I want to have my own money back.

My own money. *Own*, big and heavy.

Morad lets the little ones whine. He cannot counter their objections. Navid is right. Here or there, life will never be really good for him.

Come on. Navid takes his father's hand. Navid sets off energetically, clings to his father's big, powerful hand and pulls him along behind him. It's as though Morad is the child and Navid the grown-up, the father, the protector, who knows what is good and what is not good, who knows which is the right and which the wrong path.

Morad does not know where the boy gets all that energy from. God made little Navid that way, he says time and again. God sent little Navid so that Morad would not be alone any more. Alone with all his suffering in that wretched life.

Morad cannot help it, he has to laugh so as not to cry. The boy turns around to his father, laughs too. That feels good. Navid's eyes are full of love, his smile is all mercy. And when he sees his father's tears, tears that Morad can finally unleash, Navid wants to climb into his father's arms. He kisses him on the cheek, smiles and beams so radiantly that the glowing light of the sun seems pale in comparison. Morad's heart is filled with happiness. He presses little Navid to him, as tightly as he can. His heart is free. For one small, tiny, fragile moment that quickly passes again.

The children stand around Shirin-Gol-cloth, with the money of home in their outstretched hands, and say nothing. Three times, the much-praised country in three little children's hands. Hope, three times. Three thousand desires. They have already seen three times as many disappointments in their tiny little lives. And they will see plenty more.

They have known for a long time that this money is worthless, as worthless as the money with which their father was unable to buy them a past. They have known it for a long time, but they don't want to hear it, they would prefer to be lied to for as long as possible, hope for a miracle, believe that everything will be fine in spite of it all.

Shirin-Gol takes the banknotes, folds them, puts each

one in their trouser pockets. Morad stands beside her, looking like a child himself, as though he too had a note that Shirin-Gol was to fold up and put in his trouser pocket.

The children and Morad walk up and down, stand still, squat, look at one another, stand up, walk for another while, come back, walk again.

Poor Morad, whispers Shirin-Gol, he knows he is one of the people who will never have the right money. He knows he will never be able to buy happiness for his children.

Poor Shirin-Gol, who are you talking to?

To God, the gracious, the merciful, the one with a thousand and one names.

Shirin-Gol rubs out her name, which she has written in the sand, and writes h-o-m-e. And rubs that out as well.

Six names have stood on the platform of the truck, have swallowed the dust of the street all day. When will we finally get home? the children asked.

Home. When we hold Afghan money in our hands. Then we'll be home, and everything will be fine.

Nafass, Nabi, Navid stand there with their Afghan money in their hands. Nothing is fine. Their mother has become a cloth. The house is made of plastic. God has told the sun to turn the earth into a baker's oven.

What is fine? Nothing is fine.

The blazing heat of the sun, the dust, all the people, the shouting money-changers with their mean, slimy expressions, with their bundles of Persian money, American dollars and the holy money of home, with nothing else on their minds but cheating their fellow-countrymen as they come home again, lying to them, swindling them. The noisy truck with its platform full of dust-covered, exhausted, anxious people jumping down.

The hundreds and thousands of blue plastic tents. The new rulers of the country, the Taleban, in *shalwar-kamiz* that are far too long, with their black turbans on their heads and threatening sticks in their hands. The screaming children, the silent women, intimidated and frightened men, without honour or dignity. The net before Shirin-Gol's eyes, which her long lashes brush against each time she blinks, Shirin-Gol can no longer see neither all of this, or anything else. All she can see is the disappointment in her children's eyes.

God the merciful, murmurs Shirin-Gol-cloth and lifts her cloth-covered head to the sky as though God was up there, right over her head, only waiting for her to speak to him and send her desires and requests to him. Gracious God, have mercy. Have pity. Do not shatter our hope that everything will be fine this time. Almighty one.

Morad and the children walk up and down, stop, look around, come to Shirin-Gol, take a few steps more, come back. They all come back, time and again. Home. To God. To Shirin-Gol.

Nabi stands in front of his mother, narrows his eyes to slits, sees his mother and does not see her. If war was not raging in Afghanistan, if a just king ruled over it, who had a son, a prince, and if he was looking for a wife for the prince, a wife who would be queen, a wife with hair like black silk, with eyes like coal, with skin as tender as a fresh peach, with teeth as white as pearls, with limbs as delicate and powerful as those of a gazelle, with a voice as full and graceful as the song of a thousand *houri*, with a heart as big and warm as the light of the sun, for Nabi his mother would be that woman. Proud, honest, beautiful, poor, broken queen Shirin-Gol.

Shirin-Gol sits cross-legged. With her back upright and yet as soft as a feather, light, relaxed, proud, regal, she looks out over hundreds, thousands of blue plastic tents as though she were a ruler looking out over her army. Not like a regretful, home-coming refugee with six children who hasn't seen her oldest daughter for years, who had to leave her oldest son behind in Iran. Not one whose children were born abroad, not like someone going back to a homeland destroyed by war. Nabi sees the black cloth, dirty and dusty from the days of travelling, the hours on the platform of the truck, and does not see it. As far as he is concerned it is the queen's dress. Her cheap brass jewellery is her crown jewels. The baby in the cool hole in the ground is a princess. The last subsidised loaf of Persian bread is a feast-bread. The blue plastic tent beneath which she sits and sweats is her castle.

The eyes of her prince-son Nabi gleam and sparkle, he leaps to his feet, throws himself into her arms and cries, my queen-mother.

A man has driven his mother to hell, calls Nafass, and comes running excitedly into the tent.

What is that you say? asks Shirin-Gol.

Her family does not want her any more, I told her she could come and live with us and be our grandmother, because we haven't got a grandmother of our own.

What? Of course you have a grandmother, she is my mother, and tomorrow we will go and see her.

Then let us just keep her until tomorrow. Until-tomorrow-grandmother.

The old woman from the neighbouring tent has been cast out by her son-in-law. The United Nations only give each family eight sacks of wheat, and unfortunately the old woman is the ninth and her husband the tenth person, so the two old people get no wheat, and the old woman is seen as even more of a burden than she was already, so the son cannot carry her around with him any more, and she has to fend for herself.

Until-tomorrow-grandmother weeps and howls so much that the other women in the surrounding tents feel sorry for her, and the men shout and rage that the son-in-law has no sense of decency. They say he has forgotten what it means to be an Afghan, that he has lost his morality and his faith, and that it is the fault of the damned war that people have become like this. Soon everyone is talking at once, they are all shouting and furiously waving their arms, hurling curses and insults until Malek the official comes, followed by two Taleban with sticks in their hands and everyone calms down again. The ones standing nearest to Malek and the two Taleban with the sticks fall silent first. The ones furthest away are the last to fall silent.

Malek stands self-importantly in the middle of the furious, silent crowd and delivers a long speech, in the course of which he constantly turns in all directions so that none of those around him will miss one of his important words.

You let everyone cheat you, he says, beginning his address. Your own families, the officials in Iran who register you, the money-changers, self-appointed leaders, wheat-sellers, and then you come to us and we are supposed to put everything back in order again. Last of all we are supposed to fight a revolution for you and get rid of the government and install a new one.

Yes, that would be good, murmurs a woman in the background.

Until-tomorrow-grandmother will not stop crying. Sobbing, she throws herself on the ground, beats the dry earth with her old fists and keeps shouting, what sin have we committed that God must punish us for it? The longer the old woman weeps, the more other women, even young ones, are unable to hold back the tears, and when the mothers weep, the children weep too, and finally so do the fathers.

Malek tries to fight the weeping and sobbing, he turns around and talks and talks although no one is listening to him now. And suddenly his own throat dries up. Another Afghan, who is also wearing a blue UN cap, and who clearly has a higher rank than Malek, is unexpectedly standing in front of him.

Unlike Malek, Amjad is a quiet man, with eyes that smile with goodness even though they have seen and known grief for a very long time. His voice is soft and quiet. He takes his blue cap off, says his name and nothing else, looks at Malek, looks around, looks at Malek again. Malek opens his mouth and is about to start speaking, when Amjad discovers Until-tomorrow-grandmother, bends down to her, helps her to her feet, talks to her quietly and politely. Forgive me, mother, for talking to you. I work for the United Nations. Please, tell me. What has happened? I may be able to help you.

Poor Until-tomorrow-grandmother throws herself gratefully against Amjad's shoulder and only now starts really crying. Then she calms down again, apologises for standing too close to him, says, God will forgive me for touching a strange man. I am an old woman, destined for death, you are as young as my grandson, may God protect you both. And then she tells Amjad that her son-in-law will not take her and her husband because they don't get any wheat.

Amjad fans himself and Until-tomorrow-grandmother with his cap, scratches his sweaty head and does not know what to say.

Finally he goes with Until-tomorrow-grandmother to her son-in-law, talks to him, tells him he understands, he knows how he feels, but that he also feels sorry for Until-tomorrow-grandmother and her husband, that he too would sometimes like to leave everything and everyone behind and simply walk away. Finally he walks around with the man, buys two sacks from Shirin-Gol, who does not want to carry part of her wheat with her, gives them to the man for his old parents-in-law and extracts from him his sacred word of honour that he will take them with him and treat them well. The man is ashamed, sits on the floor, bites his lips, murmurs a promise, turns around, crouches on one of the wheat sacks in his tent, looks over at his old mother-in-law, weeps and says nothing.

The people cannot read or write, says Amjad, they are desperate and worked up, they do not understand when the authorities in Iran explain to them that they should list a maximum of so-and-so-many people as a single family. Until-tomorrow-grandmother and her husband should have been registered as a family in their own right. That is the way Afghans are, family is everyone with the same blood.

Amjad taps his blue UN cap repeatedly against his thigh, looks into the distance. Says nothing. Swallows. Swallows back tears.

Why are you crying? Nabi asks his mother and does not wait for her answer. You don't need to worry, we will never throw you out.

Amjad cannot help it, he has to laugh, he looks gratefully at the boy, puts his cap on and says goodbye.

Shirin-Gol cannot help it, she looks gratefully at her son, puts her hand on his chest and laughs, a lovely, gurgling, tearful laugh.

Why are you laughing? Nabi asks his mother and does not wait for her answer. Because we are the light of your life? he cries, putting his arms around the neck of his queenly mother and kissing her. Now it does not hurt any more, does it? *Mage na*? in Isfahan dialect.

Nabi's bright voice has lost its cheerful ring, Shirin-Gol thinks. It no longer sounds like a clear stream, welling up between the stones somewhere in the mountains of the Hindu Kush and splashing heedlessly away.

Nabi plays with one of his mother's black curls that has slipped out from under her cloth, he looks at it and is convinced that he has saved his mother's life with his questions and answers, his kisses and his love, simply by being there.

And now I am going back to Isfahan, Nabi announces, and when I've got there I'll find my Nasser-brother and buy us both an ice.

Come here, says Shirin-Gol softly. Do you want to go without Mother?

Nabi stands in front of his mother, thinks for a moment and nods.

But I am not going to let you go. Nowhere. Do you understand? You are staying with me, says Shirin-Gol and kisses her son.

Women are stronger than men, says Morad, staring at his feet.

Who says that? asks Shirin-Gol, sighs so that her body rises, her breast slips from her baby's mouth and little Nassim, with beads of sweat on her tiny brow, is startled. Shirin-Gol puts her breast back in the little one's mouth, fans her with the tip of her cloth and says to Morad, stop brooding. Stop tormenting yourself and me and the children.

Morad only nods, looks around as though trying to find something, cannot find anything, just stands there for a moment, then says, I am going.

Where? asks Nabi.

Nowhere, says Morad.

I'm coming too, call Nafass, Nabi, Navid.

No, says Shirin-Gol, you are staying here, and she says to Morad, without looking at him, just go.

Without looking at him.

The heat becomes a monster. A hungry monster with its sights on the lives of men. God has told the sun to turn the earth into a monster that wants to eat people.

Shirin-Gol breathes with her mouth open, takes off her baby's shirt, scratches a new hole beside herself in the sandy ground and lays little Nassim in the new hole.

Nafass, Nabi, Navid withdraw to the corner of the tent, lie down on the wheat sacks and doze.

Morad withdraws to some corner somewhere in the transit camp and smokes opium. For the fourth or fifth time. Fear-opium. A whole *mesqhal*. 1500 or 2000 *lak* less money for living and for his children's food. His children.

Shirin-Gol draws letters in the sand with her finger.

M-y c-h-i-l-d-r-e-n.

Do you want to sell your water container? ask two women who are already carrying eight or more plastic water containers tied together over their shoulders.

What do you want my water container for? asks Shirin-Gol.

We will buy it off you, and then you won't need to go on carrying it around with you.

And what will you do with it? You have so many already.

We sell them in the bazaar. And we will buy your wheat off you too, if you like.

No thanks, sister. God protect you, I will sell the wheat myself. You cannot pay the amount of money that I want for it, and I need the water container for the journey to my father-house.

God protect you, and may God grant that everything is fine in your father-house and everyone is in good health.

God protect you too, says Shirin-Gol.

Like Shirin-Gol, the two women have come home from Iran, they came back a year ago. They wanted to go back to their father-house as well. The Russians or somebody have bombed it to bits. Their father himself is somewhere else or dead. Their husbands are fighting somewhere else or are dead as well. So they have hung around here near the border. They live under plastic sheets and under trees, their children collect pine needles, to use them as firewood or sleep on them. The little money they have had has been used up long since. The plastic water containers and the wheat are their only source of income. They buy off the new home-comers what they can't or won't carry with them, and sell it in the city. If they are lucky, the new arrivals do not know the prices yet. Some days the women buy and sell so much that they and their children get enough to eat.

Some days.

Every day small traders buy wheat from the home-comers, there are whole truckloads of it, which they sell again in the city at higher prices. Every day money-changers come to the camp, medicine sellers, Afghans who came back from Iran at some point, hung around and became buyers and sellers. Each of them remembers his own first day on the soil of home. The hope that they have buried in the meantime. Buried hope. Buried will to start over. Dead wish for everything to be fine.

If their own brother in faith, their own countryman stands by them and says, brother I want to help you, sell me your wheat, such-and-such is the price, they believe him. If they tell him the container isn't worth more than such-and-such, or Persian money isn't worth more than so-and-so, they believe them.

And who knows how many of the people returning today will have buried their own hopes over the course of the next year. Will be buying and selling plastic canisters and wheat. Plastic canisters and wheat that the new batch of home-comers don't want to carry the whole long way into the unknown. Finally Shirin-Gol gives up, with the fourth or fifth man who wants to buy her wheat from her, negotiates briefly and sells him one of her sacks.

Who is going to carry them all? she asks herself, because there's no one else there for her to ask, and puts the money in her skirt pocket.

The beads of sweat on little Nassim's brow have children, they won't sit still, they run down her temple. Shirin-Gol holds the little one up to pee and to spit. Whitish-yellow stuff that sinks into the ground.

Father was being sick as well, says Nafass, he smoked too much opium.

How do you know what opium is? asks Shirin-Gol and wipes Nassim's mouth.

Nafass shrugs.

Go to the water pump, says Shirin-Gol to Nafass and Nabi, fill the container with fresh water and look for your father.

I'm not going, says Nafass, there's a madwoman there.

A woman walks past the tent, stumbles, almost falls,

recovers, walks on, suddenly stops as though she had bumped into a glass wall, turns around, walks in the other direction, bumps into invisible glass again, stops, squats on the ground in front of Shirin-Gol and speaks. Without reason, which she has lost, and with eyes that are open wide.

She looks at Nafass and says, give me my money back. Are you the wind? Why did you steal my money? *Salil-shodeh*. Give it back. The wind stole my money.

Happy the one who finds it, murmurs Shirin-Gol and rubs her baby's vomit out of her skirt and her cloth.

Nafass, Nabi, Navid run off in search of the woman's money. Nabi asks where she has been, Navid pulls her behind him, Nafass runs back and forth asking everyone if they have seen the poor woman's money.

That is good, the children will be occupied for a while at least, thinks Shirin-Gol.

Finally Morad comes back. Trembles. His head pulled between his shoulders. His arms folded tight in front of his chest. He drags his weary body to the tent, crouches down, sees the sick child, closes his eyes, pulls himself together, stands up again, looks like an old man and says with a heavy, paralysed tongue, the people say there is a doctor here somewhere, I will take her there.

Shirin-Gol wraps the little one in a cloth, puts her in Morad's arms, immediately takes her away again because he almost drops her, pushes Morad to the ground. Sit down, she says, you need help yourself.

As though he weren't there, as though he couldn't hear her, as though he didn't understand her, as though he had lost his mind, as though he were a little, helpless child, she puts some things under his head, takes his shoes off him, opens his belt, covers him with something.

Little Nassim spits again.

Shirin-Gol puts water in a bowl, supports Morad's head, helps him to drink, pours water into her hand, puts her damp hand at the nape of his neck, on his forehead, on his head, kneads his shoulders, helps him to huddle.

Like a baby. Morad-baby. Cowering with white stuff on his mouth.

Little Nassim spits again.

Shirin-Gol pulls her *burqa* over herself, takes little Nassim, goes out.

Where are you going? cries Nafass.

To the doctor.

I'll come with you, says Nafass, hanging on to her mother-skirt. My eyes are on fire, she says, and they hurt and they are watering and I should have gone to the doctor days ago.

Nassim lies weakly in her mother's arms. Her little babyish arms and legs dangle lifelessly from her body. Her little babyish head hangs heavily from her neck. Her breathing is shallow, her eyes are closed.

Nassim-baby. Morad-baby.

Shirin-Gol runs, not knowing where to.

A woman sees half-dead Nassim-baby in her arms and directs Shirin-Gol to the doctor.

The doctor is not a doctor. The doctor is on his way. Somewhere among the blue tents a child is half-dead and needs his help. The doctor is a nurse.

The doctor-nurse says half-dead Nassim has a high temperature, gives her an injection, presses a few pills into Shirin-Gol's hand, turns away and switches her attention to the next child, lying half-dead in his father's arms.

And my eyes? Nafass asks.

What is wrong with your eyes? asks the doctor-nurse, without looking at Nafass.

They are on fire and they hurt, says Nafass.

The doctor-nurse looks briefly at Nafass, then at Shirin-Gol and says, that little bottle, put two drops of that in her eyes, and then another two every hour.

What kind of drops are they? asks Shirin-Gol.

The only one I have, replies the doctor-nurse, gives the other child the same injection that she gave Nassim and says, and this is the only injection I have.

And I am the only nurse here, and there is only one doctor, who is on his way, and there are other half-dead children waiting outside.

Nafass is happy about the drops, happy and proud, and she feels important. To keep the drops from jumping out of her eyes, she keeps her eyes shut all the way back to the tent. At first she wants Shirin-Gol to carry her, but she understands that she is too big and too heavy for that, particularly since Shirin-Gol is carrying her half-dead sister. To keep from falling she claws her little hand into Shirin-Gol's skirt, refuses to open her eyes, even when she stumbles and nearly falls over.

Only when Shirin-Gol says, there's Until-tomorrow-grandmother, does Nafass open her eyes again.

Until-tomorrow-grandmother is sitting on a sack of wheat, with her husband sitting next to her, both of them looking straight ahead, silent, looking up anxiously when someone walks past them, then looking straight ahead again, silently.

There is my friend, calls Nafass and runs off. Nafass' friend is a young man, no older than sixteen. Nafass' friend looks like a girl, walks like a girl, has his eyebrows plucked like a married girl, wears his hair long like a girl. Nafass' friend has his little finger in his mouth, sucks on it, his other hand placed coquettishly on his hip. As he walks

Nafass' friend wiggles his bottom back and forth, forth and back. Nafass' friend twinkles at Nafass, but walks past her. I've got to work, he says. Bottom back and forth, forth and back. Nafass' friend stops in front of a man, smiles, utters two or three words, sucks on his little finger, throws back his head. Nafass' friend's hand touches the man's hand, and he laughs and disappears with him into a blue plastic tent.

Allahu akbar, says Shirin-Gol, of all the people in the world was that the only friend you could find for yourself?

Nafass shrugs, closes her eyes, clutches her mother-skirt and stumbles back beside Shirin-Gol to her own blue plastic tent.

In the tents all around everyone is packing their bags, their carpets and whatever they have brought back from Iran. Men come, carry the sacks of wheat to the buses, only Morad lies where he is, wrapped up like a baby.

Morad-baby.

Shirin-Gol sees her sacks of wheat, sees her children, sees her husband huddling on the ground, helpless, sees her half-dead baby, sees the man from the neighbouring tent, asks him to help her, presses the bags and the pretty plastic United Nations water container into the children's hands for the journey. Shirin-Gol helps Morad to his feet, pulls on her *burqa*, throws it over her face, drags herself and Morad to the bus, stands around until it is her turn to get on, pushes her children and Morad up the steps, turns her cloth-covered head around once again, and says nothing, goes in and disappears.

Chapter Fourteen

A FATHER-HOUSE, A GRAVE AND A MAD BROTHER-WIFE

Shirin-Gol is lucky. She has wheat. She has a little carpet she has made herself. She has a few dollars from coming back. She has a pretty plastic United Nations water container. She has the rock woman's necklace around her neck. She has read three-and-a-half proper books. She has, as a girl, drunk from the water of the lake. She has days that have turned into birds and flown away.

She has a father-house that she can go back to.

It has shrunk. A rocket has hit it and destroyed part of it. Her father is sick and bedridden. Her mother is no longer there. Dead.

Where the dead-mother grave is there are other graves as well.

Martyr-graves. Boy-graves. Brother-graves. Father-graves. Girl-graves. Women-graves. Sister-graves. Mother-graves.

Shirin-Gol's mother-grave.

There are long sticks in the boy- and men-graves. The people have tied rags to them. Green, yellow and red, fluttering in the wind. They are supposed to bring luck, and keep the evil spirits from disturbing the souls of the dead. To remind God that there is another dead person in

Afghanistan. For each prayer a rag. Rag-prayers flutter in the wind.

There are even more sticks in the martyr-graves. Even more green, even more yellow, even more red rags, fluttering in the wind. Even more rag-prayers fluttering in the wind.

Rags that whisper, talk, weep.

Girl-graves, without rags.

Women-graves, without rags.

Next to her dead-mother-grave is a dead Afghan Arab.

The USA flew 35,000 and more Arabs to Afghanistan, trained them and turned them into Afghan Arabs. Many of them stayed after the war as well. Dead. Dead for the Prophet. Dead for the Koran. Dead for Islam. Dead for the USA. Dead for capitalism.

Whose Prophet? Whose Koran? Whose Islam?

Whose dead Afghan Arab?

Afghans want to win, to drive the Russians out of their homeland. The Arabs came to fight, to die. To become martyrs. *Shahid*.

Does the dead Afghan-Arab have a mother as well? Is the dead Afghan-Arab's mother happy that her son has become a *shahid*? Did the hair of the dead Afghan-Arab's mother turn white? White-haired mother of an Afghan-Arab *shahid*.

Shirin-Gol had a mother with white hair.

The so-and-so many *shahid* in Shirin-Gol's life. How many? She has stopped counting.

A rocket killed her.

Do rockets have mothers?

Someone must have brought rockets into the world.

Do the men who make rockets have mothers as well? Rocket man with mother.

Do rocket men have children?

Does God have a mother? God-mother. Someone must have brought him into the world.

Shirin-Gol crouches by her mother's grave, tries to weep, but has no tears for her. Not a single one. Instead she has a thousand and one questions. A thousand and one thoughts. Instead she looks at the animals' skulls on the sticks stuck into the graves. Why have the survivors stuck animal heads on the sticks? For protection? As an omen? As a symbol? Just because it looks nice?

Why don't girl- and women-graves have animal skulls on sticks? As an omen? Just because it looks nice?

Why do women bring children into the world? *Yek ruz be dardam mikhore*, one day they might be useful to me. For what? For making war? For firing rockets at mothers?

Come back to the hut, quick, calls Nafass, the aunt has gone mad.

Why didn't the rocket kill mad Brother-wife? whispers Shirin-Gol, kisses a stone, touches it with her forehead and puts it on her dead-mother-grave.

Mad Brother-wife sits cross-legged on the floor by the tree. She has wrapped her legs around the trunk. Again and again she beats her brow against the tree. Bang. Bang. Brow against the tree-trunk. It shatters the bloody pictures in her head. Blood on her brow. Blood on the tree-trunk. Bang. Bang.

Shirin-Gol crouches next to mad Brother-wife, puts her arm around her shoulders, pulls her to her, presses her tightly to her, feels the blood from mad Brother-wife on her throat, says nothing, just holds her, rocks her back and forth.

Mad Brother-wife has lost her senses, hangs apathetically around, pulls her hair out, scratches herself bloody, tries to tear her eyes out so as not to see her husband suffering, her children starving, the hell that life has become.

Brother stepped on a mine, lost his leg. His leg and his child, the one he was holding by the hand when he stepped on the mine. Cripple-brother hangs around, has no work, screams with pain, would rather be dead himself instead of seeing, over and over again, the scraps of his leg, along with scraps of his child, flying into the air and landing with a slap on the ground.

With a slap.

One child's eye is still open and smiling. Father's hand and child's hand are torn off, lying in the dirt, still holding one another.

Brother-daughter, who was walking behind her father and her brother, was hurled to the ground by the force of the explosion. She stands up, beats the dust from her dress with the flowers that were lovely once, pallid now, takes the brother-foot, still in its plastic shoe, and tries to fasten it to the ragged brother-leg.

Cripple-brother shouts at his children. Shouts at his wife who has lost her senses. Cripple-brother throws himself on his wife who has lost her senses and impregnates her. Cripple-brother shouts. Cripple-brother stands his Kalashnikov against the wall behind him.

Shirin-Gol's father has lost his voice. Father has lost his sight. Father has lost everything. Just sits around now, only eats if someone feeds him, putting scraps into his mouth as if he were a child. Father-child. Child-father.

Nafass, Nabi, Navid, Nassim are afraid. Wake in the night.

Morad squats apathetically in the corner, smokes and smokes. Opium. Four days and four nights, then he is gone. Vanished. Without a last word. Without a last glance.

Shirin-Gol has seen nothing, heard nothing, felt nothing. She has just given little Nassim the breast and washed her because after the mother's milk she spat everything right back out again, has just put fresh bandages on Brother-wife's forehead, freshly bound Cripple-brother's stump, which has been issuing pus for months, she has just promised Nafass, Nabi and Navid that everything will be fine, when she comes into the room and sees that Morad's corner is empty.

There is no warm smoke, no fresh smell of opium in the room. The empty Morad-corner is cold.

Shirin-Gol is neither sad nor happy. She squats on the colourful carpet, gives Nassim the breast, looks at the empty Morad-corner and doesn't know how she knows he has gone and won't be coming back.

Morad, her husband, the father of her children. With a big *her* before children.

On the one hand he has been nothing but a burden lately. On the other hand, if he is sober and sensible, he is a just and tender husband. A good and loving father to her children. *Her* children.

On the one hand he is like one of her children. She must wash, feed and comfort him. On the other hand he is a man. The sole official protector. Regardless of the state he happens to be in. The main thing is that he is a man. On the one hand he is no help. On the other hand the other men leave her in peace as long as he is there.

Now Shirin-Gol is alone. Alone she looks after her children, alone she sells the wheat, alone she sells the pretty plastic United Nations water containers, alone she sells the carpet. For something decent for her children to eat. Alone she tells the mullah and the Taleb that she does not want a husband, that she has a husband who will come back. Alone she goes to the bazaar, alone she looks after Cripple-brother, Cripple-brother's mad wife, eight Cripple-brother-children. Alone she looks after her Child-father. Alone.

Every fourth day the Taleb comes to the door and wants to have Shirin-Gol. Every fourth day Shirin-Gol sends him away again.

Brother-wife, who has lost her senses, hangs apathetically around, pulls her hair out, scratches her skin till it bleeds, wraps her legs around the tree trunk and beats her brow bloody to kill the pictures in her head, tries to tear her own eyes out so that she does not have to see her husband suffering, her children starving and the hell that life has become. Bloody, mad Brother-wife says go, clear off. Go and take your children with you. Go. Go. Go. So that you don't have to look at the blood on Brother-wife's forehead, on the tree trunk. So that the stench of pus from Brother's leg-stump won't creep into your skin anymore. So that you and your children do not go mad. So that you and your children do not starve. So that we do not kill each other. So that. So that. So that. Go.

Shirin-Gol waits for forty days and forty nights. Then she grabs together everything she can carry, kisses Brother-wife's bloody forehead and goes.

Where are we going? asks Nafass.

To another village, says Shirin-Gol. To the village where your big sister Noor-Aftab lives.

Nafass thinks. That is the one with the green-yellow-orange-red, most beautiful cloud-wedding-dress in the world.

That is the one, says Shirin-Gol.

Cloud-wedding-dress-sister, calls Nafass, I want to go

there. Will I get a cloud-wedding-dress as well?

We have a sister? ask Navid and Nassim. What is a cloud-wedding-dress? Will we get one too?

Thanks be to Allah. From a long way off Shirin-Gol can see that the village that looks like a person lying on the ground with his legs pressed tightly together and his arms outstretched has only been partially bombed.

If Shirin-Gol were a bird flying in the air and looking at the village from above, she would see that the house where her daughter and the young Taleb live hasn't been destroyed either.

Along with the chants from the mosque, the wind too ventures into the street at this time of day, and into the huts, into the fields and gardens, sends the colourful heads of the poppy flowers dancing, shaking the dust of the day from their delicate blossoms.

In Afghanistan no one knows pity now, only the mosque-chant wind, Shirin-Gol thinks, squatting under the mulberry tree, closing her eyes, freeing her face from the *burqa* and yielding to it. The voice of the muezzin and the voice of the wind.

The wind knows that when the mullah's voice rings out the weapons fall silent. A small, satisfied breeze drifts quietly and inconspicuously down from the Hindu Kush, greeting Shirin-Gol and her children with the smell of snow and the peaceful murmuring of the women in the fields, down to the valley.

Shirin-Gol and her children squat in the warm evening sun and wait, half dozing, half happy, half full of fear and worry. They just sit around the way millions of other women and children are squatting and waiting somewhere in Afghanistan. Waiting. For the end of the war. For their husbands. For their sons. For something decent to eat. For this and that.

The wind merges with the scent of the apple blossom, the fine dust of the streets, the fresh grass, the poppy flowers, the brief peace, perfect quiet, the sound of the boys singing of their homeland. The wind slips through Shirin-Gol's cloths and clothes and settles on her tired skin. Eyes closed, she thinks, this could be paradise.

With the first clattering of the donkey-hoofs on the road, with the first cries of the men, with the first shots fired by the men, Shirin-Gol throws her *burqa* over her face, stands up, takes Nassim on her arm, Navid by the hand. Nafass and Nabi hold on to her skirt, and they set off down the path into the village.

The rope isn't there any more, it has turned into a barrier. The former radio-mechanic and the former women's-tailor aren't there any more. The innards of cassette tapes dangle from the barrier. Confiscated cassette tapes. The Taleban have broken them, torn out the tapes and hung them like trophies on their barrier, as a warning. Music forbidden.

The tea-house is still there, but the kind tea-house owner isn't. Where is he? asks Shirin-Gol.

Dead, says the new tea-house owner.

Who lives in the room behind the tea-house? asks Shirin-Gol.

Why do you want to know? asks the new tea-house owner.

Shirin-Gol walks on.

Down the sandy road and almost up to the light-blue iron gate, now even more pitted with bullet holes, like painful pimples and wounds. Shirin-Gol turns into the little road where her daughter lives.

Shirin-Gol's heart is dashing up and down in her body,

right to left and back again. It leaps into her throat and tries to jump out of her mouth, making her lose her voice. Voice lost. Shirin-Gol pushes Nafass forward to speak for her.

I'm looking for my sister Noor-Aftab, the little one says, beaming like the Light of the Sun.

No Noor-Aftab here, says the man, closing the wooden door.

Shirin-Gol's heart plummets into her stomach, and the world before her eyes loses its colour. Colour lost. Colour in face lost. Shirin-Gol sees black, the wind falls silent, the world turns to night.

Shirin-Gol walks on.

Puts one foot in front of the other, without knowing how she is doing it, without knowing why, without knowing where.

One foot in front of the other.

Who are you? asks a Taleb.

We're so-and-so. We're somebody or other. A woman and her children. Her children. We're looking for the Taleb called such-and-such, who used to live in such-and-such a hut.

I am new here. I do not know any so-and-so, I do not know a Taleb with such-and-such a name.

Where's Bahadur? Shirin-Gol asks the boy who opens the door.

Who?

Bahadur, the fourth wife of the second-most-important Mujahedin commander, says Shirin-Gol.

He was shot. He was a traitor.

Who did he betray? Who shot him?

The boy looks to the right, to the left and whispers, the Taleban. The Taleban shot him.

Where are his wives? asks Shirin-Gol.

They were shot, says the boy.

And their sons?

Them too.

Why? asks Shirin-Gol.

Don't know, says the boy.

Shirin-Gol walks on.

Where is the doctor, Azadine? Shirin-Gol asks the wife of the Taleb who now lives in the surgery.

Ne poyoegoem, I don't know, says the woman in Pashtu.

Shirin-Gol walks on.

The mullah's house has been hit by a rocket. Half has been destroyed, half is still standing. The mullah has been shot, the mullah's wife is still alive.

Where's my daughter? asks Shirin-Gol.

Gone, says the wife of the dead mullah.

Where to?

Herat, probably.

Herat? When? Why Herat?

Because her husband took her there, says the wife of the dead mullah, looking at the floor.

You are a mother of daughters and sons yourself, what is going on with my daughter? Whatever it is, I beg you, tell me, pleads Shirin-Gol.

Noor-Aftab and her husband, the young Taleb, had a child. The Taleb was a decent, just man. He meant well towards your Noor-Aftab, and he loved his child more than life itself, says the wife of the dead mullah.

Where is my daughter? asks Shirin-Gol.

They let your daughter live, she says, but they shot him. Because he was just. Because he resisted. Because he defended the people against the other Taleban. Because he said that what the Taleban do isn't what it says in the

Koran, it is not the law of God, it is not the word of the Prophet. The other Taleban said, even a Taleb can make a mistake, and shot him. They shot the commander, my husband, your son-in-law and many others besides.

The wife of the dead mullah looks at the floor again and says, then another Taleb took your daughter as his wife. He said he and he alone had been entitled to her from the very beginning.

Greenish-yellow. A bundle of money. Cold and bitter eyes.

Shirin-Gol has the taste of gall in her mouth. Gall-taste.

Where is the doctor? asks Shirin-Gol.

Azadine fled, says the mullah's wife. They forbade her to work. She fought against the Taleban, she told them there were women doctors in Kabul and other cities and villages as well, and no Taleb and no one would stop her from practising. The Taleban said that other Taleban made the rules in the other cities and villages. We're in charge here. For a while Azadine treated patients in secret, until the Taleban found out about it and forbade that as well. They said she needed a husband so she would not be so rebellious, so that there would be someone keeping an eye on her. Then she packed her things and fled in secret during the night.

Where to?

Kabul.

I have got to get to Herat, says Shirin-Gol. I want to find my daughter.

On your own?

With my children.

It will take weeks.

I will go.

Without a husband?

Without a husband.

Chapter Fifteen

A Queen in Charge

Asphalted roads. An airport. Trees with long, thin spikes like needles. The scent of soap. Massive great palaces and mosques that a queen commissioned, Gowhar Shad, the wife of the king Shah Rokh. Palaces that have survived all the wars. Until now.

In the Russian school Fawzi talked of Herat, and Shirin-Gol thought, I will go there one day.

One day.

Back then, before she had a daughter she would leave behind and have to search for.

Back then.

Herat, the city that was once the capital of a great and powerful empire. Herat, the city of the Teymurid kings, of Tamerlaine's dynasty, the king of the arts, the city of the great library, the school of miniature painting. Shah Rokh, the fourth son of the great Timur. The king whose power extended to Iran and as far as Turkestan. Herat, the city of blue glass. Blue like the lake that Shirin-Gol drank from as a girl. Water runs coolly down her throat.

Herat, the city of all that and much else besides.

Herat, the city where 24,000 people died when the Russian tanks rolled into the city.

Herat, today, the city of the Taleban. Taleban with black turbans. Taleban with long *shalwar-kamiz*. Taleban with strict rules forbidding women to do anything. To walk alone in the street. To go to university. Herat, a city of scholars. A city where once queens were in charge. Herat, a city of poets and writers. City of song and dance.

Back then.

Herat, the city where girls now go to school in secret, if at all.

Herat, the city with huge, crooked towers. They have survived the bombs of the Russians, the rockets of the Mujahedin.

Herat, the city of progress, formerly home to scientists and philosophers, is ruled now by backward-looking despots whose like Afghanistan has never seen before. The Taleban.

Poor Herat.

Poor Shirin-Gol, in search of her daughter, squats by the side of a street and does not know where to look for Noor-Aftab.

In the house behind her, on the first floor, sits the kind owner of the dining-room, sees Shirin-Gol, does something forbidden and asks cheeky Nabi to tell his mother to come up. The kind owner would like to please his God and give food to Shirin-Gol and her children. Do a good deed every day God gives you. A big meal and four little meals, a good deed.

That is resistance, says Shirin-Gol, freeing her face from the *burqa*.

That is resistance, says the kind dining-room owner.

Shirin-Gol, Nafass, Nabi, Navid, Nassim squat on wooden platforms, eating. Eight men sit on other platforms, watching every bite that Shirin-Gol puts in her mouth. Neither unfriendly nor friendly. Unabashed. Unashamed. Eager. Hungry.

They have the right to do so, they are men. Shirin-Gol has dared to venture into a forbidden male domain. Alone. Without protection. Without Opium-Morad.

If the *sia-sar* goes about as naked as that, she will draw attention to herself, says one. Naked.

Naked woman. Naked Shirin-Gol.

Tell her to eat rice, calls another, it makes you strong. Tell her meat is good, it gives you energy, calls another one.

Herat is no different from the rest of the country, it is dangerous here for a woman without male protection.

Let them shout, thinks Shirin-Gol, let them watch me putting my bites of food into my mouth. Shirin-Gol, Nafass, Nabi, Navid and Nassim stuff in so much that their stomachs are full and firm, that they barely have room for their breath. Stomachs full of rice, meat and vegetables, full of tea with sugar and bread.

A bird sits in the hanging cage, twittering and squawking. Neither beautiful nor ugly. Just squawking.

He wants out of his cage, says Nabi.

Where does he want to go? asks the kind dining-room owner.

Nabi shrugs.

A boy brings a bowl for them to wash their hands, puts it down by Shirin-Gol, touches her bare foot. Accidentally.

Let him touch me, thinks Shirin-Gol, washing her hands.

From the floor-length window where Shirin-Gol squats,

she sees men opening up their shops in the street. They have prayed. Eaten. Slept. They have lain beside, in, on their wives. They have washed their hands, their feet, their elbows, water behind the ears. Water, water, wash me. Purify me of my sins. Praying. Forgetting. Doing good.

Shirin-Gol slurps some tea, looks around at the men. Resistance.

It will soon be curfew, says the kind dining-room owner. Where are you going to spend the night?

Eight men stretch their necks. What will she answer, the naked woman with her stomach full of rice, meat and a good deed?

The bird twitters. Loud and quiet. Quiet and loud.

He wants out, says Nabi with a shrug.

It is not safe in the city, says the kind dining-room owner, a few nights ago the Taleban broke into a house and violated an Englishwoman. A foreigner working for an aid organisation. We have never had anything like that before in the history of our country.

A foreigner being raped.

Shirin-Gol slurps tea.

The bird wants out, says Nabi.

A Taleban rapist. A raped Englishwoman.

I will take you to my sister's, says the kind dining-room owner. You will be safe there.

We'll be safe there, says Shirin-Gol.

The kind dining-room owner doesn't want anything for his good deed. He just wants to be good.

In bad times good people must do more good, so that justice does not die, he says.

The kind dining-room owner was born in Herat, spent his whole life there, except for his studies in Kabul.

I studied jurisprudence, he says. In 1349 [in the Islamic calendar], when King Zahir Shah was in power, I started, and in 1354, when Daoud was in power, I graduated. Then I had to go to military service. I was a foot-soldier. We went everywhere on foot.

Foot-soldier with legal studies behind him, going everywhere on foot. Foot-soldier with legal studies behind him gets a medal.

I was at Russian school, says Shirin-Gol, and I got a medal, too. The other children clapped.

I worked in the finance ministry, where I was responsible for planning. I worked in the customs department, then in the city administration, first in Kabul, then in Herat.

I was at Russian school and learned to read and write, says Shirin-Gol.

If you know nothing, you tend to believe the people you think understand things better than you do, says the kind dining-room owner. If you can read yourself, you can form your own judgement, and you do not have to believe what other people tell you.

I wanted to be a doctor, says Shirin-Gol.

There aren't many women like you, says the kind dining-room owner. Where is your husband?

At first my husband was with me, but now I drag myself and my children around through life on my own.

I have known my wife since we were children, says the kind dining-room owner, who wants nothing for his kindness.

I am looking for my child, says Shirin-Gol, my daughter, Noor-Aftab, who I married to a Taleb and left at home so that I could flee to Iran with the money I got for her.

The kind dining-room owner says nothing, just nods.

The bird wants out.

And now I pray to God that she is still alive, says Shirin-Gol, and smiles so as not to weep.

We are lucky, says the kind dining-room owner. Anyone who is still alive in Afghanistan today is lucky.

Lucky, says Shirin-Gol and smiles.

The bird is lucky too, says Nabi.

I have never fought, says the kind dining-room owner. War is no solution.

There aren't many men like you, says Shirin-Gol.

In a country like ours, men who do not fight are not respected, says the kind dining-room owner. Some people do not consider me a proper man for that reason. Like all Afghans, I was against the Russians, I was against President Taraki, I was against his government because he collaborated with the Communists. I was against the Pakistanis who supported them. I was against the Americans who supported them, and I am against the Taleban. But war? That is no solution.

My father fought in the mountains, says Shirin-Gol, now he just sits around in the corner, as helpless as my little daughter. My brother stood on a mine and lost his leg. His leg, his hand and his child that he was leading by the hand. My other brother is a *shahid*, and we have buried him. I do not know if the rest of my brothers and sisters are still alive.

If I met them, says the kind dining-room owner, I would ask the leaders of the Mujahedin why they went on fighting after they had driven out the Russians. Why they left Kabul in ruins. Why they demanded tolls. Why they violated women. The wives of their own brothers in faith. The people gave the Mujahedin everything, everything, their bread and their life. I want to ask them if they are

Afghans. If this country is their home. And I would say to them that I rue and regret every day I helped them. And I would ask them, what right do you have to stay in power? And I would say to them that the Taleban came to power for one reason alone. Simply because they, the Mujahedin, went on fighting.

Shirin-Gol laughs. Our country's flag has lost its colour. Today it is white. Before it was red, white and black. And before that it was red.

The kind dining-room owner smiles and says, red, white and black.

We're like the dead, whose winding-sheets are stolen by the *kefin-kesh*, the winding-sheet thief, says the kind dining-room owner.

The *kefin-kesh* crept to the graves at night, dug up the recently dead, unwrapped the winding-sheets from around their bodies and sold them again in the bazaar.

At some point the dead got fed up being wrapped up and buried only to be dug up and unwrapped again. And as they lay so dead and cold and naked in their graves, they decided to turn to the God of the dead and ask him to free them from this shameless *kefin-kesh*. God the just listened to them, found that they were right and killed the vulgar winding-sheet thief.

The dead were happy and relieved, but their peace was not long-lasting. The *kefin-kesh*'s helper became the new *kefin-kesh*. He didn't just do what his master and predecessor had done, stealing the cloths from the dead, but had an even worse habit. After he had unwrapped the cloths from the bodies of the dead, he violated the corpses, and satisfied his contemptible lust on their bare bones.

The dead had not expected that. They profoundly

regretted their decision and asked their God to give them back their old *kefin-kesh*.

That's what's happening to us Afghans, says the kind dining-room owner. The Americans, the British and the Russians have helped themselves to our country exactly as they wished. Helped themselves to our oil. Our uranium. Our gold. Our opium. They drew up contracts with Afghanistan to their own advantage, and used us. And in future, too, they will take whatever they want. We have always suffered under the influence of the western world and will continue to do so in future. But whatever the USA and their friends and allies do to us, it is better than what their trained puppets, the Taleban, the ones they sent to us, are doing to us.

They don't just steal our uranium and pocket the profits from the sale of opium, they destroy everything as well. They are destroying millennia of our culture and tradition. They are dishonouring and insulting us.

The kind dining-room owner laughs and says, and they will kill me because I am sitting here having a forbidden conversation with a non-*marham*, talking openly with her.

I had a dream, says Shirin-Gol. I dreamed that the bombs that have been falling on our houses for more than two decades weren't bombs but books. I dreamed the mines they planted under our feet weren't mines, but wheat and cotton.

A lovely dream, says the kind dining-room owner.

For four days Shirin-Gol looks everywhere. Asks everyone. No one knows Noor-Aftab, the daughter of Shirin-Gol and Morad. Opium-Morad.

No one knows the Taleb called such-and-such, Noor-Aftab's second husband, the one she was forced to marry after her first husband had been killed. No one knows the one who spat greenish-yellow stuff at Shirin-Gol's feet so that it lay there.

No one knows her. No one has seen him.

Before the Taleban start to notice her, before they can start harassing her, before her money has been used up, before she becomes a burden to the sister of the kind dining-room owner, before, before, before, Shirin-Gol moves on.

Where to?

What difference does it make?

None at all. It makes no difference where Shirin-Gol and her children move on to.

The money that the kind dining-room owner gave to Shirin-Gol is enough for the journey to Kandahar.

Kandahar, then. The city of pomegranates. Of red, crunchy apples. The fruit of love. With a thousand and one crunchy grains. All the same size. Each one unique. Sweet and sour. It is years ago now, Shirin-Gol precisely remembers the red, juicy grains between her teeth. Sweet and sour. Noor-Aftab in her green-yellow-red-orange cloud wedding-dress had eaten of the fruit of love, the juice had coloured her lips red. Blood-like, it had run from the corners of her mouth, had dripped on to her skirt. Had become a red flower in her girlish lap. Red from the daughter-mouth, Shirin-Gol had thought.

Kandahar. Darius, the king of the Acheminids, was defeated by Alexander the Great in Kandahar. The Sassanids, the Arabs, other Persian kings, Turks, the Mongol Ghengis Khan, the Timurids, the British, the Russians and the Americans, the *kefin-kesh* and the Taleban, men spitting greenish-yellow stuff, one-eyed Mullah Omar, the famous-notorious Osama Bin Laden, they have all been here, or are here still.

But not Noor-Aftab.

No one knows her, no one has seen her.

Chapter Sixteen

SIMURG AND THE SKELETON
OF A CAPITAL

Salaam

Wa-aleikum salaam. Peace be upon you too.

The kind dining-room owner in Herat gave Shirin-Gol the address of his brother and his wife in Kabul. If my brother, my Herati brother, and his wife are still alive, and may God grant it so, they will help you, he said.

Mande nabashi, I hope you're not tired, says the Herati brother in a friendly way, puts his hand on his heart in the Afghan fashion and lowers his head.

Welcome to a city of rubble. Welcome to Kabul. Be our guest.

I lived here as a girl, says Shirin-Gol. I went to the Russian school.

There isn't much left of the city you knew as a girl, says the Herati brother. Kabul has become a city of the dead and starving.

The Herati brother has seen Kabul when the king was still ruling it, when the cannons roared once a day up on the mountain. The Herati brother knows peaceful Afghanistan, Kabul when it was not destroyed by rockets, bombs, mines, the pearl of the Orient with its blue-ornamented mosques, buildings and houses. He went to school here, too, he studied and later taught at the university until he had to go to war. Against the Mujahedin. He deserted, joined the Mujahedin, helped drive the Russians from his homeland. His homeland, which he loves like a beautiful poem, like his child, like his wife, like his own life.

Now he drives a taxi.

The Herati brother knows Afghanistan and Kabul from a time when the leaves of the trees danced in the wind along the asphalted streets and the young poplars had no idea that in less than two decades they would be turned to firewood. The Herati brother remembers the clear, bright air, full of the merry jingling and jangling of the lucky bells and the harnesses of the cabs. He remembers the soft, dreamy clack, clack of their wooden wheels, the hoofs of the horses. He still has the calls of the traders in his ear, the laughter and song of the boys. He hears the glass-clear, powerful, smiling voices singing of their wonderful homeland. He sees colourful paper kites dancing in the sky, close to God and not knowing that twenty years later the Taleban law will have forbidden the flying of home-made paper tigers and birds.

Playing forbidden.

Why?

Who knows.

Because the Taleban are the Taleban. Because they forbid all kinds of things. In the name of the Prophet, the Koran, and of Islam.

Girls and women are forbidden to walk in the street and go to school. Women are not allowed to study or work. Boys must wear caps, shave their hair, they are not allowed to play football, *wa-al-hamn-do-allah*, thanks be to God the

great, the one and only God. Men have to grow their
beards, must not wear western jackets and trousers, can
only walk in the street with their heads covered.

The Herati brother tells Shirin-Gol, as they bump along
the uneven, potholed road in his rattling old taxi, past the
wrecks of buses, cars, tanks, past people with their begging
hands outstretched, past women and children on the way
from somewhere to nowhere, past bombed-out craters,
piles of rubble, collapsed buildings, mined ruins. The
Herati brother tells her that when everything here was as
it will never be again, the stretch from their village to
Kabul, which now takes thirteen hours or more, could be
covered in four or five hours.

Kabul was full of flowers and joy, he says with tears in
his voice.

I know, says Shirin-Gol, and turns her cloth-head away,
says nothing and looks out of the car window.

Where the skeletons of the stone and mud houses now
stretch their bare, thin necks to heaven and get no reply
from God about why he let all this happen, there used to
stand magnificent old buildings with arches, arcades, brick
houses decorated with blue and green mosaics. The
bazaars did not smell of hunger, of rags, of pus-drenched
war-wounds, children with diarrhoea, of fear, of piss, of
rotten meat, of stale and mouldy drains, it smelt of
cinnamon, cardamom, turmeric, rose water, and music
and song spilling into the street from the colourful carpet
shops. At night the clear sky, with its infinite number of
stars and its unreal magnificence turned the city into a
place from a tale in the *Thousand and One Nights*.

A night like the one when Sheherezade lays her elfin
ebony body at the feet of her king. The cruel, merciless
king with the bad habit of taking a young girl as his bride

each evening and murdering her in the morning after their first night of love. Sheherezade quietly, softly starts up a little melody, falls silent, waits until her master's impatience has become infinite. The cruel king has had all his previous lovers killed after the first night, but not Sheherezade. Not her. Because she told him a tale. She didn't give away the ending. The king kneels before his beloved Sheherezade, begs, pleads for her to go on with the previous evening's tale, and he swears by his God to spare her life again, to lay jewels, gold and silk at her feet if she will just give him the end of her tale.

Sheherezade laughs sweetly, triumphantly, throws back her lovely head, her delicate fingers play angels in the air that only she and no one else can see, and goes on telling the tales that she left unfinished the previous night, so that the king must give her another day of life if he is to hear it to the end.

The same thing for a thousand and one nights. A new tale. She doesn't tell the ending.

Today, my king, my lord and master, today I am a bird, the most beautiful bird of all. So listen. This tale I shall tell you once and once only. Only this one time and this time only you will learn what God, the bountiful, whose mercy has no beginning and no end, what the Almighty can say to you through me.

One was there and another was not, apart from God there was no one, and there were his birds. Thirty in number. One day they heard the message from the bird with the name Simurg, which was supposed to live somewhere on God's great earth. It is the most magnificent of all birds, the most intelligent and the wisest of all of God's flying creatures. The sight of Simurg, the birds had heard, would blind men and women. No one could resist its beauty, its charm, its grace, its voice, bright and clear, its song, sweet and lovely.

The birds flock together at their lake, discuss the matter and decide to go in search of that one bird, the most beautiful of all birds, the Simurg, to show it their reverence and respect.

They fly over the high mountain and all the other mountains, into the deep valley and all the other valleys, cross the sea and all the other seas, the desert and all the deserts, all the cities and countries, they see all the people and all the animals, all the plants and earthly and heavenly creatures, everything good and evil, all the ages, all the wonders, all the poets, all the kings and everything else that God has made a part of life and the earth. But they do not see one thing. Simurg, the bird.

My beloved and king shares other whispers with a soft voice with which she seduces the cruel in the land of love. My beloved and king, now we may rest.

And the end of it?

Tomorrow. For my life.

The end of it.

Finally the birds return to the place where they had started their journey. Discouraged and tired. Exhausted and thirsty they draw water from their lake, look into it and see what they have been seeking throughout all those years, what they could not find.

In the lake the thirty birds see the face of Simurg. The face of thirty magnificent birds, so beautiful that the sight of them blinds both men and women.

Simurg, says God, that is you, my beloved birds. You yourselves. Because the one you were seeking all those years, the one you flew around the whole world to find, is none other than you yourselves. Thirty-birds, si-murg. Simurg.

*

What has happened to us is like what happened to Simurg, say some Afghans. Our country was the loveliest for far and wide. Our earth was fruitful. Had we known better, we would have done it properly, and no one in this country would have had to suffer from hunger. Everyone, beggars and kings, could have had a roof over his head. We could have had peace and unity. But some of us thought there was a lovelier place. A lovelier country. A better life. More power. More beauty. Greater splendour.

The story of Simurg is nothing more than a fairy tale, say other Afghans. If we were to have done it, if we could have done it, we would have done it. Neither the English nor the Russians, nor our own brothers who betrayed us, neither the Mujahedin nor the Americans, neither Osama Bin Laden nor the Taleban could have set foot in our country for a single day.

The peace of our homeland, the peace in Kabul was a lie.

The peace was made of glass.

Do you want to go up the mountain to the cannon? asks the Herati brother, and answers his question himself. The cannon is silent these days, he says. There is nothing more to see or hear. Back in the days of King Zahir Shah, the king had it fired every day at noon, so that the faithful among us were reminded to go to pray in the mosque. So that everyone who was working would take a rest. So that those who had no work were reminded that they must find work. And everyone was reminded that there was a king enthroned in his beautiful palace, holding his protecting hand over us. Today there is nothing and nobody that we would wish or need to be reminded of. That is why the cannon is silent.

So Shirin-Gol and the Herati brother do not drive up the mountain to the silent cannon. They drive on through the ruined city, where in the days of the king and his roaring cannon there were cinemas, museums, restaurants, parks, idling families, women holding their children by the hand, women and men walking along the canal, dreaming of a lovelier future. In the Kabul of those days, when the Russians had not yet invaded Afghanistan, when the rich were rich and the poor were poor, when the powerful had power and the weak obeyed. When people still had dreams, when the flowers still blossomed, the trees were still alive, the houses still had walls, roofs, doors and windows. When the fountains in the squares and at the crossing of the city had water that danced in the air. When colourful lights decorated the shops and stalls. When there was still not a hint of war, no one was afraid they might at any moment stand on a mine, no one was afraid they might at any moment transgress arbitrary laws and be arrested. Back when God still held his protecting hand over Afghanistan and the people still had all their pride and all their dignity. Back then.

The Herati brother has known an Afghanistan where he was not constantly afraid of being robbed by bandits. He was in Kabul at a time when women and children did not beg at every street corner, breaking his heart. He saw the country when no one was one-armed, one-legged. He knows the old Afghanistan and its capital the way it was and never will be again.

Shirin-Gol envies him that.

*

Shirin-Gol has heard that there are foreign aid organisations in the capital which distribute wheat and fat to widows and inoculate their children against the most serious diseases.

Her. Her children.

And maybe give her a job. People say there are schools in Kabul, even for girls. Secret ones, but they exist. Maybe Shirin-Gol could train to be a teacher. Maybe she could make carpets in the carpet workshop for widows.

Maybe. Maybe.

You are not a widow, says her daughter Nafass.

Your father is not here, says Shirin-Gol. What is the difference?

There is a difference, says Nafass.

What use is a father who is not here? asks Shirin-Gol. What use is a man who leaves his wife on her own? What am I to do? Am I to watch us die one after the other?

Die. Dead of hunger. Hunger-death.

No, says Nafass, I want to live.

Yes, says Shirin-Gol, we will say Morad is dead.

Morad is dead. Dead-Morad.

What difference does it make whether he is alive or dead?

No difference at all. None at all.

Fine, says Nafass, then I will say my father is dead.

Fine, says Shirin-Gol.

Shirin-Gol is afraid. Afraid of the capital. Of the ruined streets. Afraid of *tanhai*, of being alone. Afraid for four fatherless children. Afraid of lies. Afraid of thieves. Afraid of men. Afraid of the Taleban. Afraid of mines. Afraid of the skeletons of the houses.

She recognises the canal. She cannot find the way to the Russian school any more. She recognises Bazaar Street. It was here that Morad laid his handkerchief on a stone. It was here that he told her he would marry her. Here that she said it made no difference. She cannot find the room where she lived with Morad. The bombs have devoured it.

Women move facelessly past Shirin-Gol. Shirin-Gol moves facelessly past other women. They do not notice one another. Not as people.

One cloth walks past her, two. A cloth talks to her, begging for money or bread. Asks if she has work for her. Sometimes Shirin-Gol hears a voice and thinks, I know her. At one point a cloth grabs her by the arm, pulls her to one side, greets her, embraces her, kisses her. Then the cloth realises she has made a mistake. The cloth thought she had found a lost sister again.

At Shirin-Gol's feet a little boy lies in the dust. Apart from a grey, dusty rag that he has wrapped around his hips, he is naked. The whole person is so covered with dust and filth that he barely stands out against the sand and gravel of the street. He has only one leg, it is skin and bone and so crippled that it's more of a burden than a help.

On the same side where the boy's leg is missing, he has no arm. His other arm is just a stump. He lowers his wounded stump, concentrates and pulls his rump and the rest of what he has left behind him.

Shirin-Gol has to make an effort to see the child in the confusion of skin and bone, rags and dirt. He only remotely resembles a human being, he looks more like a big insect. An insect that has been half crushed underfoot, but is still alive. Half dead, half alive, it lies there and wriggles. And no one has the mercy to release it from its half-life.

Shirin-Gol concentrates on the boy's eyes, his beautiful, dark, joyfully radiant eyes, which give Shirin-Gol-cloth an open smile. The loveliest child's smile in the world.

Shirin-Gol buys bread, squats down, throws back her veil, tears small pieces from the bread, feeds the insect boy.

While rummaging through rubbish, the insect boy found a toy mine. A mine made specially for children. A mine that looks like a toy. The insect boy saw the box, it was beautiful, it glittered and sparkled.

It sparkled and glittered so much that he could not help himself and absolutely had to open it to see what was inside. The force of the explosion was not particularly great, but it shredded his hands, his arms, his lips and hurled him into the air. It was as though he was flying. And then, when he fell to the earth, there was another explosion, then he could not remember anything. People later said he had been hurled on to a second mine.

Men walk past Shirin-Gol, who is squatting on the ground by the insect boy, and look at her pityingly. Women under their cloths stop, shake their heads walk on. Other cloths whisper, stroke Shirin-Gol's arms, her head, her cheek. One cloth speaks to her, it is hungry, it wants bread, it wants work. Another cloth puts its hand on her back, pulls her up, wipes tears from Shirin-Gol's eyes and says, do not show weakness, that is all they want. They want us to show weakness so that they feel strong. The cloth embraces Shirin-Gol, hugs her. It is a powerful embrace. The cloth calms Shirin-Gol's shivering and trembling.

Shirin-Gol bends down to the insect boy, kisses him on his half-cheek, strokes his head, gives him money.

You are the most beautiful woman I have ever seen, says the insect-boy.

Shirin-Gol laughs and says, and you have the loveliest eyes I have ever seen.

The insect boy bashfully lowers his eyes and says, I

would like to give you a present. I will give you a little tale.

The insect boy looks at Shirin-Gol's unclothed face and tells his story. A girl falls into a well. A boy is walking past, he jumps in after her and saves the girl. The girl thanks him and asks, why did you do that? The boy says, because my life would have been worth nothing if I had watched you die. Because there is no difference between you and me. Because we are all God's creatures. Because every time one of us dies, we all die a little.

That was a lovely tale, says Shirin-Gol. You are a real story-teller.

I am, says the insect boy and smiles. The loveliest child's smile in the world. That is how I earn my living.

May God protect you, little story-teller.

What is your name?

Shirin-Gol.

I will never forget you, Shirin-Gol, says the insect boy, lowers his stump and pulls his rump and the rest of what he has left behind him and disappears among the cloths and legs in the bazaar. And no one has the mercy to release him from his half-life.

Shirin-Gol, veiled from head to toe, walks on through the streets of the city where she was a girl. The city of which little remains. Kabul, the city of the dead and the starving, the stinking, the insect boys.

There is hair on the ground. Men's hair. The Taleban have been publicly shearing men.

The lanterns are draped with the guts of tapes. Music forbidden.

A corpse hangs from a tree. Someone is hanging from the tree. The Taleban have hanged him. As a warning. A dead man as a warning to the half-dead.

Women cower in the corners. They smell of hunger.

They whimper and beg. Kabul, the city with forty-thousand widows. Shirin-Gol is not a widow. Shirin-Gol has Morad. Opium-Morad.

In the ruins, children with bags on their little backs look for things to burn, things to eat. Shirin-Gol looks at her feet. She does not want to be looking if one of them finds a mine.

Kabul, the city of hungry mines, waiting to swallow, to shred, to shatter one of the fifty-thousand starving street children.

Shirin-Gol walks through the streets of the city of her girl-years. Past the stinking canal. Past the tired and the exhausted. Past the starving. The half-dead.

Past the stadium.

First the Taleban forbade football. Instead of playing, the men were to come to the stadium to pray on Friday, and hear the speeches of the self-appointed rulers. And they were to watch. As a warning. Chopping off hands. Stoning. Head-crushing. Chopping off legs. In the name of the Prophet, of the Koran, of Islam.

The men did not come. Then the Taleban allowed football again so that the men would come back to the stadium. *Allahu-akbar* and *la-elaha-el-allah* was a duty. At the start and in the end prayer was a duty. In the half-time of football without applause, with *allahu-akbar* and *la-elaha-el-allah*, the Taleb chopped legs off. Hands off. Shot women. Men. Girls. Boys. Stoned people to death. People-stoning. Smashed heads. Head-smashing, so that the blood from the heads splashed on the executioner's shirt.

Today it's Aisha's turn. Aisha. Lovely little Aisha.

Two Taleban have sat the cloth-woman on a donkey because she can no longer walk. It is as though there were nothing and no one under the cloth. It has collapsed in on itself. Aisha the whore has lost her bones, says the Taleb who is allowed to play executioner today, laughs and spits. Greenish-yellow stuff.

May God protect you, her mother said when she drew the girl from her body and gave her, for her protection, the name of the Prophet's wife. For a long life. For a healthy life. For a free life. *Salaamho-aleihe-wa-allehi-wa salaam*. Aisha was six years old. Six, when the Prophet in the house of his friend and patron Abu Bakr saw his daughter Aisha and sensed the man in himself. Male Prophet-lust. Abu Bakr understood and promised the Prophet to give him his daughter in marriage once she reached the age of sexual maturity. Aisha's mature sex. Three years later, Aisha is nine years old when the Prophet takes her as his wife in Medina.

Aisha is nine. Nine little girl years.

The Prophet is fifty. Fifty big Prophet years.

Mothers call their daughters Aisha so that the Prophet will be reminded of his favourite wife and protect the daughters.

Aisha the whore sits on the donkey, sees the men through the net in front of her eyes. Net-men.

Starving whore, who has lost her bones, sees net-men.

Aisha cannot control her trembling. Aisha has the taste of death in her mouth. Her tongue is stuck. Leaden it sticks in her jaw, making her ill. Her stomach is an empty cave. The child is gone. Her cloth sticks to her frightened, sweaty skin. When she breathes she pulls it into her mouth. All Aisha can hear in her head is the knocking, the hammering of her own heart and the first cries of the child she pulled from her body yesterday.

Where is my child? thinks Aisha. Why did God give it to me? thinks Aisha. Is God watching? thinks Aisha. Where is he? thinks Aisha. The only one. The single one. The one with the thousand names.

This woman has broken God's law, shouts the Taleb in the middle of the playing field. She has sinned. She has sold her body. She has brought shame upon us and upon our Prophet.

The Taleban are merciful, they have waited until pregnant Aisha has brought her child into the world before killing her. The Taleban are just. They do not kill pregnant women. Aisha kneels on the ground. Before her executioner. Sees the executioner's hand holding the stone. The executioner's hand draws back. Comes closer. Closer. Aisha throws back her veil.

Look at me, she whispers. Aisha looks into her executioner's face.

That is resistance.

Stone-hand stops in the air. The executioner spits greenish-yellow stuff. Draws back again. Strikes.

Stone-hand cracks against Aisha's whorish head.

Twice. Four times.

The blood from Aisha's head washes the whore's shame and the greenish-yellow stuff from the executioner's mouth into the soil of her homeland.

Washing shame. Washing greenish-yellow stuff.

Allahu-akbar and *la-elaha-el-allah* is duty.

Football men come back on to the playing field.

First one game, then the other.

The spectators have lowered their heads. They do not want to see either one game or the other.

Football men fall to the ground. Mime injured knees and joints. They do not show injured hearts. They do not show their shame and nausea. That would be resistance.

The players avoid stepping on the blood from Aisha's

head. Sacrificial blood. Head-blood. Holy ground. Blood-drenched ground. Blood-ground.

Taleban stand at the edge of the game swinging sticks. Go on playing. In the name of the Prophet.

Allahu-akbar.

Taleban stand with sticks among the spectators. Stay here. Heads up. Watch.

Allahu-akbar. Allahu-akbar. Allahu-akbar.

They are all there. Only one is not there. The only one. The single one. The one with a thousand names.

Shirin-Gol walks through the streets of the city where she was a girl.

The dead want their old *kefin-kesh* back.

Simurg looks into the lake. Simurg sees its reflection.

That is resistance.

Pictures are forbidden in Taleban Afghanistan.

Why?

Who knows.

Because the Taleban are the Taleban.

Arabs have taken over the city. They have everything painted white. All the facades, all the walls, all the huts, shops, buildings. White for peace. White for purity. White for virginity.

An Arab Taleb shoves a little boy into his gleaming, glittering four-by-four. The little one screams, fights back, struggles, kicks, cries.

Shirin-Gol shouts, what are you doing with him?

The Arab reaches into his crotch, weighs his balls and his cock. Slavers, laughs, drives off.

Shirin-Gol stops in her tracks.

The boy was as small or as big as Sarvar from the poppy village behind the pitted light-blue gate, who lived with the Taleban. Sarvar the little boy who does everything imaginable for the Taleban because they are nice to him and give him food to eat. Little street boy shoved into the car, little boy behind the gate, who gets something to eat. What will become of these children when they aren't children any more? thinks Shirin-Gol.

Ce hal dari, how are you?

Tashak-kor, thank you.

Two women, two friends, two sisters hold each other in their arms. In silence.

Shirin-Gol has found Azadine.

Azadine treats women. Officially in the hospital and secretly at home.

Secretly.

Azadine's house is full of women. Other doctors. An economist. A biologist. Teachers. An engineer. Nurses. Women who can read. Women who cannot read. Secret women. They flock together in Azadine's house. According to the law of the Taleban that is forbidden. The women do it anyway. That is resistance.

They help one another to find work. To earn money. To find a place where they and their children can live. They help other women to drag themselves and their children through life. That is resistance.

They have taken everything from us, says the biologist. Everything. Our little rights, which we had just won from our rulers. They have taken our work from us, our children, our husbands, fathers and mothers, our houses, our fields, our home, our honour, our pride. Even our dreams. But we have something they cannot take from us.

I have nothing left, says Shirin-Gol, nothing at all. I have nothing that anyone could take from me. Only my life and the lives of my children.

Our hope, says the biologist, they cannot take our hope from us.

Can't they? asks Shirin-Gol.

They can't, says the biologist. Not as long as we stand together. Not as long as we help each other and other women. Not as long as we live and breathe.

I did not know there were women like you in our country, says Shirin-Gol. You have gone through school, you have studied, you are good at thinking, you are good at talking, you have each other. I have been alone for most of my life.

Azadine embraces Shirin-Gol, laughs and says, just wait, you will see. We all belong together, we share our every joy and our every suffering. Now you are not alone.

Being alone is a great enemy of girls and women in Afghanistan, says the biologist, giving Shirin-Gol a smile. Now you are not alone.

Women, whatever country they live in, whatever language they speak, whatever religion they have, must stick together and resist the oppression and the nonsense that men spread, says the teacher.

But we made the men what they are, says a nurse. After all, we women bring up our sons, who turn into men.

We are under the thumb of our husbands, we are afraid of them, says a woman who cannot read.

That will change, says the biologist, proudly raising her head. Yes, she says, I am convinced that our work will be successful. We started three years ago, and we have already found work for five hundred women. It is not enough, but it is a start.

Wherever we live and how we live, however difficult it is, says Azadine, we have to fight.

That is resistance, says Shirin-Gol.

That is resistance, says Azadine and laughs.

There aren't many women like you in Afghanistan, says Shirin-Gol.

There are more and more of us, says Azadine and laughs. And all the other women laugh too, until they have tears in their eyes. Tears of joy. Grief-joy.

That afternoon Shirin-Gol and Azadine know nothing of what is shortly to happen in their homeland. The women doctors, the economist, the biologist, the teachers, the engineer, the nurses, the women who can read, the women who cannot read, the women who have gathered in Azadine's house, still do not know that in less than a year the Americans and Europeans will finally come to their aid in their struggle against the Taleban. That afternoon the women believe, for the umpteenth hope-filled time, that a better future is on the way. That afternoon they still know nothing of the many friends they have in far-off America and Europe. They still do not know that terrorism can only be fought with bombs and rockets.

That afternoon the women still do not know that bombs will soon be falling again, on them, on Kabul, on all the other cities, on their country.

That afternoon they do not know that the Americans are going to come and liberate them. That many of them, for the umpteenth time in their life, will have to leave everything behind and flee.

That afternoon they still do not know that a few of them will be dead a few months later. Hit by the bombs of the Americans who came to free them.

Chapter Seventeen

OPIUM-MORAD AND AN ORPHANAGE

She does not ask him why he left her on her own, or where he has been all this time. Neither does she ask him how he found her. She just gives him a glass of tea and asks if he is tired. Then Shirin-Gol sends Nafass to get fresh bread for her father.

Morad still needs opium every day. He is incapable of working. In particular, he cannot set foot outside the door because in an attack of insanity he shaved his beard off and the Taleban would throw him into prison.

Shirin-Gol is neither happy nor unhappy about Morad's return. By now she is coming to terms with not being allowed to walk in the street and having to be veiled from head to foot. She has learned how to get around the Taleban's prohibition on women working, and to find food for herself and four children. And now that Opium-Morad is with his family again, she will manage to feed him, too. If she has to, she will pay for his opium as well. Even if she doesn't yet know how she will do all that. But somehow she has always managed.

Shirin-Gol has, with the help of Azadine and her new friends, found a paid job as a cleaning woman. The foreigner works for an American aid organisation in Afghanistan, and is glad that Shirin-Gol is working for her, because she is the only personal contact she has with Afghans. Secret contact.

Shirin-Gol likes the foreigner and isn't only grateful to her for the work, but also for the courage that the American woman shows. Because just as the Taleban forbid foreigners to enter the houses of Afghans, according to the law of the Taleban Afghan women are forbidden to go into the houses of foreigners. Quite apart from the fact that women are forbidden to work, unless they are working as doctors and nurses.

Shirin-Gol brings her children into the foreign woman's house, sits them on the lawn in the lovely garden, looks at them over and over again and is happy that her children have a little peace among the flowers and bushes and trees, that they can run around without fear of stepping on a mine. Shirin-Gol is happy that her children and she get something decent to eat every day.

Shirin-Gol is happy to be able to look into the eyes of a woman who comes from a free world and has everything she needs for life and happiness.

The foreigner is a good, hard-working and smart woman. And she knows how to live.

Every few weeks she employs a second cook in addition to her own, has them prepare a royal feast and invites her foreign friends, who work in Kabul for other aid organisations.

With the help of the happy gardener, Shirin-Gol carries the carpets out into the garden. She arranges them under the trees, puts cushions and little mattresses on them. Among the bushes and flowers Shirin-Gol puts candles and thin sticks which, when you light them, emit a wonderful scent.

There is enough food all evening. Each of the guests can help themselves to the delicacies as they feel like it. All evening there are all kinds of drinks, some of which smell horrible but which the guests seem to like anyway. All evening not only the men, but the women, too, smoke cigarettes. Shirin-Gol soon gets used to it, even if she thinks the women who do not smoke are prettier.

The first time Shirin-Gol did not really know what to make of the fact that strange men and women were embracing, sitting side by side, putting their heads together, even exchanging a kiss from time to time. Shirin-Gol always tried to look away. But wherever she looked, lightly dressed women were sitting close beside men who looked at them unashamedly, held their hands, were tender towards them. Not even her own husband Morad has ever held Shirin-Gol's hand so long in his and caressed and stroked her, played with her and looked her tenderly in the eyes, smiled, stolen a loving little kiss. The God of foreigners must be a good and free God, thinks Shirin-Gol, to allow people to do all that without punishing them for it.

Shirin-Gol likes to watch the happy gardener, the sad driver and the other Afghans going from guest to guest with their trays and asking, *Saheb*, excuse me, another slice of fish? *Saheb*, excuse me, another piece of chicken? *Saheb*, excuse me, another drink? *Saheb*, excuse me, another coke? Coke from Pakistan.

Saheb here, *saheb* there. As they would have done a century ago, under the British colonial rulers.

Saheb, the owner. *Excuse me.*

The lords prefer to stay in England now, and the new *sahebs* come from all around the world. They work for the

UN, for the Red Cross or the other non-government organisations. They are young, they have hardly any money, they are esoteric, democratic, harem-pants-wearing, alternative, adventurous, helpful, self-sacrificing. Most of the *sahebs* did not fit in at home, or wanted out of the regulated, secure, boring, meaningless run of things.

Saheb, another coke?

The next morning Nafass is the first on her feet. The previous evening she set aside an empty cardboard box. Even before the cocks crow in the neighbours' gardens, Nafass creeps into the garden and crawls among the bushes, looks behind the trees and into the flowerbeds, collects the empty cans in her box and feels as rich as a queen when she sees how many there are. She will get so much money for them in the bazaar that she may finally fulfil her great dream and buy a pair of used rubber shoes, to keep her feet dry and warm. She may even be able to buy a pair for herself and another pair for her little sister Nassim. Two pairs of rubber boots for a whole cardboard box full of empty coke cans. *Saheb*, excuse me.

Shirin-Gol picks up the butts of the stinking cigarettes that the *sahebs* have thrown into the flowerbed, on to the lawn, into the paths. She collects the cushions the *sahebs* have been sitting and lying on. In particular she is already looking forward to telling her friends about the women who are courageous and free. Who show their skin. Who talk in public with men, touch them, allow themselves to be touched and do all sorts of things. Shirin-Gol will tell her friends that she has looked into the eyes of women who have everything in life that you need to be happy and contented. She will tell her friends that she has found new hope. As long as there are women somewhere in the world who aren't hungry, who are free, as long as that is the case Shirin-Gol and her friends will have hope.

After the stinking cigarette-butts in the flowerbeds come the plates. Plates smeared with valuable fat, leftover bread, leftover meat, leftover rice. Good food for a few days. For Shirin-Gol, the children and Morad, for the happy gardener, the sad driver and the other Afghans who work for the foreigner.

The happy gardener clears the cushions, mattresses and carpets back into the house, always with a smile on his face, and says, as long as we are working we don't have to think about the war or the mines, or all the other misery in our homeland. Come, children, give me a hand. That's a help. One cushion, two cushions, who can carry three?

Me, me, calls Navid.

Me, me, calls Nafass.

Proud, honest, happy gardener with all his muscles, grabs the children along with their cushions and carries them into the house. Oh no, look, those aren't cushions, those are children.

Nafass, Nabi, Navid, Nassim laugh, bringing tears to Shirin-Gol's eyes. Tears of joy.

Now comes the best part of our work, says the jolly gardener.

Nafass, Nabi, Navid, Nassim clap their hands, jump up and down. Water. Water. Plastic hose water.

The happy gardener loves his plastic hose, the very idea that he is about to wash away all the dust and dirt with his water puts him in ecstasy. His back, his muscles relax as he goes to the tap, turns it on, not too much. Not a lot of pressure. It is a matter of getting the dosage right. Water. Water. Clean, fresh water.

Nafass, Nabi, Navid, Nassim crouch in a row, quiet as

little mice, watching the happy gardener as though he were telling a fairy tale, as though he were performing a trick.

Look, says the happy gardener, the water does exactly what I want. Look. It follows my instructions. Absolute control.

With thumb and forefinger he presses the end of the hose together. As though the water were a fan, it bursts powerfully out of the hose and washes away everything the happy gardener aims at. With a *bismi-allah* he drives everything in front of him and washes it into the flowerbed. Everything. Dust. Sand. Ashes. Sin.

Only the sins of the Taleban remain.

Shirin-Gol is caught. She cannot work for the American woman any more.

Shirin-Gol is caught. She cannot teach in the secret school, the home-school, any more.

Shirin-Gol is caught, she cannot sell the carpets she has made in the bazaar anymore.

Azadine is caught, the Taleban put her in prison.

The biologist cannot stand it any more. She takes her children and everything she can carry and flees.

The nurse has to marry. Her husband will not let her out of the house any more.

The American woman gets a new job in another part of the world where there is also a war on.

Shirin-Gol squats in the corner of the bazaar, thinks, so there are other countries with wars, sticks her hand out from under her cloth and begs. She is allowed to do that. It isn't work. The Taleban will cope with that. Because they don't want to pay out for Shirin-Gol and the other however many umpteen-thousand beggar women. Begging permitted.

Shirin-Gol is grateful. She still doesn't have to sell her body.

Her children are a great help. Nabi, cheeky Nabi, cleans shoes, little Nassim burns incense in an old coke can and gets money from passersby for whom she says a little prayer.

May God the merciful protect you against all ills, all sicknesses, all suffering. *Al-hamn-do-allah*. Navid scours the rubbish for anything that might be burned and sells it. Nafass already has the beginnings of breasts, her hips are round, she has reached the age of sexual maturity. Nafass is nine, perhaps even ten or eleven, at any rate she is too old to walk in the street. Shirin-Gol has forbidden her even to step outside the door. The danger that a Taleb or some other man might see her and want her for his wife is too great.

Nafass crouches all day in the skeleton hut, beside Opium-Morad, stares straight ahead into the air, waiting for her mother and brothers and sisters to come back.

One day Nabi comes into the skeleton hut with a black turban wrapped around his head.

I want to be a Taleb, he announces proudly, then I will go to war and defend my home and my religion against the godless ones and the enemies of the Prophet and Islam.

On the first day Shirin-Gol tells him in a nice manner to abandon this nonsense. On the second she threatens to throw him out if he doesn't stop. On the third she beats him black and blue.

Nafass hurls herself at her mother, frees her brother from her mother's mad claws and shouts, what do you expect? He is out there all day. All day he hears the nonsense that the Taleban are bellowing through their megaphones from the mosques. He is just a child. Are you surprised he believes what they are telling him?

Shirin-Gol looks at her daughter, her little Nafass, who is still a child herself, and doesn't know what to say.

Nabi presses himself against his big sister, weeps, is happy that she has stood up for him, unhappy about his unjust mother. Happy-unhappy.

Shirin-Gol crouches in the corner, sees Opium-Morad in the other corner. Hates him. Hates herself. Hates the Taleban. Hates hunger. Hates the rags on the bodies of her emaciated children. Hates the stench that enfolds everyone and everything like a cloud. Hates everything. Hates everyone.

What kind of God is that? asks Shirin-Gol. Why doesn't he free me from this life and take me to him?

Nafass casts hate-filled glances at her mother, laughs at her and asks, why should he take you to him? What would God want with anyone like you? He is happy not to have to look at you.

What do you know about God? asks Shirin-Gol with the taste of hatred in her mouth.

God.

The next evening Nabi, Navid, Nassim come back to the skeleton hut from shoe-cleaning, rubbish-collecting, incense-burning, begging. Nafass comes back from begging which she, too, has had to do lately. Shirin-Gol is lying on the floor with two red bracelets on each wrist. Blood-bracelets.

Shirin-Gol has opened her veins.

Nafass, Nabi, Navid, Nassim crouch by their mother.

Nassim dips a finger in her mother's blood, draws a blood-bracelet on her own wrist.

Nafass tears up scraps of fabric, wraps them around her

mother's wrists. Mother has gone mad, she says to her brothers and sisters.

For four days and four nights Shirin-Gol lies there with scraps of fabric around her wrists.

Then she opens her eyes, sees her daughter Nafass crouching by her and wiping the sweat from her mother's brow.

Shirin-Gol smiles at Nafass. It was lovely, she says, I have seen him.

Who? asks her daughter.

God.

Shirin-Gol lies awake. All night. She neither weeps nor complains nor moans. She just lies there awake. Before the sun casts its light into the skeleton hut, she gets up, climbs over sleeping Opium-Morad, wakes her children and says, let's go.

Where are we going?

Somewhere.

We're frightened.

So am I.

Where are we? asks Nafass.

Shirin-Gol says nothing.

What kind of house is that? asks Nabi.

Shirin-Gol says nothing.

It smells of shit here, says Nabi.

Shirin-Gol says nothing.

Your children will live well with us, says the Taleb. As soon as we get money from a foreign aid organisation again, we will introduce physical exercise and sport for the boys, says the young Taleb crouching by the blue *burqa* under which Shirin-Gol is happy to be able to hide her face.

The Taleb is twenty, maybe even twenty-three. His shirt

and his pearly teeth are almond-blossom-white. His turban, his long beard and his long, shining hair are pitch black.

He's a handsome man, thinks Shirin-Gol and asks, what about the girls?

Sport is a free physical activity, says the handsome Taleban, that is too dangerous for girls. Islam decrees that girls at the age of puberty should not move violently. They should not jump or run, so that no damage is done to their bodies. After all, if they moved violently they could lose their virginity or maybe lose the chance of getting pregnant. And then they will not find a husband.

Shirin-Gol cannot believe that a Taleb is sitting in front of her, a strange man, talking to her about the virginity of girls, her daughters.

Will they learn to read and write? says Shirin-Gol.

The divine law of the Sharia is our law, according to which we bring up the children put in our care, says the Taleb impatiently, ringing a bell that stands on the table to fetch the old servant with the crooked back, puts the piece of paper with the four names of the new arrivals in his hand and sends him out again.

A piece of paper with four names. Nafass, Nabi, Navid, Nassim. The children of Shirin-Gol.

You were at the Russian school, says the Taleb, furiously sending his prayer-beads back and forth.

Shirin-Gol says nothing.

I haven't learned chemistry or biology, says the Taleb, all I have learned are the words of God. The Taleb looks at Shirin-Gol-cloth, bores his kajal-black painted almond-eyed gaze through the blue, holed material and says, but it doesn't mean I am a savage. It is your decision. Either you leave your children here or you take them away with you.

I am leaving them here, says Shirin-Gol.

The Taleb rings for the old bent-backed servant. Bring the children of this *sia-sar* to the refectory, he orders.

The bent-backed servant waits by the door until Shirin-Gol comes out, says nothing, just waves to Shirin-Gol to follow him.

Further back, when they go along the dark, long corridors, past the rooms without doors and windows, when they pass the stench of shit and the lakes of piss, when they pass children's eyes staring dead ahead of them, when they pass all that and much else besides, the bent-backed servant says, at least your children will get enough to eat here.

Only Nabi and Navid are allowed to eat in the refectory.

The girls have to eat in their rooms. Girls do everything in their rooms. Sleeping, drinking, eating, living.

From morning to evening. From evening to morning.

Twenty girls and more in each room.

The whole year, summer and winter. In the name of the Prophet, the Koran, Islam.

Girls are not allowed to go into the courtyard or on to the flat roof. They are not allowed into the refectory or the internal courtyard.

Why?

Because girls are girls.

At least they will get enough to eat here.

May God's protection be with you, say Nafass, Nabi, Navid, Nassim.

God's protection be with you, says Shirin-Gol.

Where are the children? asks Opium-Morad through his opium cloud.

In the orphanage, says Shirin-Gol. At least they will get enough to eat.

Shirin-Gol sits in the corner of the bazaar, stretches her hand out from under her blue, ragged *burqa*, falls over, lies where she is.

Shirin-Gol does not stir.

All that moves is her blood. Only her blood stirs. Comes out of her stomach. Washes out the baby. Dyes her blue, ragged *burqa* red.

The dead wish they could have their old *kefin-kesh* back.

Simurg looks into the lake. Simurg sees his reflection.

Shirin-Gol goes to a foreign aid organisation.

I need help, she says.

The translator translates.

You are not eligible for help.

Shirin-Gol is not disappointed or surprised. She understands.

Hardened professional aid workers who do not see individual fates like that of Shirin-Gol. Cannot see them. Mustn't see them. It would destroy them. That wouldn't help anyone.

The aid organisations are concerned with so and so many tons of wheat, so-and-so many hundreds of thousands of dollars of subsidies, refugee areas of so-and-so many thousand families. They are right, thinks Shirin-Gol, their mission is to look after the big, the whole, the mass. Anything else would be ineffective, unjust, not right. In the evening they sit in their stone houses, for which they pay their rent in dollars, and weep their tears there, quietly, so that no one can see. Shirin-Gol has seen it when she was working for the American woman. And the next morning she was back out there, with her barrels and masses and wheat and donor countries and recipient countries. Afghanistan.

Shirin-Gol crouches in front of the woman and shows her her veins. The fresh scars. Shows her emaciated, starving bony body.

The foreign woman believes in her desperation, gives her a piece of paper. The man who takes the piece of paper gives Shirin-Gol wheat. Shirin-Gol gets money for the wheat in the bazaar.

Shirin-Gol collects her children from the orphanage.

Nafass, Nabi, Navid, Nassim hold each other by the hand, stand in front of their mother.

Ce hal dari, how are you?

Tashak-kor, thank you.

Chapter Eighteen

A RAGGED WOMAN AND A BIT OF GOAT-MILK

Ragged Shirin-Gol with her opened veins and miscarriage-stomach, Nafass, Nabi, Navid, Nassim and Opium-Morad have nothing to pack together.

They set off.

Ragged Shirin-Gol does not know whether she can survive another flight. Ragged Shirin-Gol does not know if the rumours are true that Cheeky-twin is living in the north. Ragged Shirin-Gol does not know whether they will be able to cross the front. Ragged Shirin-Gol does not know all those things, or anything else.

Who knows anything at all in this godforsaken country?

On the fourth day God feels like weeping again. He comes to Afghanistan, sees ragged Shirin-Gol, barely recognises her, hears her prayers and sends a caravan of nomads past, who pick up ragged Shirin-Gol, her children and Opium-Morad.

Nafass, Nabi, Navid, Nassim help them drive and milk the sheep, collect camel dung, sheep dung and donkey dung that they dry and use to make fires. Nafass, Nabi, Navid, Nassim carry the little lambs and babies, knot amulets out of threads. Four colours. Red, white, green, black. Nafass, Nabi, Navid, Nassim sing loud songs, run, drive sheep together. Shirin-Gol changes her black skirt for colourful nomad skirts. Red, white, green, black. She opens her plaits, weaves many thin plaits that she ties over her brow, hangs jangling brass jewellery around her neck, drinks goat-milk, fires a rifle, learns how to defuse mines, rides on horseback, hammers posts into the ground with a big stone.

For forty days Shirin-Gol and her children cross the desert, climb over mountains and wander through valleys. They eat and sleep well, they are contented, and Nafass, Nabi, Navid and Nassim even laugh. They cross the front, hike through ice and snow, climb up the mountains of the Hindu Kush and finally reach Fayzabad.

Chapter Eighteen

Two Brothers, the North and a Sweet Grandmother

Shirin-Gol's brother, now a commander, is fighting in the mountains, in the north of the country, against the Taleban. He is a respected man, and for miles around the best rider in the game of *bozkeshi*, the game in which men on horseback fight over the corpse of a sheep. The game that is centuries old. The game that the king invented to strengthen his men and prepare them for war.

Commander-brother cannot remember how many enemies he has killed. How many Russians. How many Arabian and Pakistani soldiers paid by Saudi Arabia, Pakistan and the USA. And he does not count his dead Taleban either. He only knows that whatever he has done, he has done for his homeland. For his children, so that they will have a better future. For freedom. For his God. For the Prophet. In the name of the Koran.

His life had just begun, he had just learned the Koran, he had just learned to plough the field with oxen, he had just discovered the first fluff under his chin, he had just become a half-boy-half-man, he had just thought, soon I will be a whole man, when the Russians invaded his village. The brother had to go into the mountains with his father and his other brothers. For ten years they fought in the resistance, until they had driven the Russians from their homeland. Then they fought for power with other groups of Mujahedin. So-and-so many years later the Taleban came and drove the exhausted Mujahedin further to the North. Again enemy groups of the Mujahedin joined together. To form the Northern Alliance.

At some point Shirin-Gol's brother himself was appointed a commander with the task of protecting such and such a mountain against enemy attack. In the name of the homeland, of freedom, of the Northern Alliance, the Prophet, the Koran, Islam.

At some point a young man came into the mountains, introduced himself to Commander-brother and said, my teachers have wrapped a turban around my head, have said I am a Taleb, sent me off with other Taleban, said I was to free my homeland and kill the Mujahedin. But I fled, now I am here and want to kill the Taleban.

That is a good and wise wish, says the commander, embraces the deserter, presses him to his heart and feels a strange pain. He doesn't understand why his eyes are swimming with tears.

A number of days pass before Commander-brother understands the pain and the tears. The deserter is one of his younger brothers. His blood brother. His father's son. Cheeky-twin.

The enemy? They are the Taleban. The Afghan Taleban. The Pakistani Taleban. The Arab Taleban. But sometimes the enemy is the other commander who wants to extend the sphere of his power.

Commander-brother does not know how long he will still be fighting. Cheeky-twin will fight as long as Commander-brother fights. As long as necessary. As long as it takes. What else is he going to do? The fields are mined. The villages are destroyed. What else is he going to do?

Cheeky-twin has not married yet. Commander-brother has two wives. Commander-brother's two wives and eleven children are happy with their lives.

At some point Shirin-Gol's daughter, Noor-Aftab became a widow for a second time. She and her two children came to stay with Commander-brother in the mountains so that he would look after her too. He married her to one of his young fighters, and if God wills it she will soon be bearing him a son.

And now God has shown Shirin-Gol the way to the north. Shirin-Gol, Nafass, Nabi, Navid, Nassim and Morad, who is still smoking opium but not as much. Half-Opium-Morad.

At long last we are back together, says Commander-brother, looking at his sister, who he hasn't seen for so-and-so many years.

Shirin-Gol is just taking off her headscarf, loosening her plaits, leaning her tired back against the cushion, she is just slurping hot sweet tea, Noor-Aftab's first child, Shirin-Gol's first grandchild is just running from right to left and Noor-Aftab's second child, Shirin-Gol's second grandchild is running from left to right, they bump their heads together, fall over, start crying, both look to their grand-mother Shirin-Gol for help, when Noor-Aftab utters a cry, bends double with pain, looks over to her mother, lies down on the floor and says, it is time.

Shirin-Gol knots her hair together, pulls on her headscarf, ties it tight, takes her sickle out from the niche beside the door, holds it in the fire, immerses it in boiling water, throws back her daughter's skirts, inserts one finger into her daughter's birth-passage, feels the child's little soft nose, its ears, its mouth, places her fingers around the tiny, slippery baby's head and pulls out her daughter's third child.

May God never abandon you, says Shirin-Gol, places the boy's umbilical cord over the sickle and cuts it through. With a *bismi-allah*.

Shirin-Gol kisses the child on the forehead and says, may God send you good fortune. Always enough to eat. Contentment.

Shirin-Gol puts her third grandchild, which she has just pulled from the body of her first daughter, into the arms of his mother and says, may Allah grant you a life of peace and tranquillity. May he grant that your homeland, Afghanistan, is finally free.

Shirin-Gol takes off her headscarf, brushes back her white hair, slurps the rest of her sweet tea and asks her daughter, what are you going to call him?

Shir-Del, like my first husband, the one they killed, says Noor-Aftab, kissing her son on the forehead.

Shir-Del. Lion-heart. That is a lovely name, says Shirin-Gol.

Your hair has lost its colour, says Noor-Aftab, it has turned white. You've become a *bibi*.

A *bibi*. A grandmother.

Sweet grandmother.

Bibi-Shirin.

THANKS

Afghanistan, the Hindu Kush, the desert, the rivers, the mountains and valleys, Kabul, Mazar-e-Sharif, Herat, Fayzabad, Baharak, Jalalabad, Kandahar, Sorubi . . . the people of Afghanistan have changed my life. I owe you a great deal. A very great deal. Thank you, my Afghan friends.

May there come a time when I can mention your names with all the pride, respect and love that I feel for you, without endangering your lives.

I thank everyone who has made it possible for me, time and time again, to travel to this wonderful country. Above all, Inge von Bönninghausen and Jürgen Thebrath, my editors at WDR. In spite of war, and although I wasn't even sure I would be able to take my camera to the country, let alone film, they let me go and gave me all their confidence.

I thank Helmut Grosse and Albrecht Reinhard, my editors at ARD Weltspiegel, and Heinz Deiters and Birgit Keller-Reddemann from Kinderweltspiegel, who let me go there time and again. Thanks to Maria Dickmeis for her devotion. Thanks to all the editors and cameramen who have made my films what they are.

Uli Fischer, to you I owe many places, people and friends in Afghanistan. Uli Fischer is another of those people under the spell of the land below the Hindu Kush. He looks like an Afghan when he slips into his *shalwar-kamiz*. He once said I'd be an Afghan in my next life. I hope the war's over by then.

I thank Abed Naib, who first introduced me to Ahmed Shah Massoud, the charismatic warlord who fell victim to a cowardly attack two days before the inhuman attack on the World Trade Center.

I thank Rita Griesshaber, Gerd Poppe, Claudia Roth, Angelika Graf, who allowed me to accompany them on their journey through Afghanistan.

I thank Mullah so-and-so who broke many laws for me, protected me and warned me and only really became a Talib because he thought if he was part of it he could change the Taliban. May he have got out in time to serve the cause of homeland.

I thank Malalai and her brother, who saved my life.

I thank Rahmat, who protected me from stepping on a mine.

I thank Fatane, you gave the girls their dreams back.

I thank Ulla Nölle and Tine for allowing me to see your schools where women work and girls can study.

I thank Deutsche Welthungerhilfe; Ellen Heinrich, who wouldn't leave me alone until I started collecting stories for my book two years ago, alongside my film work; Erhard Bauer, Robert Godin, who stood by me; Ingeborg Schäuble, chairman of the board of Welthungerhilfe, who leaves no stone unturned in her efforts to make Afghanistan popular. My special thanks to the Afghan friends who cooked for me, looked after me and drove me, and very special thanks, again and again, to my friends

Anita and Richard for your friendship, your love, your support. Without you many things would have been impossible.

I thank my friends at the United Nations and other aid organisations who have helped me time and again and strengthened my will.

I thank my friend Eli Holst, who introduced me to the world's best agent.

For giving me strength, I thank Joachim Jessen of the Thomas Schlück Agency and all his colleagues.

I thank everyone at Bertelsmann, particularly as represented by Margit Schönberger, who pampers me and tends to my every need; Klaus Eck, who bought my book before September 11th, when the world wasn't interested in Afghanistan, and demonstrated once again that men can sometimes have sound gut instincts; Claudia Vidoni, my mercilessly good editor, who steered me in the right direction and did everything she could to ensure that I stayed true to my language and my rhythm; Anna Cherrett, from Century, thank you for the most beautiful phone call ever.

Samantha and Rahela, thanks for everything I learned from you. If he really exists, may God grant you, and all the women, children and men to whom you have devoted your lives, a long and peaceful life.

Karla Schefter, thank you for the other way of helping and for the other Afghanistan.

Mary-jan, thank you for your courage and your love. May you soon return to Afghanistan.

I thank Rüdiger König, who has understood Afghanistan and its people like no other Western diplomat, and has always put them and their interests first.

Thanks to Irene Salimi, caretaker of the former German

Embassy, for contact with the Taleban, the armoured cars and the white table-cloth.

I thank my friends in New York, who went to the mosque in defiance of everything after September 11th, and who, with the action group www.ourgriefisnotacryforwar.org are fighting for a peaceful solution in Afghanistan. And I bow to the parents, relatives and friends of the victims of September 11th who took an eight-day march from Washington to New York to demonstrate their will for peace and an end to the bombing and dying of even more innocent people in Afghanistan. My heart is torn when I think of the pain you must have gone through. May it be your last.

Thanks to Arundhati Roy, you always remind me that courage is worth it.

Thanks to Shirin Neshat for your friendship, that gives me wings.

Roland Suzo Richter and Peter Hermann, thanks for the inspiration, and for believing in my compatriots and me.

Thanks to Sonia Mikich, from you I have learned to think big.

Thanks to Adrienne Göhler, from you I have learned that it is worth being true to myself and the things I believe in.

Thanks to Jürgen Domian for your friendship, and your way of reminding me where I come from.

Thanks to Brigitte Leeser, you saved my soul.

Thanks to Thomas Leeser and Rebecca van de Sandt for Ava, for inspiration and the Sunday breakfasts in New York.

I thank my parents, my brother Arian, his wife Karin, their son Tarek, my brother Omid and his son Julian, simply because you're always there for me. From you I learned to look behind every surface to find my own truth.

Thanks to my cousin Bahram Beyzai, without you none of this, and nothing else, would have happened.

Arman, you left us too soon.

Madjid, stay alive.

Thanks Biggi Müller for being an example.

Tom Schlessinger and Keith Cunningham, thank you for infecting me with the right virus.

Thanks Judith Weston for the insights.

Jean Houston, thank you for the heroes.

Thanks Julia Cameron for the right path.

Without friends, life is not worth it.

Thank you Angel for the angel, Teresa for the mosque, Gail for the quilt, Persheng, Dicki and Marie, Arde, Farahad, Birgit, Anita, Lucia, Karin.

Thanks Uli for the years, the passes and everything.

Ashkan and Kim, thank you for you and for Ananda and Jaya.

I thank my family, my friends and the people in my homeland, Iran. You have taught me that there is a future even for countries that God forgot, where he comes only to weep.

And I thank all those whom I can't mention here, but who are important for me, my life and my work. You know already:

Everything is part of everything.